THE ANGLO-AMERICAN PREDICAMENT

The Anglo-American Predicament

Predicament

*The British Commonwealth, The United States
and European Unity*

By

H. C. ALLEN, M.C.

*Commonwealth Fund Professor of American History
in the University of London*

ST MARTIN'S PRESS · NEW YORK

1960

MACMILLAN AND COMPANY LIMITED

London Bombay Calcutta Madras Melbourne

THE MACMILLAN COMPANY OF CANADA LIMITED

Toronto

ST MARTIN'S PRESS INC

New York

PRINTED IN GREAT BRITAIN

For

JULIA, GIANA and FRANKLIN

To Whom The Future Belongs

' There must be room within the great world organization for organisms like that British Empire and Commonwealth, as we now call it, and I trust that there will be room also for the fraternal association of the British Commonwealth and the United States . . . and besides this—I, for my part, hope to deserve to be called a good European—we have the duty of trying to raise the glorious continent of Europe, the parent of so many powerful States, from its present miserable condition as a volcano of strife and tumult to its old glory as a family of nations and a vital expression of Christendom. I am sure these great entities which I have mentioned—the British Empire, the conception of a Europe truly united, the fraternal association with the United States—will in no way disturb the general purposes of the world organization.'

Winston Churchill, 1944

Preface

THIS is a tract for the times, and is not therefore a 'work of scholarship', though I hope that it is not totally devoid of scholarly qualities. It was written as swiftly as possible, and without doubt therefore has its full share — and perhaps more — of the errors of fact, deficiencies of argument and infelicities of style to be expected in such circumstances. No one beside myself read it before it went to press, so that it is not even necessary to declare on this occasion that I alone am responsible for its shortcomings. I hesitate to mention any person or institution in the preface to such a work, but I feel that I must express my sincere gratitude to the Institute for Advanced Study, for providing so splendid an opportunity to write it. I trust that it may not be regarded as too ephemeral, opinionated and unworthy a product of that hospitality.

Princeton,　　　　　　　　　　　　　　　　　　　　H.C.A.
New Jersey　　　　　　　　　　　　　　　　*December 1959*

Introduction

THIS book is addressed equally to the British and the American peoples. They read many identical works in their common language, but few of these are aimed directly and impartially at both of them. Part One is especially addressed to Great Britain; Part Two to the United States; and Part Three to both nations, as well as to the free world in general.

The thesis of the book is the imperative necessity for a federal Atlantic Union, both to strengthen the West in its struggle with Communism, and to fortify the democracy, and develop fully the prosperity, of the free world. Such a Union should not be an exclusive organization, but should be a step — the first practicable step — in the direction of a world society combining order with liberty.

Because of Britain's unique international political and economic position, such a Union alone can reconcile her different ties with The Commonwealth, the United States and continental Europe. The United States needs such a Union because of the cold war — and even the struggle for peaceful co-existence — with Soviet Russia and Communist China, and because of her determination to ensure the survival, and indeed the triumph, of her democratic way of life. Europe, too, for many reasons, should welcome this wider Union. But only a united Anglo-American determination can actually bring it into existence. It is to this end that the national policies of the two peoples should be urgently directed.

Contents

xiii

PART III

THE ANGLO-AMERICAN PREDICAMENT

PART I

The Dilemma of Britain

'. . . each time we must choose between Europe and the open sea, we shall always choose the open sea.'

Winston Churchill, 1944

CHAPTER I

The International Position of the United Kingdom

T HE position of Great Britain among the nations of the world is unique in two important respects; first, the extent, dispersion and complexity of her Empire, which she is now in the process of transforming into a Commonwealth of associated but free and independent nation-states; and second, the degree of her dependence on international trade, with manifold and distant parts of the world, for her very life. These two facts present her with special problems which do not face any other great power in like degree. The foreign policy of the United Kingdom is, and must be, essentially conditioned by these two vital factors, imperial and commercial.

(A) The Commonwealth and Empire

Any real comprehension of the grave dilemma which confronts Britain in international affairs today must begin with some consideration of the great historic fact of British imperialism, for it has been the Empire, more perhaps than anything else, which has dominated, and indeed conditioned, her relationship with the outside world for the past three centuries. Of no other power in Europe — or elsewhere — has this been so true, for the historical and geographical position of the British Isles made trans-oceanic expansion natural, and even easy, for her, once the geographical discoveries of the fifteenth century began to open up the vast expanses of the whole globe to trade and settlement. Until that time a remote, 'under-developed', raw-material exporting kingdom off the northwest shores of the European mainland, she soon became a great commercial, and later industrial, power; when the Atlantic replaced the Mediterranean as the maritime heart of the Western world, her central position enabled her to lead, and for a period almost to monopolize, the startling economic progress of Western man in the eighteenth century and the first three-quarters of the nineteenth. This unprecedented leap forward in human material potentialities, which for want of a better term we call the Industrial Revolution, was intimately associated with the opening up of new markets and new sources of commodities throughout the world, and these Britain chiefly found within the borders of an Empire which was acquired and protected by her dominant sea power. The United Kingdom was no longer, in its foreign and dynastic policies, exclusively or even primarily concerned with Europe; after the loss of Calais in the sixteenth century Gibraltar was her only lasting acquisition on the European mainland, and even wars which were of European origin seemed to become for her, when her leaders knew their business, chiefly wars for colonial objectives. Thus she came to be subject to two magnetic attractions, one from Europe and one from her Empire; after the most important part of that Empire had broken off and become the United States in 1783, a third force was added. In many ways the most powerful pull historically has been that of the Empire, which is now being, not without tribulation, converted into the Commonwealth. It is for this reason that we must, in order to understand the problem of Britain's international position, look first at the history of British imperialism.

The Empire was the product of three motives, not by any means confined to the British but common to men everywhere. First in time and importance was economic, the fundamental urge for trade and wealth; this led to the foundation of the earliest British colony, at Jamestown, Virginia, in 1607. Second came a religious motive, showing itself at first in a desire to quit the mother country in order to seek religious freedom in new lands; this was exemplified in the second American settlement, that of the Pilgrim Fathers in New England in 1620. Religious zeal was to show itself in a much more positive way later with the growth of the great missionary movement, which reached its height, as far as Britain was concerned, in Africa in the nineteenth century. Thirdly and lastly, there was a political motive for British emigration, an ardent desire to seek freedom from the political and social restraints of the old world. By the time that the Second British Empire was coming into existence in the nineteenth century, there was added to this negative motive, too, a positive political imperialism, which had as its ostensible object the spreading of the orderly civilization of Western man to all the quarters of the globe, and which was probably best embodied in the often selfless work of the old Indian Civil Service.

These three strains, each taking many forms, are all apparent in the long and complex history of British imperialism. Though the desire to escape from the restrictions and difficulties of a hide-bound Europe was always strong, and often predominant, in the minds of successful colonists (becoming indeed transmuted into perhaps the most important underlying motive of the makers of the American Revolution), to the authorities at home in Britain the First British Empire, which was brought to an end in that Revolution, appeared essentially as an economic structure. In common with their contemporaries in all the countries concerned they held views about the nature of empire which historians have, significantly enough, called Mercantilist. Devoted to the idea of national power, rather than to that of popular welfare in the twentieth-century fashion, they none the less grasped fully the importance of economic development, and of economic regulation as a means to it, and considered that the economic life of colonies should essentially be organized to add as much as possible to the strength of the whole empire. In practice, however, this came to be interpreted as meaning the subordination of the interests of each colony to the needs of the central government, that is to say of the mother country. Ultimately, the stifling social effects of the economic straitjacket which the United Kingdom Parliament tried to apply to the thirteen American colonies, when combined with the long-standing and steadily increasing desire of the Americans for political rights and self-government, led to the explosion of the War of American Independence.

The immediate effect of the American victory in 1783 was to reduce the power and prestige of the British Empire to a lower level than it had reached for many years, or was to reach for many years to come; it needed all the perseverance Britain displayed in the twenty years of war against Revolutionary and Napoleonic France (in which she became involved ten years later), and all the fruits of victory in 1815, to restore her standing in the world. This long struggle, too, concealed from Britain's rulers for several decades the profound effects which the American Revolution must necessarily have on their own ideas about their remaining colonies, but in due course it came to be apparent to them that they could no longer wholeheartedly believe in either the economic or the political benefits of the British imperial system. If the only result of building up the strength of colonies was to be a series of bloody, expensive and heart-rending wars in which they exacted their independence at the cannon's mouth, was it really worth while having an Empire at all? On the whole it seemed wise to let dissatisfied colonies depart in peace when they demanded to do so, and it certainly began to seem less than desirable to trouble to acquire new ones. At the same time, the rise of British industry, and the spread under its influence of the idea of international free trade, removed, in the eyes of contemporaries, the chief economic motive which had led to the growth of the First British Empire. If there be added to this the development, first clearly marked in 1832, of the idea of democratic self-government at home in Britain, and the resultant difficulty, in all conscience, of refusing similar democratic rights to Britons in colonies overseas, the curious history of British imperialism in the middle years of the nineteenth century may be more readily understood.

This was the era when statesmen (and even politicians) expected colonies to 'drop off like ripe plums'; when, so far from seeking to conquer fresh colonies, Britain began, with the publication of the Durham Report which followed the Canadian rebellion of 1837, to grant self-government to her more advanced possessions, such as Canada, Australia and New Zealand; and when, in fact, the principles which now underlie the free association of member nations in the British Commonwealth were first being slowly evolved. Awareness of this recession in the tide of British imperialism is essential to an understanding of its later history, but it should be noted that effective measures of self-government were only applied to 'white' communities in the Empire, in the belief that they alone were fitted to exercise political rights and perform political duties.

And the tide of imperialist sentiment was not at the ebb very long. By the 1870s under the leadership of Disraeli the Conservatives had begun to develop into the party of Empire, and the entry of Joseph Chamberlain into the Conservative and Unionist government in 1895 as Colonial Secretary marked perhaps the high-water mark of this revivified, and in some respects new, imperialism. But the disillusion which followed the Boer War of 1899 and which was to a considerable extent responsible for the great Liberal victory in the election of 1906 marked the beginning of another, this time much more gradual, decline in British imperialism. Symbolized at first in a generous policy towards South Africa, this new Liberal spirit became submerged in nationalist sentiment during World War I. At the same time, Conservative efforts, led by Chamberlain, to revive the old partnership between economic and political imperialism by a policy of imperial preference and tariff protection had made no real headway against the dominant doctrine of free trade, which was still most strongly espoused by the Liberals. The United Kingdom, in fact, paradoxically appeared to emerge from the war in 1918 still a strongly imperialist as well as a free trade country.

But under the post-war leadership of Stanley Baldwin two important, and in a historical sense contradictory, developments took place. Under the impact of the Great Depression in 1929 Britain adopted for the first time for three-quarters of a century a protectionist policy which included substantial measures of imperial preference, but while strengthening the bonds of Empire economically, the Tory governments of these years appeared to some to weaken them politically by explicitly accepting the ultimate goal of self-government for India. This vital step in the application of the doctrine of self-government to other than the 'white' Dominions was taken against the persistent opposition of Winston Churchill; and it was under his leadership that Britain was fighting for her life against Germany within four years of the passage in 1936 of the crucial Government of India Act. This fact put a virtual stop to the growth of colonial self-government for the duration of the struggle, and might well have delayed it after the return of peace had Labour not swept into office in 1945 and given to the process of self-determination in the Empire the greatest impetus that perhaps it had ever received.

The whole Indian sub-continent was granted full self-government (at the cost of political division and a multitude of lives lost in Hindu-Moslem riots) and yet chose to remain within the Commonwealth — one of the most remarkable tributes ever paid to the liberal evolution of British imperialism. Ceylon, too, remained as a Dominion, but Burma chose complete independence. The new arrangement by which the Crown remained the sole constitutional link between all the member states of the Commonwealth was applied without distinction of race, colour or creed; indeed, in what seemed to some critics an excessive watering down of Commonwealth cohesion, India, although recognizing the Crown as the symbol of the free association, became herself a Republic. Thus the Labour party, by the time it left office in 1951, had firmly established the goal for Britain of a multi-racial Commonwealth of free, self-governing nations.

The Conservative governments which succeeded Labour continued to seek this goal, albeit sometimes with less resolute single-mindedness than their predecessors. Thus they granted full self-government to Ghana and to Malaya, although in the latter a long preliminary military campaign against Communist terrorism had been necessary. Even after the suppression of Mau Mau in Kenya, grave racial difficulties hindered progress in East Africa, while in the Mediterranean island of Cyprus (and it sometimes seemed likely that Malta would follow suit) serious disorders further complicated already highly awkward problems, for even when the main units of the Commonwealth had gained their independence a number of very intractable, if relatively minor, conundrums would remain to be solved, particularly in the case of small strategic colonies, such as Gibraltar and Aden. But with Nigeria scheduled for independence in 1960 and the West Indies in the throes of confederation, the main direction of the line of march continued the same under the Conservatives as under Labour.

Thus the development of the British Empire and Commonwealth over the last two centuries has not been the monolithic imperialistic venture that its critics, particularly the Marxists, would like to have it seem. In the last three-quarters of a century, it is true, the Tories have been the party of Empire (in sharp contrast to the seventeenth and early eighteenth centuries when they were its opponents and the Whigs were its supporters), while the Liberal and later Labour parties have been the prime movers in the direction of colonial liberty; but in mid-nineteenth century Tories were as ready as anyone else to accept the trend towards the independence of powerful colonies, while in the last twenty-five years they have on the whole loyally promoted the development of the free Commonwealth.

But this vast operation, of voluntarily granting self-government to the members of an immense empire, is in many respects totally unprecedented in human history, for man has in general been profoundly reluctant to surrender the power, the riches and the pomp of great empire. It is in fact a strategic withdrawal on a gigantic scale — and retreat without rout is notoriously the most difficult of the operations of war. This huge process of political disengagement has thrown a serious strain on the balanced judgment of many Britons, and particularly on members of the Tory party, for it was made difficult, even hazardous, not merely by the practical problem of timing — of planning and effecting each step towards independence in the various colonies in such a way that it both prevented an explosion of hope too long frustrated, and warded off the threat of ultimate disaster through local unreadiness to assume effective control — but also by the more subtle problem arising from the emotional sensibilities of Britons about their declining influence and prestige in international affairs. This adjustment to the second rank of world powers was far from easy for a people accustomed for more than two centuries to an international position of the greatest eminence.

Their feelings came to centre in the 1950s upon British

policy in the Middle East, where Anthony Eden as Foreign Secretary manfully granted a perhaps premature independence to the Sudan, in order finally to settle the long-standing difficulties with Egypt over the Suez Canal, from the military occupation of which Britain agreed to withdraw in the treaty of 1954. These measures were bitterly denounced by a few rebel Tories, who struck a deep vibrating chord in the hearts of many ordinary Conservatives, and even a number of others who were not party men, particularly perhaps those of the older generation. They had, these elders, been born in the very different world of 1914, at a time when Britain had recently been the greatest, and was still the equal of any, power, and when the impalpable and sometimes lukewarm concept of Commonwealth had not yet replaced the solid yet glittering idea of Empire; when self-government was a reality only to the colonies of Western European and predominantly British stock, and when self-determination for 'lesser breeds without the law' was only a very distant aspiration. Throughout the adult lives of this generation the power of Britain relative to other nations had remorselessly declined, and the sense of political frustration of many Conservatives was exaggerated by economic difficulties, not merely those arising from the dwindling of the Empire, but also from the increasing burden of the measures of working-class advancement and social security which was placed upon middle-class shoulders in post-war years.

These manifold irritations and frustrations, coming on top of the strain of the Second World War — victory in which produced only a prolonged period of austerity — had a profound effect. No single internal measure, no single external action was in itself enough to produce a really violent reaction, but each and every one added to the increasing psychological tension. Thus all unrecognized, the electric charge built up, and the Suez crisis was the lightning flash that heralded the unexpected, violent, astounding storm. The British decision to intervene with France in the Middle East by force of arms after the Egyptian nationalization of the Suez Canal in 1956 was not a purely rational one, and perhaps the most important of the underlying emotional causes was that a long-sensitive nerve, that of declining imperial greatness, lay exposed, and was touched upon the raw by this threat to the Canal, which still loomed so large in the inner recesses of most British minds as the 'life-line' of Empire. The situation was exacerbated by the prolonged, highly emotional, very generalized, and often quite inaccurate 'anti-colonial' and 'anti-imperial' criticisms, not merely of Britain's enemies and the neutral nations but also of some of her friends, such as the Asian members of the Commonwealth and the United States. Yet the idea that imperialism has been exclusively harmful to the colonial peoples cannot be sustained; they have in fact derived considerable immediate and enormous ultimate benefits from the Western commodities, ideas, techniques and capital of which the British Empire was perhaps the greatest bearer. On balance Conservatives could not but regard British Imperial achievements with real pride.

It is true that other consciences were more tender. Socialists and Liberals, being in most cases less directly involved in the overseas Empire and drawn from sections of society which had grievances of their own against what they had been brought up to consider the 'governing classes', felt more acutely the passion of the Afro-Asian peoples for complete and rapid independence; any appearance of hesitation or delay in the implementation of the policy of swift self-determination filled them with misgivings. They abhorred the use of violence, of terrorism, by colonial peoples, but were anxious lest, in the Tory desire in traditional fashion to preserve order and stability in the Empire, Britain should find herself fighting some genuine national revolt. And there appeared to them to be, in Malta, in Aden, in the Gulf Sheikdoms, in Singapore, and above all in East and Central Africa, plenty of situations, both chronic and acute, to make difficult for many years to come the operation of imperial disengagement. In fact, their fears were, it may seem, exaggerated. The Macmillan government not only repaired, in amazingly successful fashion, the disastrous Anglo-American breach over Suez, but within a reasonably short space of time was the coadjutor of the United States in strengthening pro-Western influences in the Middle East by forceful intervention in Jordan and the Lebanon. Furthermore, in the internal imperial sphere things moved forward, for, despite some fumbling in East Africa, progress towards Nigerian independence continued apace, and, as by a miracle, a solution to the Cyprus problem seemed to have been found at long last.

But in any case, swiftly as the process of granting self-government to the constituent elements of the British Empire may proceed, it cannot with the best will in the world be accomplished overnight, for that Empire is still a body politic of remarkable size, astonishing spread and astounding complexity. British public opinion before the First World War was fully aware of the form and vast extent of that Empire upon which, as the more flamboyant of Englishmen were wont to say, the sun never set; one suspects that the British people today, and particularly the British youth, inured to the idea of imperial transformation if not dissolution, have very little idea how large and widespread it is. Indeed, in some respects there appears in modern British attitudes something that looks like a new parochialism, or at least the rebirth of an old English instinct to withdraw as much as possible within her island shell; isolationism, in a sense, was invented in Britain and had, as one of its more shameful manifestations, prompted the dishonourable abandonment of her European allies at the time of the Treaty of Utrecht of 1713. In its heyday the imperial spirit had the great advantage that it kept the United Kingdom acutely aware of its world-wide interests and responsibilities; with its decline and with the increasing embroilment of Britain in European affairs in the twentieth century, there has been an inclination, very apparent in recent years, for Britons to fix their gaze upon matters of immediate import to them in northwest Europe and to neglect, in a quiet way, their wider concerns.

This can be plainly seen in, and has been exaggerated by, recent trends in British education, and particularly in the history studied and taught by Englishmen in this century. Along with the English history which is the basis of instruction in their schools and universities, Britons have customarily studied both Imperial and European history. But with the decline of Empire, Imperial history has, understandably perhaps, become steadily less and less popular; it would not, for example, be entirely true to say that, as India left the

Empire and discarded all but the sometimes nebulous-seeming ties of the Commonwealth, Britons ceased to be interested in Indian history, but there would be an element of truth in the statement. And as concern with the story of the Empire waned, so in some ways does concern with that of Europe seem to have waxed; indeed it can be maintained that the great vice of British historical education at this time is its excessive concentration on Europe, to the grave neglect of the affairs and culture of the Commonwealth, the United States and the wider world. This has been reflected in, as well as being in part the result of, the distorting Eurocentricity of many British attitudes. At the very least a reborn awareness in Britain of the importance of her social and political bonds with the English-speaking peoples is necessary to wise judgments in international affairs.

This new awareness might begin with a revival of interest in the life of the Commonwealth, and even more of that inner core of Empire lying within it, which is still the direct and peculiar responsibility of the United Kingdom. In the history of the last four centuries the Empire has not been unrivalled in kind and in stature, but it has been very much larger and has lasted very much longer than any modern empire, and indeed in some senses it would be true to say that for a period of almost a century the other European overseas empires only survived through British good will and the strength of the Royal Navy. British sea power, which began to be important at the end of the sixteenth century, which became increasingly so during the next two hundred years, and which in effect controlled the oceans of the world throughout the nineteenth, gave to the British Empire (which was acquired entirely within those three centuries) its unique character, and particularly its global ramifications.

There had been instances of overseas expansion in other ages — that of the Greeks in the ancient Mediterranean world for example — and there were similar modern empires, such as the Portuguese, with possessions scattered throughout the world, but when, beginning in the late sixteenth century, Britain defeated Spain, then Holland and then France — the leaders of their day in nautical power and overseas empire — she made possible not only the unmatched extent but also the unequalled spread and diversity of British trans-oceanic possessions, acquired as they were in such manifold and different ways and for such complex and varied reasons.

From the very beginning, many of them were acquired simply by settlement; of this method perhaps Australia, penal colony though it was, provides the clearest example. Many, too, came from a combination of settlement with conquest from the native inhabitants, as was the case in New Zealand. Other colonies (beginning with Jamaica, which had been Spanish) were conquered from rival European powers, as was Canada from France. Some possessions, such as Egypt, were occupied to forestall similar action which it was feared might be taken by one or other of these rivals. Some, such as Gibraltar, were seized for strategic reasons. Others again, such as those in West Africa, were trading posts and came under political control in the course of actions taken to protect economic interests. Yet others, and above all India, were conquered in pursuit both of trade and political dominion, the latter being in part a by-product of a genuine search for social order. Still others, such as a number of Britain's African possessions, became protectorates, for the establishment of which British motives were, at least in part, good and disinterested. League of Nations Mandates and United Nations Trusteeships, of which Great Britain was given a number, were partly a method of making the possession of colonial territories respectable in the twentieth century, and partly a real attempt to control internationally the progress of backward areas toward independence. Though there was frequently a strong vein of imperialist sentiment, as well as economic desire, behind British expansion, there is also some truth in the old dictum that the Empire was acquired in a fit of absence of mind.

But whatever its history and whatever its future, the British Commonwealth and Empire still lies sprawled across the page of political reality in all its complexity, and this fact can only be ignored, by either its people or its critics, at their peril. Merely to peruse a list of its component parts, with a brief description of their status, is to bring this fact inescapably home — particularly when one remembers also the existence of those one-time members, such as the United States, on which British beliefs and habits have left a permanent mark. But it is big enough in any event, for in 1959 it was composed as follows:

The Commonwealth

The United Kingdom
Canada
Australia
New Zealand
South Africa
India
Pakistan
Ceylon
Ghana
The Federation of Malaya

These nations, together with their dependencies, form a free association of sovereign independent states, certain of them owing no allegiance to the Crown but all accepting it as the symbol of that free association.

The British Empire: colonies and protectorates of the United Kingdom

Aden — colony and protectorates. The Governor is also responsible for Kamaran Island

Bahamas — colony

Bermuda — colony

British Guiana — colony

British Honduras — colony

British Virgin Islands — colony

Christmas Island — colony

Cyprus — transitional status

Falkland Islands — colony with dependencies

Fiji — colony. The Governor is also responsible for the Pitcairn Islands Group and for relations with the protected state of Tonga

Gambia — colony and protectorate

Gibraltar — colony

Hong Kong — colony and leased territories

Kenya — colony and protectorate

Malta — colony

Mauritius — colony

Nigeria — federation of colonies and protectorates moving swiftly towards final independence

North Borneo — colony

St. Helena — colony with dependencies

Sarawak — colony. The Governor is also High Commissioner for the protected state of Brunei

Seychelles — colony

Sierra Leone — colony and protectorate

Singapore — special status

Somaliland — protectorate

Tanganyika — Trust territory

Uganda — protectorate

Western Pacific High Commission — the British Solomon Islands Protectorate, the Gilbert and Ellice Islands Colony, Central and Southern Line Islands, and the New Hebrides Condominium

West Indies Federation — a federation of the colonies of Antigua, Barbados, Dominica, Grenada, Jamaica, Montserrat, St. Christopher-Nevis and Anguilla, St. Lucia, St. Vincent, and Trinidad and Tobago, the federation moving towards full independence

Zanzibar — protectorate

In a special position are the Basutoland, Bechuanaland and Swaziland protectorates in South Africa.

The Federation of Rhodesia and Nyasaland is still not fully and entirely independent of Colonial Office control.

Such a list must make it clear beyond a doubt that Great Britain is not today (and never has been since the fifteenth century) purely a European power. Indeed, she is not even, as we shall shortly see, primarily a European power: she is essentially a world power — a nation with unrivalled political connections dispersed throughout the whole globe. No future which does not safeguard these world-wide interests is one which the United Kingdom can contemplate with satisfaction, or even equanimity, let alone with enthusiasm.

(B) Foreign Trade

If the world-wide extent of the British Empire is still unequalled, so also is the global spread of British commerce.

The heart of that Empire, the United Kingdom, is probably unique among the enduring empires of history in the degree of her dependence upon international and particularly distant overseas trade for her existence; she is certainly unique among modern nations in combining widespread political and imperial responsibilities as a great power with remarkable wealth built almost entirely on foreign commerce. Until recent years absolutely the world's greatest trading nation, she still, despite the fact that her population is much smaller than that of the greatest national Leviathans of today, both imports and exports more than any other country except the United States.

The 'white' British Commonwealth (the United Kingdom, Canada, Australia, New Zealand and South Africa) approaches the United States as an exporter and substantially surpasses her as an importer. The Commonwealth as a whole both exports and imports considerably more than America, though the value of this economic classification is very doubtful, since these countries do not all share even the common bonds constituted by membership of the Sterling Area or by the Ottawa Imperial Preference agreements made between the Dominions of 1932; furthermore, the Commonwealth as a whole shows few signs of developing any greater exclusive economic cohesion. There are many smaller nations which are relatively more dependent upon international commerce than Great Britain, but no great power equals and few great powers approach her in the extent to which she relies upon overseas, and especially trans-oceanic, trade.

This extraordinary dependence upon her economic relations with all quarters of the globe is the most important fact of her political and economic existence. It must be the first and fundamental consideration in all her national policies, political, economic and military, for it is at once the well-spring of her strength and the source of her peculiar weakness.

How did this state of affairs come about? In a manner closely linked with that in which she acquired her great overseas Empire. By the early years of the eighteenth century her maritime strength, both naval and commercial, had begun to outstrip that of her greatest erstwhile nautical and commercial rivals, the Dutch, and it did so under the shield of the Mercantilist system of imperial trade protection. Not only did this mean a great absolute increase in the quantity of her commerce, but it also meant a decisive increase in the proportion of it which was with her Empire in America, at the expense of the proportion of it which was with Europe. Thus in the years 1698-1701 19·6 per cent of British imports came from America and 64·8 per cent from Europe, while 11·9 per cent of British exports went to America and 80·8 per cent to Europe; a century later, in 1801-2, 45·4 per cent were from America and 32·7 per cent only from Europe, while 33·5 per cent went to America and 55·2 per cent to Europe.[1]

Even despite the shock of the loss of the Thirteen Colonies and the theoretical onslaught of Adam Smith on mercantile imperialism in *The Wealth of Nations*, Great Britain prospered and grew in economic strength under the Mercantilist regulations as she had never done before; more than that, she developed commercially and industrially as no other power in history had ever done. In these first throes of the gigantic economic upheaval of the Industrial Revolution the national income of Britain increased very rapidly; all estimates at this time were very unreliable but contemporaries gave the following figures: 1688 £43 millions, 1776 £100 millions, in the 1820s £300 millions, in the 1840s £500 millions.[2] As the pre-eminent industrial power, she established in these years an economic ascendancy over the other nations of the world that endured until almost the last quarter of the nineteenth century.

This produced by mid-century what even Adam Smith himself had despaired of seeing, free trade policies enacted in Britain. So much more important than the strictly mercantile interest of the eighteenth century did the great manufacturing interests of the nineteenth become that their incessant demand for larger and larger markets to absorb their unprecedented and increasing floods of manufactured goods became the dominating factor in British economic life. If Britain was to be able to export freely, she had to import freely, not merely to provide raw materials for the industrial machine and food for its growing armies of workers, but simply in order that her customers could afford to buy her exports.

(This was also made easier by Britain's large-scale export of capital, mostly derived from the profits of industrial development.) As it became more and more impossible to feed the growing urban population from domestic agricultural production, the demand for free trade became less and less possible to resist, and after the enfranchisement of the industrial middle class by the Great Reform Bill of 1832, the citadel of protection fell with the repeal of the Corn Laws in 1846. In a very few years Britain became a fully free trade country.

The implications of this fact and of the situation of which it was the outcome were of overwhelming importance for Great Britain, and its results are still at the heart of her international position today. The economic growth of which free trade was the result had been accomplished in a period during much of which Britain had been at war with France. For a short time, indeed, her trade with Europe had been to a great extent cut off by Napoleon's Continental System, but her trade with the rest of the world (which constituted, even in the breathing space for European trade provided by the peace-time year 1801-2, some $\frac{2}{3}$ of the whole) was continued and expanded under the protection of the British navy, whose virtually absolute maritime supremacy was signalized by the Battle of Trafalgar in 1805. Without that supremacy not merely Britain's victory but also her continued expansion in power, wealth and greatness would not have been possible. This is often concealed by the fact that the nineteenth century was a peaceful century, particularly for Britain, for whom it was once again an age of very rapid economic growth, matching under free trade what had been accomplished under Mercantilism; thus by the outbreak of World War I British national income was probably approaching £2,500 millions, roughly a five-fold increase since the middle forties, approximating to the five-fold increase then since the middle 1770s.[3] Fundamentally, this expansion was made possible by the freedom of the seas which the British fleet guaranteed, in the same way that the maintenance and indeed expansion of her great overseas Empire was made possible by its protection.

The essence of Britain's economic development in the nineteenth century was that it was an *overseas* expansion, for the

C

British people had outgrown their domestic base. Nor was
trade within the Empire, as permitted in the Mercantilist
system, any longer sufficient for British needs, particularly
after the loss of the American colonies; thus for a period in
the early nineteenth century, for example, much was hoped
of expanding British trade with Latin America. In any case,
with the coming after the Napoleonic wars of a stable peace
(in some respects the most stable in modern history), it seemed
unnecessary any longer to cabin and confine British commerce
within what now appeared an outmoded imperial mould.
Mercantilism had always been predominantly a means to
'power' and now forward-looking men were primarily concerned with questions of 'plenty'. So it was that, from the
1820s onwards, moves in the direction of the liberalization of
British trade began.

Complete free trade was accomplished essentially under the
leadership of those who were to become the Liberal party,
but before long the Conservatives, too, came to accept it, and,
despite some attempts to alter it, it remained the fundamental
economic policy of Britain for three-quarters of a century. It
tended to be with the Liberals, however, far more than an
economic doctrine: it was nearer to an article of faith or an
ideal, associated in their minds with the hope, and indeed
expectation, of the spread of enlightenment, democracy and
peace. It was no coincidence that the great leaders of the free
trade movement were also in the van of other liberal causes;
that Bright was the apostle of peace, Cobden the advocate of
arbitration, Gladstone the exponent of morality in international affairs. The marvels of the new industrialism, it was
thought, would be matched by the progress of mankind
towards international order and the rule of law between states.
The long years of peace and the consciousness of British
strength, and particularly of British power to maintain the
freedom of the seas upon which her new dominance essentially
depended, gave colour to this sanguine belief, and it was
fortified by calculations of self-interest. Acting, consciously
or unconsciously, on these basic assumptions, the British
people embraced free trade, and pressed on with the expansion of their economy upon the developing foundation of an
ever widening commerce.

Between 1801 and 1921 the population of England, Scotland and Wales quadrupled:

1801	10,500,856
1821	14,091,757
1851	20,816,351
1881	29,710,012
1901	36,999,946
1921	42,769,196

During the period between 1820, just before the first liberalization of trade was effected, and 1933, just after the reimposition of protection, the national income increased more than sixfold. The figures on this occasion are in terms of pounds sterling of 1913 purchasing power.

Average Annual National Income

	£ million
1820-9	460
1830-9	464
1840-9	534
1850-9	650
1860-9	780
1870-9	1,022
1880-9	1,318
1890-9	1,684
1900-4	1,903
1910-3	2,016
1927-9	2,550
1930-3	2,893[4]

It is apparent from both sets of figures that at the end of the nineteenth century the British people had little reason to question the efficacy of free trade.

But at this juncture it became apparent that the Liberal vision of international peace and plenty through free trade was not going to be fulfilled, whatever the prosperity of Britain. The Hague Conferences on International Peace in 1899 and 1907 were shortly followed by the cataclysm of World War I; and it had become quite clear even earlier that the rest of the world was not going to follow the example of Britain, and usher in the millennium by adopting universal free trade. It became obvious, for instance, that in a United

States of vast continental dimensions it was not necessary to worry about the classical arguments in favour of international free trade, the limited extent of the market or of the division of labour within merely national boundaries; from 1861 until 1914 America became an increasingly protectionist country. It became plain, also, to take the next most important example, that the newly united Germany, with its arrogant sense of national power, would not be content to accept for economic reasons a system which might ensure for many years to come the industrial supremacy of Britain, for such supremacy implied in the modern world an ascendancy in military matters also. Finally, it became obvious that backward nations would not be willing indefinitely to receive the manufactures of Britain in return for the raw materials which they could most easily produce, even at an economic profit: this system made them far too dependent upon a commodity market over which they had little or no control, and they very soon became acutely aware that it was in rapid industrialization that their hope of swift economic expansion lay. By 1914 the idea, conceived by Adam Smith, of a 'great mercantile republic' of the peoples, without trade barriers between them, was as patently doomed by conflicting economic interests as it was by the breakdown of international peace.

Yet during the century from 1815 to 1914, in the course of which she had fought no really great war and through some half to two-thirds of which she had enjoyed unfettered international trade, the United Kingdom had given hostages to fortune on a scale which it is almost hard to credit. The policy of free trade was an extraordinary act of faith, and though it achieved its immediate object of making Britain wealthy in a way that neither she nor any other power had ever been before, it left an immense and troublesome inheritance, with the difficulties, and even perils, of which the British people are still struggling today. Every year of her expansion meant that a greater proportion of her men, women and children became directly dependent on imports of raw materials from overseas to enable them to earn their living, and on imports of food from distant lands to enable them to survive. Broadly speaking, after 1850 the net quantity of food actually grown at home in Britain did not increase greatly till 1939, except in special and temporary circumstances, despite the fact that the population far more than doubled; and it was in the three decades between 1850 and 1880, when the first full impact of free trade was being felt, that the greatest relative increase in Britain's importation of foodstuffs took place. The annual average percentage of all Britain's imports constituted by imports of foodstuffs was 24·4 per cent from 1814-45, 32·1 per cent from 1854-60 and 44·7 per cent from 1875-1933.[5] At the present time the United Kingdom produces almost exactly half of the food which her population consumes: that is to say, every other person in the islands might be reckoned to live on food imported from overseas, much of it from great distances.

Britain's dependence upon imports of raw materials for her industry is almost as great: between 1875 and 1933 her gross imports of raw materials constituted on the average 41·6 per cent of her total imports.[6] The purely economic difficulties arising from this dependence on imports of both food and raw materials, which between them constituted, from 1875 to 1933, more than four-fifths of all her imports, are ones with which she became, between 1945 and 1955, all too familiar, particularly in the ominous shape of the dollar gap. Before the Second World War Britain was able to meet her bills without excessive difficulty owing to her economic services to foreign customers, to the existence of her long-standing over-seas investments, and to favourable terms of trade, but when after the war was over the last two factors no longer existed, she was faced with the necessity of enormously increasing her exports of goods and services to pay for her vital imports of food and raw materials, and of doing so in an increasingly competitive world.

The political and strategic, as opposed to economic, dangers of her situation had been much more dramatically and suddenly brought home to her in the two world wars, when her control over the vital sea lanes of her commerce was imperilled by the actions of her enemies. The U-boat attacks of World War I and the imminence of starvation in 1917 starkly illustrated the extent of her dependence upon these imports;

and the lesson was reinforced in 1940. On the second occasion it was made much more vivid by the fact that she was able to survive totally cut off from almost the whole of Europe, but that she never could have done so cut off from her other, extra-European, sources of supply. Even so, the second German war of attrition against her merchant fleets came at one time within measurable distance of strangling the United Kingdom. No inhabitant of those islands should ever need to be reminded of the vulnerability of their overseas trade to any attack from a considerable naval power.

It would be wrong, however, to give the impression that Britain alone has developed this dependence upon maritime commerce; Europe as a whole has followed in her footsteps as it became more and more industrialized. Thus in 1913 Europe, including Russia, accounted for 55·2 per cent of the world's total exports and 61·5 per cent of its total imports. Of this import total of 61·5 per cent, intra-European trade accounted for 40 per cent and imports to Europe from outside the continent for the remaining 21·5 per cent. In 1938 the position had not changed radically, for intra-European trade constituted 29·1 per cent of world imports and European imports from outside for 26·6 per cent, a total proportion of 55·7 per cent of the world's imports.[7]

There are also a number of powers, both in Europe and outside, which are in some senses more dependent on foreign trade than Britain, according to the method of computation. Perhaps in theory one of the most satisfactory ways of assessing reliance on international trade might seem to be by calculating the relationship which the foreign trade of a country bears to its national income. When this is worked out (for the year 1951, by W. S. and E. S. Woytinsky) small countries, with only one industry or with industries controlled by foreign capital, head the list; the highest of all is Indonesia, whose foreign trade constituted no less than 244 per cent of her national income, and all those countries which show a foreign trade-national income proportion of over 75 per cent have one-sided and poorly balanced economies. Those whose foreign trade constitutes between 50 and 65 per cent of national income tend to be countries which are highly industrialized but small in population, such as the Netherlands (63 per cent), New

Zealand (62·6 per cent), Australia (61·1 per cent), South Africa (58·7 per cent), Canada (51 per cent) and Denmark (50·6 per cent). In the group between 30 and 40 per cent are to be found those highly industrialized countries, such as Britain and France, which have fairly large populations; the figure for the United Kingdom is 39·4 per cent and for France 30·3 per cent. In large countries with large populations but relatively little industry — in other words with subsistence economies — the ratio of foreign trade to national income is very low; India's, for example, is 14 per cent and China's 4·4 per cent. Owing to the special circumstances of the post-war period, the figure for West Germany in 1949 was 22·2 per cent and for Japan 17 per cent, but between 1949 and 1951 the international trade of these two countries revived very rapidly and raised their ratios to levels similar to those of Britain and France. Germany's in 1959 may still perhaps be lower than Britain's and possibly than France's, but Japan's may well exceed both, as it did before the war, when it was more than 40 per cent. The United States, a very highly industrialized country which also has a large population combined with a very large terrain rich in resources, is an exception to this as to so many other economic rules, for its foreign trade represents only 9 per cent of its national income. There are no sufficiently reliable figures for that great unknown, in this as in so many other equations, the U.S.S.R.[8]

In practice, however, the relative position of Britain in dependence upon foreign trade can be shown more clearly by another set of figures, those of *per capita* foreign trade (i.e. exports *plus* imports) for a selected list of countries, which gives the ratio to population rather than to wealth or national income. For the sake of interest, however, the *per capita* income is also given in each case.

	1949	
	Per capita Foreign trade $	Per capita Income $
Iceland	712	476
New Zealand	536	856 (1949-50)
Canada	444	870
Australia	415	679 (1948-9)
Belgium-Luxemburg	415	582

	1949 Per capita Foreign trade $	Per capita Income $
Norway	363	587
Denmark	349	689
Netherlands	318	502
United Kingdom	305	773
South Africa	155	264
France	146	482
United States	131	1,453
Ceylon	80	67
West Germany	71	320
Italy	58	235
Japan	17	100
Pakistan	11	51
India	8	57 (1948-9)
China	1·2	27

Once again West Germany and Japan have since 1949 made rapid strides in *per capita* foreign trade, though perhaps less in *per capita* income; and once more no reliable figures are available for the U.S.S.R.[9]

What does all this, in fact, mean as far as the United Kingdom is concerned? It means essentially that no great power, with the possible exception of Japan, is as dependent, or even anything like as dependent as she is upon foreign trade. The largest and strongest nation which is more dependent is Canada, which has less than a quarter of her population although enjoying a substantially higher standard of living. Britain is only approached in the degree of her dependence on foreign trade, and then not closely, by two great powers besides Japan, West Germany and France. Japan is the power whom Britain most resembles in a number of ways, for as with the British Isles the relatively small geographical base constituted by the Japanese homeland forced the Japanese to rely increasingly on overseas trade if they were to expand their population, which they have in fact done a great deal faster and farther than Britain. But they have done it by combining a Western industrialism with an 'Oriental' standard of living. The relatively high ratio between foreign trade and national income in Japan is explained largely by the smallness of the income; so also, because the population is large, *per capita* foreign trade is low. The most startling proof of this is the figure of Japanese *per capita* income, which in 1949 was not much more than one-eighth of that in the United Kingdom. Japan is indeed a most ominous illustration of what might happen to Britain's standard of living if, for economic or political reasons, the British people fail to earn enough to pay for the imports that they must have.

Japan also serves as a pointer to another vital feature of Britain's situation; that all her foreign trade is overseas trade, which is in some respects more vulnerable in time of war than commerce over land frontiers. Sea power is much more flexible and manoeuvrable than land power, and thus it is that a relatively distant enemy may be able to endanger British commerce, where it could not damage the trade of a land-locked power. (On the other hand, of course, the land powers are much more vulnerable to their immediate neighbours, both economically and militarily. Napoleon's Continental System was a nice illustration of both the advantages and disadvantages of land and sea power.) Many of the small powers whose dependence on foreign trade is greater than Britain's conduct a good deal of it across their land frontiers; this is illustrated by the proportion of the trade of the following countries which was with Northwest Europe in 1952 (even though these figures include the substantial maritime trade of these countries with Britain) — Belgium-Luxemburg 53 per cent; Netherlands 55 per cent; Denmark 76 per cent. In the same way, in 1927, for example, 65 per cent of Canada's imports and 40 per cent of her exports came from or went to North America, and 52·9 per cent of Germany's imports and 74 per cent of her exports came from or went to Europe.

Furthermore, some powers conduct a high proportion even of their overseas trade along coastal waters or across narrow or semi-inland seas, where, particularly in these days of air power, attacks upon it can be more easily prevented. Thus in the years 1949-52, for instance, the Western Hemisphere accounted for 40 per cent of America's exports and 55 per cent of her imports; in 1952 62 per cent of Norway's trade was with Northwest Europe; and in the same year 51 per cent of France's exports and 24 per cent of her imports came from Northwest Europe and a further 38 per cent of her imports from Africa or the Middle East. But even this modification does not apply to Britain, for in 1952 only 34 per cent of her exports and 31 per cent of her imports went to or came from Europe; 19 per cent and 26 per cent respectively were with the Americas, and 47 per cent and 43 per cent with Africa, Asia and Oceania. In other words, more than two-thirds of all British trade is across the broad oceans.[10]

The extent to which the United Kingdom is unique in this is illustrated by the following table of the distribution of overseas trade for a number of countries in the period between the wars; this distribution has not altered drastically today.

Foreign Trade of Selected Countries: Percentage Distribution of Exports and Imports by Continent, 1927.[11]

	N.Am.	Middle Am.	S.Am.	Europe	Asia	Africa	Oceania
U.S.A.							
Imp.	11·6	12	12·4	30·5	30·0	2·2	1·3
Ex.	17·4	8·4	9·0	47·5	11·5	2·2	4·0
Canada							
Imp.	65·1	2·6	2·9	24·5	2·9	0·4	1·6
Ex.	40·0	2·2	2·2	46·9	5·4	1·2	2·1
U.K.							
Imp.	21·1	2·2	9·3	39·3	13·0	6·9	8·2
Ex.	10·7	1·8	8·4	34·0	22·3	11·3	11·5
France							
Imp.	14·1	2·4	8·6	44·3	13·1	13·2	4·3
Ex.	7·3	1·3	4·7	63·6	7·3	15·1	0·7
Netherlands							
Imp.	12·2	2·6	11·1	62·0	9·1	2·5	0·5
Ex.	6·1	0·9	2·0	76·4	11·1	2·9	0.6
Germany							
Imp.	17·9	1·6	10·8	52·9	10·0	4·3	2·5
Ex.	7·8	1·1	6·3	74·0	7·6	2·4	0·8
Japan							
Imp.	33·6	0·5	0·5	17·9	40·2	1·7	5·6
Ex.	43·2	0·3	1·0	7·4	42·4	2·6	3·1
Australia							
Imp.	27·9	0·1	0·1	53·0	14·7	0·7	3·5
Ex.	13·7	0·0	0·3	63·5	13·8	4·4	4·3

No other country had so wide a distribution of trade or so little concentration of it in one area as Britain, and few had to trade over such great distances.

The only one in the list to have such long sea routes is Australia, more than three-quarters of whose trade was either with Europe or with North America. The same sort of figure applies in the trade of New Zealand, some two-thirds of which in 1952 was with Europe alone. Most of Canada's trade, as we have seen, is with America, but in 1927 about a third of it was still with Europe. These things underline the fact that the Commonwealth and Empire as a whole are almost as dependent on overseas trade as is the mother country. Indeed these ocean trade routes are vital links of the Commonwealth, and their importance is reflected in the strength of the currency trading bloc which has come to be called the Sterling Area. But at its heart is the United Kingdom with a widespread distribution of overseas trade unparalleled in the world. A final table once more makes this abundantly clear, showing as it does the percentage distribution of British exports and imports in 1952.

	Exports	Imports
Western Hemisphere	19	26
Northwest Europe	24	23
South Europe	6	3
East Europe and USSR	4	5
Middle East	6	9
Other Asia	14	10
Other Africa	15	12
Oceania	12	12

Well may W. S. and E. S. Woytinsky sum the matter up: 'The United Kingdom holds a unique position in the world market. Its commercial interests and operations are dispersed over the whole globe.'[12]

But the story does not stop even here, for Britain is also uniquely vulnerable strategically, as we have seen in her history, because of the kind of imports she takes—because of the high proportion of them that consists of raw materials and above all food. The figures (for a number of selected countries) of the percentage distribution of exports and imports by main commodity groups around 1937 are very illuminating.[13]

	EXPORTS			IMPORTS		
	Food-stuffs	Mater-ials	Fabricated articles	Food-stuffs	Mater-ials	Fabricated articles
The Commonwealth	28	33	39	24	40	36
U.K.	6·9	18·3	74·8	41·5	42·0	16·5
France	15·2	29·4	55·4	25·7	58·8	15·5
Netherlands	36·6	31·1	32·3	17·8	41·5	40·7
U.S.	8·0	42·1	49·9	29·5	50·2	20·3
Germany	1·4	16·5	82·1	29·1	60·2	10·7
Japan	9·4	19·8	70·8	17·0	63·3	19·7
New Zealand	64·8	34·9	0·3	10·9	11·0	78·1
Australia	38·7	57·0	4·3	6·7	21·1	72·2
U. of S. Africa	30·9	60·0	9·1	6·1	10·5	83·4
Canada	32·6	38·8	28·6	14·4	30·3	55·3

It is the food figures which are the core of the problem. A nation which exports foodstuffs, like Australia or New Zealand, can in time of emergency live, even though at a reduced standard of living; a nation which earns a living by selling exports made from imported raw materials but which imports relatively little food, like France, or eats relatively little, like Japan, can also survive, though often at the cost of greater hardship; but a nation which imports as high a proportion of its food as Britain is uniquely vulnerable. No other country among those for which figures are given in the table (and probably no other country in the world) approached at the beginning of World War II within 10 per cent of the proportion of Britain's total imports which was constituted by food. It is true that Germany exports a higher proportion of fabricated articles but she produces much more of her own food; and Japan, because of her low consumption, imports a much smaller proportion of foodstuffs, even though her situation is not unlike the British and her population much larger. But the United Kingdom stands quite alone in the degree of her dependence on the importation of food.

Among the great nations of the world, then, Britain is unique in the degree to which she is dependent upon com-

merce with distant quarters of the globe not only for raw
materials, but even more for food; not merely for the maintenance of a high standard of living for her people, but also for
their very life. She is thus even more of a world power
economically than politically; her trading life-blood dictates
as clearly as her connections with the Empire and the
Commonwealth that she can never be an exclusively, or even
predominantly, European power. Her statesmen and her
people must never permit to be absent from all their calculations, social, economic and political, an awareness of the
essentially global ramifications of Britain's international
position.

NOTES

[1] Werner Schlote, *British Overseas Trade from 1700 to the 1930s*, Oxford
1952, p. 80.

[2] E. Lipson, *The Growth of English Society, A Short Economic History*,
London 1949, p. 393.

[3] W. S. and E. S. Woytinsky, *World Population and Production, Trends
and Outlook*, New York 1953, p. 385. I have quoted here the figure in
'current prices' which can be roughly compared with the contemporary
estimates given for the earlier periods by Lipson (see note 2 above).

[4] Schlote, *op. cit.*, p. 49.

[5] *Ibid.*, p. 53.

[6] *Ibid.*, p. 53.

[7] W. S. and E. S. Woytinsky, *World Commerce and Governments, Trends
and Outlook*, New York 1955, pp. 71, 80.

[8] Woytinsky, *World Commerce and Governments*, p. 65.

[9] *Ibid.*, p. 66.

[10] *Ibid.*, p. 105.

[11] *Ibid.*, p. 75.

[12] *Ibid.*, p. 105.

[13] *Ibid.*, pp. 119, 122-3.

CHAPTER II

European Economic Unity

O N 19 September 1946 Winston Churchill, speaking at Zurich University in neutral Switzerland,
declared:

'I wish to speak to you today about the tragedy of Europe.
This noble continent . . . is the home of all the great parent
races of the western world. It is the fountain of Christian faith
and Christian ethics. It is the origin of most of the culture, arts,
philosophy and science both of ancient and modern times. If
Europe were once united in the sharing of its common inheritance, there would be no limit to the happiness, to the prosperity
and glory which its three or four hundred million people would
enjoy. Yet it is from Europe that have sprung that series of
frightful nationalistic quarrels, originated by the Teutonic
nations, which we have seen even in this twentieth century and
in our own lifetime, wreck the peace and mar the prospects of
all mankind. . . .
'Yet all the while there is a remedy which . . . would as if by
a miracle transform the whole scene, and would in a few years
make all Europe, or the greater part of it, as free and as happy
as Switzerland is today. What is this sovereign remedy? It is to
re-create the European Family, or as much of it as we can, and
provide it with a structure under which it can dwell in peace,
in safety and in freedom. We must build a kind of United
States of Europe.'[1]

This suggestion of European unity fell on fertile soil —
indeed upon ground already sown with similar seed by less
illustrious hands. In a Europe shattered, impoverished, low in
spirit, and increasingly conscious of the swelling threat of
Soviet Communism, a Europe whose three leading nations
(each utterly defeated at one stage or other of the great war
from which they had just emerged) were highly receptive of
novel political remedies, the miracle occurred, and from this
time forth the idea of European union, in one form or another,
never ceased to work upon the imaginations of men. More

than that, what had been before World War II considered
merely as the fanciful whim of a single French statesman,
Aristide Briand, began to assume practical shape. It did so in
the way which Churchill had predicted when he said in that
same speech in Zurich:

> 'I am now going to say something that will astonish you.
> The first step in the re-creation of the European family must be
> a partnership between France and Germany.'[2]

With the growth, among an able group of French statesmen,
of a feeling for the unity of Europe, and a perception of its
great advantages for their country, and with the rise to power
in the shortly-to-be-created West German Federal Republic
of a Christian Democratic party dedicated to a democratic
pro-Western policy, the unification of Western Europe began
to move, with astonishing swiftness, towards reality.

This rapid materialization of what many of Churchill's
countrymen had regarded as no more than a pious political
aspiration faced the British people with a challenge, or rather
a series of challenges, of a gravity and importance seldom
equalled in their long history. But for some time it did not
become clear in what particular shape the new Europe would
emerge, and thus in what form the challenge would be finally
presented. Indeed, the immediate reactions of the British
people and government to the early manifestations of the new
spirit in Europe were themselves important in determin-
ing what were the first actual steps which the European
nations took to construct their union. In the event, it was
really in the economic sphere that progress was initially
consolidated; common economic institutions were the first
material clothing for the skeletal idea of the European
community.

That this was so resulted partly from the active intervention
of the United States. America, alone among the participants
in the Second World War, whether victors or vanquished,
emerged from it economically strengthened rather than weakened. When Europe was in the throes of a severe economic
crisis in the spring of 1947 — a crisis 'above all ... of food and
dollars '[3] — the Truman administration, already alerted to the
dangers of Communist expansion in Greece and Turkey,

became aware not merely of the human misery among the European peoples but also of the risk of the spread of Communism amidst conditions of such economic distress, and proposed what later came to be called the Marshall Plan, which, with superb generosity, offered to the European nations massive financial aid 'against hunger, poverty, desperation and chaos'. In the same speech in which this proposal was made, General Marshall, the Secretary of State, had also laid it down that 'The initiative . . . must come from Europe,'[4] that it must be a joint European programme which administered the aid that was offered.

Accordingly, Ernest Bevin, the Foreign Secretary of Britain (which, it should be noted, had received special and unique aid at an earlier date by means of the Anglo-American Loan of 1946) 'grabbed the Marshall offer with both hands'.[5] Under his active leadership the European powers met in Paris and established the Organization for European Economic Recovery (O.E.E.C.), which handled the aid which began to flow in after President Truman had signed, on 3 April 1948, an Act appropriating $5.3 billion for the European Recovery Programme (E.R.P.). These funds were administered at the American end by the Economic Cooperation Administration (E.C.A.). Under this splendid stimulus the productivity of the European participants rapidly increased and their trade began once more to expand. But O.E.E.C. did not rest here; it further promoted the economic co-operation of the member states, consisting of most of the European countries west of the Iron Curtain, by getting the bulk of the national trade quotas, which had hitherto hampered their European commerce, removed, and by setting up in 1950 (under the impulse of a grant earmarked for the purpose by E.C.A.) the European Payments Union (E.P.U.). This body very successfully promoted financial stability among the European states, and became, in association with the Sterling Area, a currency clearing centre not only for Europe but for much of the non-dollar world. These achievements went some way to alleviate the main international symptom of European economic deficiencies, the shortage of so-called 'hard' currencies which came to be known as the dollar gap.

But the symptom constantly tended to recur, and the

majority of influential and knowledgeable Americans believed in their hearts that a real European union was the only permanent and complete cure for the ills of Europe's separate nations. Considering the vast sums of money which they poured across the Atlantic, the American people were remarkably restrained in the use they made of their economic influence to impose their own particular solution upon Europe, but they did press continually for a hastening of European unity. With a great deal of justice, they looked upon the huge free trade area of their own continental nation, with its unified currency, stable social and political institutions, and great resources, as one of the principal causes of their unequalled economic prosperity. They could not help but feel — and it fitted in well with their deep preconceptions about the virtues of their new world and the vices of the old world which they had shrugged off — that only the senseless national divisions of Europe prevented her from enjoying a magnificent economic resurgence. And this sentiment now found a ready response among a number of great European leaders, whose minds had already begun to move in a similar direction — Spaak of Belgium, De Gasperi of Italy, Adenauer of Germany, and Schuman and Monnet of France.

In May 1950 Robert Schuman, then French Foreign Minister, proposed the setting up of what came to be called a High Authority to control the entire West European production of two basic commodities, coal and steel. This proposal was from the beginning presented as the first step towards a European federation. It marked the real beginning of that Franco-German rapprochement which Churchill had suggested at Zurich and which has been one of the most remarkable developments of the last decade. Inspired though a number of these leaders were by the highest pan-European idealism, other motives were also present. France, conscious of her long-apparent political and economic weakness *vis à vis* Germany (particularly in the event of German reunion) sought to render German strength more amenable by clutching it to her bosom; Germany sought that re-entry into the Western comity of nations which she so much desired by accepting the idea of European union; both peoples honestly sought to avoid a recurrence of their fearful traditional

D

hostility by submerging their separate sovereignties in the unity of a wider body politic.

The first practical move in this direction was this limited proposal for economic unification, which was so strongly supported by the United States. It was at this juncture that the initial challenge was presented to the United Kingdom. The double fact, that it was an economic one and that neither of the great European protagonists had a Socialist Government, may well have been one of the reasons for the cautious, if not suspicious, reaction of the Labour government in Britain, but there is no real evidence that a Conservative government would have acted differently. The French invitation to Britain to take part in the talks on the 'Schuman Plan' made it clear that pre-acceptance of the goals of a supra-national authority and ultimate political union was a condition of participation; the British government, disliking this unusual prior commitment, declined to attend. In her absence the six-nation Coal and Steel Community, consisting of France, Germany, Italy, Holland, Belgium and Luxemburg, came into existence, and began operations in 1953. Britain linked herself to it only, in reality, for consultative purposes. As a result, mistrust of British motives commenced to grow among continental advocates of European unity, even though Britain had always been one of the most active of the 17 members of O.E.E.C.

In 1955 some of these seventeen, which had low tariff barriers, began to feel that O.E.E.C.'s work, in the liberalization of trade through the removal of quotas, did not go far enough, and urged that it should also tackle the lowering of tariffs. But Britain, now under a Tory government, again blew cool, and the Six, determined not to allow the movement towards economic unity to lose its impetus, arranged a meeting of their own ministers at Messina in June 1955, without the other members of O.E.E.C. The Six then set up the 'Spaak committees' to work out plans both for a customs union and for an atomic community. Even as late as the autumn of 1955, however, there seemed some chance that Britain might join in; at the suggestion of France, she consented to send experts to sit with the Spaak committees in Brussels. But when in November work had gone so far that M. Spaak felt impelled to ask for a commitment of some kind from Britain, she decided to withdraw her representatives. This was the moment when all real hope that Britain might join the nascent European union came to an end. In the course of the next year the Six governments began in earnest to negotiate the treaties which were to set up their united economic and atomic organizations — the European Economic Community and Euratom.

These challenges of the growing European union to Great Britain now at last, after more than five years, began to elicit an active response. Peter Thorneycroft at the Board of Trade and Harold Macmillan as Chancellor of the Exchequer showed themselves sensitive to the alterations which, willy nilly, a united Europe might produce in the British way of life and to the risks inherent in the growing division in Europe between the Six and the rest. Accordingly, in July 1956 Britain proposed to the nations of O.E.E.C. the creation of a European 'free trade area', and in September 1956 explained the plan to a Commonwealth finance ministers' meeting and to the public. Now, therefore, two proposals for the promotion of economic unity had been put before the peoples of Europe — that for a 'common market' of, in the first place, the Six powers (France, Germany, Italy, and the Benelux countries) who were already actually operating the Coal and Steel Community, and that for a free trade area of a larger group of the members of O.E.E.C. including, at first, not only the Six, but also in all probability Britain, Austria, Switzerland, Sweden, Norway and Denmark. The British government were at great pains to maintain from the beginning that the Free Trade Area was not regarded by them as an alternative to the Common Market, but rather as a complement to it, which would prevent the disruption of O.E.E.C. and the economic division of Europe into two camps. To many, however, particularly of the 'Europeans' on the continent, the scheme looked like a plot to destroy the Common Market even before it had come into existence.

This belief, that Britain disliked the whole idea of a Common Market, which she herself was not willing to join, because it would place her at a considerable disadvantage in the competition for international markets, and that she therefore desired to prevent its formation without incurring the odium of trying to do so directly and openly, did the British government less than justice. On the other hand, observers were right to suppose that the British proposals did not proceed from a deep conviction of the necessity — let alone a genuine passion — for the creation of a United Europe, similar to that which moved a number of European leaders. The Free Trade Area proposal was a realistic British attempt to prevent the economic division of Europe which the creation of a Common Market of only Six nations was producing and to enable the good work done by O.E.E.C. within the framework of a broader Europe to be continued, by taking particular care of the two main obstacles to closer British association with European economic institutions, the Commonwealth and the British farmer. In its lack of formal regulations and institutions and in its practical flavour, it rather too obviously breathed the pragmatic constitutional atmosphere of Britain; it would have done much to merge the national economies of the larger Europe, but it was too plainly tailored to Britain's peculiar needs to meet with an enthusiastic response, except from some of the smaller nations of Europe which had reservations of their own about the Common Market.

The plans for the Free Trade Area and the Common Market differed in a number of very important respects, but the spirit which each exuded formed an even more striking contrast, demonstrating, indeed, how far Britain's instinctive preconceptions were from those of the great European powers, and particularly France and Germany. Not only was the one vague, permissive and flexible and the other documented, organized and precise, but where Britons thought, naturally enough in the light of their nineteenth-century history, of free trade as their immediate as well as ultimate goal, the European nations thought essentially of a Zollverein, such as that which had laid the foundations of unity in Germany during that same nineteenth century. British attempts to establish any real form of customs union in the British Empire in the past had signally failed: to the European powers, and particularly to France, on the other hand, the idea of free trade not merely lacked appeal but was even actually distasteful. The fundamental approach of the two parties was quite distinct, and so were their proposals.

Both were plans for the abolition, by stages over a period of years, of quota restrictions and customs tariffs between the participating states. The most important difference by far between the two schemes was that *the Common Market would come to be in a specified time a complete customs union or Zollverein, with no restrictions on trade between its members and with a common external tariff wall against all other countries. In the Free Trade Area, on the other hand, while member nations would in due time remove all restrictions against trade with other members, their existing tariffs against third parties, which were not members of the Area, would be retained.* Two other differences were of importance; first, the Free Trade Area, as originally envisaged by Britain, was to apply fully only to industry and was to make special arrangements about agriculture, and, second, the Common Market includes the overseas territories of members, which was not planned in the case of the Free Trade Area. Both, it was recognized, would entail an increasing political co-operation, but it appeared that this would probably be very much more rapid and more complete in the case of the Common Market; in the Free Trade Area, for example, unanimity would be required in the Council of Ministers, so that every member state would have the power of veto.

At the end of 1956 a working party of O.E.E.C., representing all its members, agreed that a Free Trade Area was possible. Thus the two plans were now formally under consideration, and in January 1957 the newly inaugurated Macmillan government proposed immediate negotiations between the Six and the other nations most interested in the Free Trade Area. At the request of M. Spaak, however, Britain agreed to wait until the Common Market treaty— negotiations for which had now reached a decisive stage— was signed; meanwhile, in February, technical discussions on a Free Trade Area arranged by the O.E.E.C. Council, (preliminary it was hoped to the taking of major decisions in July) proved inconclusive. On 25 March 1957 in Rome twin treaties were signed by the Six, setting up a European Economic Community and an atomic community; but Britain again consented, as a demonstration of the fact that her motives in proposing it were not aimed at the destruction of the Common Market, to delay real negotiations for the Free Trade Area until the Rome treaties were ratified by France and Germany, which was done in July 1957.

The British government had by now become aware that these persistent delays were based on outright but covert opposition, particularly among ardent 'Europeans' and in France, to the whole notion of a Free Trade Area, which still appeared to many of these enthusiasts as an effort to dilute the pure milk of the gospel of European unity. Britain therefore considered carefully once more the idea of actually joining Euratom and the Coal and Steel Community, but decided against it and in favour of a really vigorous drive for the Free Trade Area. Under this renewed British pressure the O.E.E.C. Council, of which of course the Six were members, approved in October 1957 the creation of a Free Trade Area in parallel with the Common Market, and set up a committee, under the chairmanship of Reginald Maudling, the British Minister charged with the affair, to open negotiations. At this juncture prospects for a broader framework of European economic unity than that of the Common Market appeared rosier than either before or since, for, once the committee met, the real extent of the obstacles in the path of the creation of the Free Trade Area became fully apparent for the first time.

On 1 January 1958 the Rome treaties went into effect. It then became clear that the institutions of the Common Market and Euratom (to which the governments, in their laudable enthusiasm, had sent many of their ablest men), with their growing, if still limited, power to overrule member states, were fostering still further the already admirable solidarity of the Six, whose eyes appeared fixed on further measures of unification among themselves. To this process, the Free Trade Area seemed to many of them to add nothing. Therefore, during 1958,

'French opposition to the free trade area plan changed from a combination of lip-service with reservations and delaying tactics into a much more explicit resistance. Although much of this opposition arises from sheer protectionism, the painful medicine of the common market, which is already laying France open to foreign competition, has nevertheless been accepted — on political grounds. France's young " Europeans " see European institutions as a means of regenerating both their country's economy and its political life; and the common market has also appealed to them . . . as a means of harnessing German energies to European ends. The free trade area, in contrast, has seemed to them to jeopardise these political aims.

'Thus, behind the French case against the free trade area, which was first expressed in a memorandum to the other members of the Six in March, 1958, there has lain a strange alliance between destructive nationalist protectionism and the forward-looking idea of European unity.'[6]

As the O.E.E.C. committee continued its deliberations during 1958, despite very considerable British concessions to French protectionism, the representatives of the Six, led by France, moved closer and closer to a common position of direct and overt opposition to the realization of the plan for a Free Trade Area. When this became unmistakably clear, the British chairman broke off talks on 15 November 1958.

In effect, any hope of the early creation of a European Free Trade Area was at an end, and many believed that now it would never come into being at all. But the Common Market was in existence already, and on 1 January 1959 — a date of whose vital significance all concerned had been well aware — the actual process of tariff and quota dismantling within the Common Market began. There could be no concealing the fact that this was a resounding defeat for the British proposals for a wider and looser European economic grouping, and a victory for the 'Europeans' who pinned their faith to the narrower, but to them much more practical, and valuable, unity of the Six. To all men everywhere who had feared that the nations of the West, if not of all the world, were incapable of rising above their parochial national prejudices and creating wider unions, the European Economic Community could not but be a cause for rejoicing. Yet because it was also accomplished at the very real cost of splitting Europe into two camps, through economic discrimination by the Six against their fellow members of O.E.E.C. — a broader organization which had already contributed much to the economic development of Europe — that joy was in many cases necessarily mingled with sorrow and apprehension. It was readily understandable that some European, and even American, observers sought to put the blame squarely on the shoulders of the British, who had, by refusing to join the Common Market itself, made the fuller integration of the wider Europe impossible. The position of Britain, however, was far more difficult and complex than was usually realized by outsiders; her real fault, as we shall shortly see, lay, not in her refusal to join the Common Market, but in her lethargic reluctance to go far enough or fast enough in the search for a real solution to her dilemma.

But now, in early 1959, she did begin once more to bestir herself and to put forward further positive proposals. It is true that these proposals, like those for the Free Trade Area itself, were simply reactions to the actions of others, the creators of the Common Market, but at least they came with rapidity and were pressed forward with energy and conviction. Less than a month after the breakdown of negotiations in November 1958, the British government had put forward in O.E.E.C. proposals of a temporary nature to prevent the actual occurrence of discrimination between its members on 1 January 1959, when the first 10 per cent lowering of Common Market internal tariffs took place; and the Six did consent in fact to extend certain liberal measures to O.E.E.C. members and even to all members of G.A.T.T., the much wider International Agreement on Tariffs and Trade. But the French representatives at the O.E.E.C. meeting in France on 15 December, believing in fact that discrimination against European nations who would not join the Common Market, far from being reprehensible, was a necessary means of rewarding its members for the political obligations they had assumed and the economic risks they had run in joining it, refused to accept a further British proposal which would have prevented any discrimination at all between O.E.E.C. members on 1 January. In a heated exchange between Sir David Eccles and M. Couve de Murville, the French representative, Britain bluntly declared that if there was no change in the attitude of the Six, she would take 'defensive measures'.[7] For almost the first time, the passions that bubbled below the crust of Europe's co-operation were plainly audible.

When nothing emerged in the following weeks, except these

temporary accommodations (the French going some way further still to alleviate, but not remove, discrimination) and agreement all round to consider the long-term prospects for a wider European association, the British government put forward publicly at the beginning of May proposals for what came to be known as the Little Free Trade Area, a new grouping of the outer European powers, technically called the European Free Trade Association, which might have some effect in creating new trade between its members and which would certainly make retaliation against the Common Market easier if that came to seem desirable. In other words, Britain intended this as a means of bringing pressure to bear on the Six to take seriously once again the question of their relations with the Western European nations which were not members of their union, and also as an instrument which might be of some economic assistance to its participants in case they were adversely affected by the growing strength of the Common Market. During May and June such progress was made in informal and technical discussions between Britain, Sweden, Switzerland, Austria, Norway, Denmark and Portugal that on 20 July 1959 a meeting of their Ministers gave definite instructions to its experts to draw up a convention. On 20 November the convention was initialled by the Ministers of the Seven; it bound them to a mutual 20 per cent reduction of tariffs (to keep pace with that of the Common Market) on 1 July 1960. The institutions and the broad policy of the new organization seemed likely to follow very closely those proposed for the original Free Trade Area, though with some changes. But essentially it was still an arrangement by which members would enjoy free trade with one another, but would retain their own individual tariffs against the outside world.

Three of the Seven, Britain, Sweden and Switzerland, had always been more enthusiastic for the plan than the others, but they had been able to win them over, including the most serious doubter, Denmark, by concessions such as the important ones made by Britain in agriculture. The speed of their work owed a good deal to the groundwork laid, quite unintentionally of course, by the Scandinavian powers in their thorough but abortive negotiations in the post-war years for a Nordic Customs Union, as well as to those for the European

Free Trade Area. But by any standards it constituted a remarkably rapid diplomatic achievement.

What the long-term effects of this energetic action may be is, of course, highly speculative, and it is by no means clear what its immediate effects will be upon the Common Market countries. There are some signs that it may have surprised them, and even made them more conscious of the need for broadening the basis of their economic association in Europe, quite apart from their renewed assertion — and in this they have always been consistent — that other powers in Europe could, and in the end would, join the full Common Market. There are contrary signs that it may have spurred them on to hasten the integration of the Six. But the signs are not in any case easy to read. Even admitted that in 1958 the 'Europeans' won their great battle and brought the European Economic Community to real life, yet there were those who believed that many difficulties lay ahead for it and who thought that they detected a certain, albeit enforced, tendency among the Six to rest for the present upon their oars. The main French impulse to union had, after all, arisen during the days of the Fourth Republic, and in 1958 De Gaulle came to a plenitude of power. Most of the indications in his history were that, single-minded devotee as he had always been of the unique destiny of France, his ear would not too easily be gained by passionate advocates of European unity, let alone his heart won to a belief in the sovereign remedy of indissoluble union with Germany. But in fact he implemented loyally the economic and institutional commitments undertaken by his predecessors; indeed, he went further, and seemed to form an unexpectedly cordial and close personal relationship with Chancellor Adenauer. But 'Europeans' still wondered, even now, how far he would go beyond the economic steps he had already taken, how far he would ever be prepared for the political integration of the European community which had never ceased to be their ultimate, their final objective.

In some sense the situation may have been saved by the greatest 'European' of them all, Adenauer himself, for whom the winning of De Gaulle had many of the aspects of a great personal triumph. But even here there were problems, for it became clear in the course of 1959 that there were real differences of emphasis, in their attitudes towards European unity, between Adenauer and the man who had generally come to be recognized as his heir apparent, Dr. Erhard. This situation was dramatically emphasized by the Chancellor's sudden and unexpected retraction during the course of the year of his decision to accept the German Presidency in place of the influential Chancellorship, apparently in his uneasiness as to whether his successor would be 'sound' enough on European unity. In fact Adenauer's motives for cleaving to the idea of European unity were almost entirely political, and he was anxious to press Germany's partners, and particularly France, onwards to full political union. Erhard, on the other hand, with his triumphant economic *expertise* was much more sensitive to the British economic arguments in favour of a wider European economic association; this great advocate of free enterprise, more perhaps than any other leading continental figure, was capable of being drawn to the idea of a Free Trade Area in which the size and efficiency of German industry would reap its fullest reward. For the moment Dr. Adenauer, with his accustomed political mastery, remained in power, but even he is mortal, and Dr. Erhard is still very much alive.

These were only the most dramatic of the internal tensions within the Common Market, and there were others, as for instance the constant struggle between little low tariff Holland at one end and highly protectionist France at the other. Whatever their effect, some evidence did appear that the Six, and even France herself, were aware of the gravity of the European split. In bilateral talks between France and Britain in the summer, necessitated by the refusal of France to accept the original British proposals to prevent intra-European discrimination on the previous January 1, the French seemed to be going out of their way to be conciliatory. More important in a sense, the Commission of the European Economic Community submitted to its member governments at the end of September 1959 concrete proposals for the reduction of tariff barriers against other countries. If—and it is an important if—the governments concerned, and particularly France, react favourably to them they may, in the words of the Chairman of the Commission, Professor

Hallstein, 'without compromising the positions of principle'[8] of the Common Market materially ease the problem of association between the Six and the Seven. On 24 November the Six decided to give other Western nations on 1 January 1960 the benefit of the import quota liberalization due within the Common Market on that date.

Yet these were diplomatic signs, which could be seriously misleading, whereas the fact was that, with the steady consolidation of the institutions of the Six, an increasing number of vested interests, mergers, consortiums, and perhaps cartels, were being created, which favoured the continued existence, without fundamental changes, of the Common Market. The vital significance of this division of Europe brought about by the union of the Six is shown by the increasing tendency of European powers which are neither of the Six nor of the Seven to feel forced to commit themselves to one side or the other. Already there has been a natural attraction between the Seven and those comets of the Scandinavian system, Finland and Iceland; on the other hand Greece and Turkey have got as far as concrete negotiations with the Six. Though Ireland still tries to keep a foot in both doors, even Spain, long the pariah of Europe, felt impelled to declare in August that, when her stabilization plan had taken effect, she would consider the advisability of joining one or the other. Furthermore, the fact that G.A.T.T., to which all the powers concerned are parties, allows only customs unions and free trade areas, but not 'preferential zones', prevents at the moment the creation of special relationships for any of these states with either the Six or the Seven. These might have been desirable in the case of countries which are much less wealthy than the rest. This situation strengthens still further the tendency to polarization and clear-cut division between the two groups in Europe.

This increasingly deep cleavage may yet be prevented from growing worse, and it may even be bridged, as Britain with the Seven has from the beginning hoped and proclaimed that she hoped. But it is the most unhappy result of the otherwise admirable creation of two new economic supra-national groupings in Europe. And this profoundly important division of Europe is certainly epitomized in, and was to a considerable extent the result of, the refusal of the United Kingdom to enter the European Community with the Six. A recent student of the European Free Trade Association[9] envisages the ultimate possibility of a free trade or partial free trade area, embracing both the Six and the Seven, but with each bloc working as an independent group. But whether such is the outcome or not, she concludes, perhaps with great prescience, that recent developments may be most important to historians because they marked the point at which it became increasingly difficult for Britain to forge any *political* relationship of an integral kind with Europe, even should she desire to do so. And in a very real sense it was the refusal of Britain, first under Labour and later under the Conservatives, to enter the Coal and Steel Community, and then Euratom and the Common Market, which divided Europe against itself.

Why did she refuse to enter a European economic union, and how far did her real interests justify that refusal? There were two main reasons for it, apart from a general conservatism and the Socialist fear during their years in office that intimate economic association with a largely free enterprise Europe would undermine and frustrate their programme in Britain. These two reasons are illustrated by the nature of the proposed Free Trade Area itself. The first and much less important was concern for the special position of the British farmer, who is on the whole much richer and much more productive than his peasant counterpart in Europe. Yet, because there are so few farmers, relatively speaking, in this 80·8 per cent urban country, the British farmer is politically in many respects weaker than his European opposite number. The concern of politicians to safeguard this special interest in Britain is not purely a result of its votes, but is connected with the long — and in the first years of this century far from happy — history of British agriculture, which languished under the competition of the outside world in free trade Britain. The two world wars, however, clearly demonstrated (though the lesson was not well learnt in the first one) how desperately important strategically a flourishing British agriculture could be, and post-war governments have done a great deal to preserve, largely at the present time by a policy of subsidy, the strength of the British farmer. As a result,

Britain now produces a much higher proportion of her own food than before the war — approximately 50 per cent rather than something nearer to 40 per cent. Thus the British government's concern to protect the farmer in the United Kingdom is by no means unconnected with that extraordinary dependence of Britain upon trade with the outside world which we have already observed.

Nevertheless, as subsequent negotiations between Britain and Denmark over the Little Free Trade Area have shown, the special position of British agriculture (which was one of the reasons for its complete exclusion, later substantially modified, from Britain's original proposal for a Free Trade Area) was not likely indefinitely to have prevented Britain from entering a European economic union if it had seemed desirable for her to do so. Even if no satisfactory compromise could be found and it proved impossible in any way to compensate the farmers, it is very doubtful if they would have had the political influence at their command to prevent the government from adhering to the new European economic grouping.

The second reason advanced by Britain's government for her refusal to enter the Common Market was not unconnected with this but was very much more important — it was Britain's special relations with the Commonwealth. This long-standing and still very important British economic association, which has had a preferential protective character since the Ottawa agreements in 1932, was partly responsible not merely for the exclusion of agriculture from the proposed Free Trade Area but also for the whole basic idea that each country in it would retain its own tariff wall against non-members of the area. Britain would thus be able to maintain her large preferential imports of primary products from the Commonwealth and her corresponding exports of manufactured goods thereto. In this way the British government, believing that the task of marrying so diverse a structure as the Commonwealth and Empire to the European Economic Community (as France had done in the Common Market by gaining initial support for the idea of 'Eurafrica') would prove far too complex and difficult, hoped to preserve her special economic relationships with the Commonwealth, while associating herself in a real way with Europe, by putting forward the idea of the Free

Trade Area. To 'Europeans' this seemed a not uncharacteristic example of Britain's desire to have the best of both worlds: to enjoy the fruits of a large market for the products of her powerful industry without running any corresponding risk to her agriculture, and to gain the benefits of close economic association with Europe without either losing that with her Empire or giving Europe any chance to benefit from its existence. Many critics regarded the British plea of the existence of special economic bonds with the Commonwealth as a mere pretext for inaction and even as a conspiracy to destroy the embryo of European unity.

Some colour did seem to be given to this view by the subsequent attitude of certain Commonwealth countries and by the fact that the most important of these, economically, to Britain, such as Australia and New Zealand, were industrializing fast. Thus one could envisage a time, in a dozen years or so (and the Common Market itself was scheduled to come into existence only by slow stages over 12 years), when their desire to continue the preference they now give to British manufactured goods might well have diminished or disappeared altogether. Furthermore, these countries might in any case be agreeable to immediate arrangements by which they gained access freely for their agricultural produce to the great Common Market, with the members of which, for example, New Zealand already had a thriving trade, even at the cost of losing their special position in the United Kingdom market. Thus during 1959 the New Zealand government, and somewhat more cautiously the Australian government, appeared to be pressing Britain towards a reopening of negotiations with the European Economic Community. The theoretical, as well as practical, arguments for this also seemed apparent to many, and the unofficial Commonwealth Conference held under the auspices of the Royal Institute of International Affairs in 1959 unanimously recommended a renewed British approach to the Common Market countries.

But in considering how far Britain's plea of special ties with the Commonwealth justified her in refusing to enter the Common Market there is no substitute for the figures. We have already noted when discussing Britain's dependence on foreign trade that as an importer and exporter she is only surpassed, among the nations of the whole world, by the United States. But it is necessary to emphasize here how very large the foreign trade of Britain is, relative to her size, resources and population. In 1957 her total foreign trade, exports *plus* imports, was greater than that of any power except the United States, totalling $20,348,000,000 compared with an American figure of $33,721,000,000. The population of the United States is, of course, three times as big. The next largest was West Germany which, with an approximately equal population, had a total of $16,074,000,000 of foreign trade,[10] or 20 per cent less than that of the United Kingdom.

But it is the distribution of Britain's foreign trade — so much more vital is it to her than to any other country — which is important to us here. We have seen clearly enough the ancient link between Britain's commerce and her Empire, and the marked tendency of her trade with Europe to decrease in favour of trade with her Empire in America in the eighteenth century. Despite the loss of the American colonies, it has been estimated that the Empire still absorbed between 25 and 30 per cent of Britain's exports during the first half of the nineteenth century,[11] while the figures of British exports sent to Europe sank from 55·2 per cent in 1801 to 39·4 per cent in 1854. In this latter year, the first for which we have comprehensive figures, the British Empire took 34·8 per cent by value of British exports, and provided 22·4 per cent of Britain's imports, and this was five years after the repeal of the Navigation Acts, the centrepiece of imperial trade protection. In the same year the United Kingdom sent 39·4 per cent of her exports to Europe and received 42·3 per cent of her imports therefrom.

During the next sixty years, until World War I, even with Britain in the full flood of free trade, her proportion of commerce with the Empire remained relatively stable, although her trade with Europe (particularly her exports thereto) diminished somewhat and her trade with the Americas more markedly, while her commerce with those parts of the other continents which were not in the Empire became steadily more important. In the period 1909-13 the Empire provided 24·7 per cent of the imports of the United Kingdom, and took 35·4 per cent of her exports. Over the same years,

1909-13, the continental distribution of Britain's trade was as follows (percentage of actual values).

	Imports	Exports
Europe	40.8	35.3
America	32.3	23.5
Africa	6.4	10.1
Asia	12.4	22.3
Australia	8.1	8.8[12]

But after this date a much more pronounced change set in, for Britain's trade with the Empire steadily, and after the Great Depression and the coming of Imperial Preference in 1932 sharply, increased. Thus the figures for the trade of the United Kingdom (that is to say, Great Britain and Ireland, the area of 1801-1923) with the Empire were as follows:

(Percentage of Total Trade)

1914-18	29.6 per cent
1919-26	30.7 "
1927-29	31.6 "
1930-32	30.8 "
1933-35	37.2 "

There was a greater increase in the proportion of her imports from the Empire than of her exports to it. By contrast, Europe's share of the exports of Great Britain and Ireland in the years 1927-29 was down to 35.6 per cent, and that of her imports stood at 37 per cent, while in 1936 the former figure was virtually unchanged at 35.8 per cent but the latter had sunk somewhat to 34.3 per cent. Thus, very approximately, before World War II one-third of the trade of the United Kingdom was with Europe, a little over a third was with the Empire, and something under a third was with the rest of the world. And by 1949-50 the trend had gone much further, encouraged by the distortion of war-time trade with Europe, which was for so long largely isolated from the outside world, for the percentage of Britain's exports was as follows: to the Overseas Sterling Area, most of it in the Empire and Commonwealth, 48 per cent; to Canada, 5 per cent; to O.E.E.C. countries, 24 per cent. That of her imports was as follows: from the Sterling Area, 37 per cent; from Canada, 9 per cent; from O.E.E.C. countries, 21 per cent.

In reality, it is the proportion of Britain's commerce which

E

is with Europe, contrasted with that which is with the non-European world, which is most significant for us here, although something like a half of this remainder may be with the Commonwealth. As we have observed, it is the extraordinary world-wide spread of British trade which is unique, so that in 1952 no single one of the great regional markets cited by Woytinsky accounts for as much as one-fourth of her foreign trade.[13] Thus in this same year, if we exclude that part of Europe which was under the domination of the U.S.S.R., the two great European markets, the Northwestern and the Southern, account for 24 per cent and 6 per cent respectively of the exports of the United Kingdom and 23 per cent and 3 per cent of her imports. *In other words, in 1952 when the first stage towards European economic unity, the Coal and Steel Community, was just being reached, but four years after O.E.E.C. had come into being to stimulate the revival of European commerce, the total trade of the United Kingdom of Great Britain and Northern Ireland with free Europe was only 28 per cent of her whole commerce.* This compares with 22½ per cent with the Western Hemisphere, 4½ per cent with Eastern Europe and the U.S.S.R., 7½ per cent with the Middle East, 12 per cent with the rest of Asia, 13½ per cent with the rest of Africa, and 12 per cent with Oceania — a balance of 72 per cent.

Here is graphic evidence indeed that the United Kingdom could again, as she has before, live cut off entirely from trade with Europe, but that she can never survive without commerce with the outer world. By way of comparison with the 23½ per cent of Britain's trade (exports *plus* imports) that was with Northwestern Europe at this time, the proportion of Belgium-Luxemburg trade with the same area was 53 per cent and of Dutch trade 55 per cent, while that of Western Germany was not far short of a half. Even the proportions of Italian and French trade with Northwestern Europe were not, respectively, much above or much below a third of the whole. *Finally, and perhaps most conclusive, in 1958 only 14 per cent of the trade of the United Kingdom was with the Six countries of the Common Market, whereas, even with the much smaller nations of the ' Outer Seven ', the figure was 10 per cent.*[14]

Over the last three centuries, therefore, the proportion of Britain's trade which has been with Europe has, broadly speaking, declined, while that with the rest of the world, and particularly with the Empire in the eighteenth and early twentieth centuries, has greatly increased. Even during the heyday of free trade (which Adam Smith himself expected greatly to augment the proportion of European — 'short-haul' — trade) this trend was not reversed. It does not logically follow from this that the proportion of Britain's trade which is with Europe must necessarily continue to diminish, or even to remain unchanged; to some extent the increases in Commonwealth trade in the thirties of this century were the result of the special protective measures inaugurated in 1931, although the trend was noticeable before the return of protection. We must certainly not underestimate the effect of political actions in altering the channels of trade, but the political effects of the strict enforcement of Mercantilist legislation in the years leading up to the American Revolution were not such as to encourage Britons to undertake fundamental efforts to change the whole course of their national commerce for purely economic reasons — unless these are of a perfectly overwhelming urgency — until they are quite clear in their minds as to what the ultimate political as well as economic consequences of these efforts are likely to be.

For, all in all, the far-flung nature of British commerce, whatever its particular disadvantages for her, has not only been of great benefit to herself but also to mankind as a whole, for it constitutes the prototype, it demonstrates the pattern, of that expanding international trade which all wise students of our interdependent world — and even all economists — agree to be essential to human welfare. The whole magnificent history of the rise of material standards of living in the Western world in the last four centuries is intimately bound up with the ever widening limits of international trade. The great British free trade experiment of the nineteenth century was nothing of which to be ashamed; all the complex and increasingly bureaucratic present-day apparatus of political protection of trade and industry has its place in our world no doubt, but we must never allow ourselves to forget that, all things being equal, increasing, and increasingly general, free trade is still the condition under which the human economy will expand most rapidly. All substitutes for freedom in trade, however necessary they may be, are, in ideal circumstances, inferior as well as substitutes.

On purely economic grounds, Britons may justifiably be reluctant to enter a group of only Six nations in Europe, with whom at present they carry on only one-seventh of all their trade, and in which they would lose a substantial measure of their control over their own economic destiny; on purely economic grounds, they may justly claim that the Six should consider with much more sincerity than they have so far done the advisability and wisdom of forming some much wider economic association. On purely economic grounds also, he would be an inaccurate man who declared that Britain's hesitations about joining the European Common Market, because of her special and vital commercial ties with the Commonwealth and extra-European world, had no real justification; on purely economic grounds, he would be a rash man who would advocate that Britain unconditionally join the Common Market now, without the fullest exploration of every possible alternative.

NOTES

[1] Randolph S. Churchill (Ed.), *The Sinews of Peace, Post-War Speeches by Winston S. Churchill*, Boston 1948, pp. 198-9.

[2] *Ibid.*, p. 201.

[3] John C. Campbell, *The United States in World Affairs, 1947-1948*, New York 1948, p. 52.

[4] Raymond Dennett and Robert K. Turner (Eds.), *Documents on American Foreign Relations, Vol. IX*, 1947, Princeton 1949, pp. 10-11.

[5] Campbell, *op. cit.*, p. 418.

[6] *The Economist*, 10 January 1959, "The European Rift", p. 134. I am in debt to the whole of this article for much of the material in this section of the book.

[7] *The Economist*, 20 December 1958, p. 1089.

[8] *The Economist*, 3 October 1959, p. 70.

[9] Miriam Camps, *The European Free Trade Association*, London 1959.

[10] See also Chapter VI below.

[11] Schlote, *op. cit.*, pp. 79-80, 88-94, 156-163.

[12] It has been necessary here to amend certain of Schlote's figures which appear to be self-contradictory.

[13] *World Commerce and Governments*, p. 105.

[14] *The Economist*, 30 May 1959, p. 867.

CHAPTER III

European Political Unity

W AS it, however, on purely economic grounds that Britain decided not to throw in her lot with the Common Market, or Euratom, or the Coal and Steel Community? The answer is, ' No '. Behind all the proposals for economic unity, there lay always the openly avowed intention of the 'Europeans' to move on, as soon as might be, towards political unification. Indeed, the curious manner in which the negotiations for the first positive economic step, the Schuman Plan of 1950, were launched rendered this abundantly clear, with the invitation of the French government to participate in the talks making the unusual request that the governments concerned should immediately indicate their general acceptance of the principles of the plan, including the establishment of a High Authority with power to make binding decisions. It may have been the fear of a supranational authority's absolute control over two of Britain's key industries which was uppermost in the mind of the Labour government at this time, but their refusal was certainly also influenced by apprehension about the as yet vague foreshadowing of similar institutions in the political sphere. When the most crucial decision had to be made by Britain, that concerning entry to the Common Market, it was made by a Conservative government. Once more it was the request that Britain should give some firm undertaking about the long-term purpose of the discussions which led to the withdrawal of the British representatives, and in effect to Britain's decision not to enter the Common Market. Because in fact these, and other similar decisions, were ostensibly merely decisions on whether or not to negotiate — that is to say procedural decisions, and not fundamental decisions on whether or not Britain would participate in the European institutions — the precise reasons which at bottom have moved the British governments have never been fully and clearly stated.

This disinclination to go to the roots of the matter and if necessary to proclaim unpleasant facts openly was not an isolated occurrence. Reluctance to state hard truths of this kind without ambiguity and without understatement amounts in the British to a habitual vice; it is the national character, almost, by now to speak in what *The Economist* once called a 'muffled' voice, to avoid giving offence by not telling the whole truth, to leave underlying meanings to the unaided and instinctive comprehension of those concerned, to trust that unpleasantness may thus be avoided, and even to hope that the need for positive, far-reaching and disturbing action may disappear altogether in the onward surge of events. In foreign affairs this course can very easily be defended on the grounds that it is 'diplomatic', but it can also very easily do profound harm, because usually, such is the way of the world, 'foreigners' do not easily grasp the subtle implications of the actions of other 'foreign' nations. Without doubt the reputation for hypocrisy so long borne by Perfidious Albion owes much to this habit of mind. Thus the ostensible reasons given by Britain's governments (where given outright at all) for her refusal to adhere to the institutions of the Six have almost always been economic — principally the extent of her overseas trade, particularly with the Commonwealth. But there can be little doubt that much more important, if much less formed, has been her deep mistrust of being in effect committed to the loss of her national political sovereignty, her nearly millennial tradition of political independence.

That there were political implications in all the moves for economic unity, and that fear of political commitment was a powerful motive for their rejection in both Labour and Tory governments is abundantly demonstrated by the course of events, for it was not in fact in the economic but in the political sphere that the first actual moves towards Europe's unity were made. In fact, at each stage, economic proposals were made only when no advance was possible, or even when outright retreat had been necessary, on the political front.

It was to the political fears and aspirations of Europe that, characteristically, Mr. Churchill had first appealed in 1946, and the earliest plans put forward by the advocates of European unity were those, aimed by their extreme proponents at the ultimate creation of a 'United States of Europe', which resulted in the signature of the Statute of the Council of Europe, on 5 May, 1949, by Belgium, Denmark, France, Ireland, Italy, Luxemburg, The Netherlands, Norway, Sweden, and the United Kingdom. But, though Britain signed this instrument, a divergence of views between herself (supported in large degree by the Scandinavian countries) and some of the other continental nations became clearly apparent, for she now first aroused the suspicions of the ardent 'Europeans' by working resolutely to keep the new institutions under tight national governmental control. In this she was successful, for the Committee of Ministers, who were delegates of their national governments, was bound to unanimity on all major decisions, while the Consultative Assembly, which some had hoped would be an epoch-making constituent assembly, or constitutional convention of the American type, was strictly limited to the function of debating and making recommendations to the Committee of Ministers. Thus, though a number of interesting ideas had their public origin in the Council of Europe in the years to come, the British Labour government had effectively strangled this direct attempt at European political unity at birth.

'Europeans', however, did not yet despair of the British, for even though their next and much more successful advance — the Coal and Steel Community — was not joined by the British government, the Leader of His Majesty's Opposition was still in the forefront of the movement for European unity. (Many people, indeed, perhaps mistakenly, thought that one of the main reasons why Labour blew so cold was that Churchill blew so hot.) In truth it was he who, harking back to his original thesis that European unity must be built on a Franco-German *rapprochement*, first put forward in the Assembly of the Council of Europe in August, 1950, the idea of the creation of a joint European army, as the only satisfactory path, in view of French mistrust of Germany, to German rearmament, now so necessary in the face of the Russian menace. It was even his son-in-law, Mr. Duncan Sandys, who drafted the first plan for it. From this arose the

projected European Defence Community with its integrated
European army, which was the embodiment of the second and
very formidable drive of the 'Europeans' towards the political
unity of Europe, designed to follow up on the political front
the remarkable success of the Schuman Plan on the economic.
When Mr. Churchill returned to office in October, 1951,
hopes were high among the 'Europeans' that Britain would
unreservedly join E.D.C., and they were correspondingly
disillusioned and angry when, within a few months, the
British Tory government intimated that she would not enter
the nascent European union.

The 'Europeans' had allowed themselves to be too
sanguine, for, although his free use of the editorial 'we' in
this context had always been confusing, Mr. Churchill had
clearly implied in the last sentence of his original Zurich
address that Britain would support European unity—but
not for herself. Perhaps, with the freedom of a statesman in
Opposition, he may subsequently have allowed himself
seriously to consider British participation, but a very short
period back in office with a Cabinet of Conservative politicians was quite sufficient to make its political impossibility
clear to him. Nor can the British refusal to join E.D.C. be
ascribed merely to a recrudescence of British isolationism, to
a revulsion from any international responsibilities whatever
on the European mainland, for Britain (in one of the few
veins of genuine spontaneous initiative she has shown in the
whole of her post-war relations with Europe) had taken the
lead in the foundation of the two basic Western alliances of
the post-war world, the Brussels Pact of March, 1948, and
the much more important North Atlantic Treaty, bringing
N.A.T.O into existence, which was formally proclaimed on
24 August, 1949. Clearly, what Britain feared here, though
once again it never seems to have been clearly enunciated,
was the political commitment involved in E.D.C. This was
spelled out with the utmost clarity in the first article of the
Treaty, which called for 'a European Defence Community,
supra-national in character, consisting of common institutions,
common armed Forces and a common budget'.[1] There is no
real doubt that here we have struck the rock on which all
plans, whether large or small, to gain the adhesion of the

United Kingdom to European institutions were to founder — her fundamental fear of submerging her national sovereignty in a European political union.

This was forcibly illustrated by her immediate and energetic actions when (basically because she herself had refused to join it) the E.D.C. Treaty was in effect rejected by the French National Assembly on 30 August, 1954, thus putting in jeopardy the essential West German military contribution to the defence of Europe. Here was a traditional international problem, one that could be dealt with in the conventional way which Britain liked and to which she was accustomed. On the swift initiative of Foreign Secretary Anthony Eden, a treaty was negotiated providing for the rearmament of Western Germany and for her entry into N.A.T.O.; in it Britain bound herself to maintain a substantial body of troops upon the European mainland, thus providing a counter-balance, of which the French were naturally very desirous, to the new armed forces of Germany. Since Britain had never before undertaken such a specific long-term commitment, this was hailed as a great concession on her part, but in fact it was a practical, limited and not totally irreversible step of a kind which carried no risk whatever for Britain's cherished freedom of national action. As a result she was content to undertake it.

But to the devoted 'Europeans' this orthodox alliance of sovereign states seemed a shoddy edifice indeed to have erected on the noble ruins of European unity, even though it was grandiosely, and somewhat absurdly, called Western European Union. (In this they were right, for it remained in fact largely moribund until, six years later, Britain characteristically suggested that it should — since it consists of the Six *plus* the United Kingdom — be used to ensure regular political consultation between herself and the continental powers. Britain became increasingly sensitive on this score as France in 1959 made efforts, as yet not very successful, to take the first steps towards political unification of the Six.) When, however, *reculer pour mieux sauter* after their defeat on E.D.C., the leaders of the movement for a real European union turned their attention once more to the area of their one great success, economics, and set in train in 1955 the proposals for the Common Market, they were no longer in any mood to consider very tenderly the sensibilities of Britain, nor to pretend that they did not regard their economic proposals as merely the groundwork on which their political dream of true European unity might, one day in the not too far distant future, be realized.

It is against this political background that the present situation of the Common Market and the proposed Little Free Trade Area, as well as the actions of Britain which have led up to it, must be judged. The British people must be aware, as their governments have shown themselves to be, that behind the specific commitments of an economic character which would be demanded of her in the European Economic Community there lies in fact a general commitment to ultimate European political union. They must not imagine that they would be taking a purely economic step, if, for the sake of argument, they joined the Common Market. Quite apart from the avowed intentions of the powerful 'European' group, whose strength is likely to grow by what it feeds on as European institutions take root, it would be very misguided to assume that even strictly limited economic commitments to Europe could be undertaken without any risk to Britain's political, as well as economic, ties with other parts of the world.

The history of the Mercantilist era, when, for more than two centuries, the growth of the British Empire (and of all the other European empires) was directed, controlled and encouraged by national political legislation, affords us ample evidence of the extent to which economic and political developments are inextricably interdependent. The great switch in British commerce, which we have observed, from European to American trade in the eighteenth century, was in large degree the direct result of political regulations devised to increase the trade of the United Kingdom with her imperial possessions. That without those regulations this development would have been vastly slower, and perhaps very different, is the whole theme of that first, and perhaps greatest, of economic treatises, Adam Smith's *Wealth of Nations*. But once such a new pattern of trade is created, huge economic vested interests come into being which make it a task of immense difficulty to alter and reshape the design once again. It was in this fashion that the German Zollverein in 1833 prepared the way for the political unity of Germany. If, by deliberate political action now, Britain binds herself, by special, and in some senses exclusive, economic arrangements, to the Six nations of the Common Market, she is likely, slowly perhaps at first, but very surely, to divert the currents of her commerce towards Europe and away from the rest of the world. In so doing she will create a thousand economic bonds with Europe which may in the future limit her national freedom of political action almost as surely as if she joined an outright political union. She is likely, by a process of symbiosis, to 'grow into' the European community in the same way that she 'grew into' the life of her Empire in the eighteenth century.

This may or may not be a good thing in itself, but what Britons must avoid above all else at this juncture — and their governments have acted wisely in this respect in this last decade (although they have perhaps failed to show the same wisdom in not explaining fully to their people the fundamental reason for their actions) — is the illusion that to join an economic organization of the type of the Common Market (and even, it could possibly be — if the greatest care is not taken — one as loosely organized and pragmatically conceived as the Free Trade Area) would involve purely economic commitments. From such an economic decision, political consequences would follow, as certainly as the night follows the day.

Britain therefore must at all costs be sure that she is ready to accept the *political* consequences of entering a European *economic* union before she takes irrevocable steps to do so.[2]

NOTES

[1] Richard P. Stebbins, *The United States in World Affairs*, New York 1952, p. 159.

[2] In April 1960 with the Hallstein Plan the Six seem to be reacting very strongly to the formation of the Seven, by rapidly accelerating their economic unification, but to be moving much less decisively towards political unity.

CHAPTER IV

Great Britain and European Union

T HE British people, then, must face and answer the question, 'Shall we join a European political federation?' For them, as for any self-governing people, this is not merely a question of the size, geography and constituent elements of the proposed union, of whether their interests are sufficiently close to and have sufficient in common with those of its other members, it is also — and perhaps this is even more important — a question of the type of government which the federation is likely to have.

Our world is one riven in two by the struggle — vastly more important than the internecine divisions in the West itself — between our way of life and that of Communism, between freedom and arbitrary rule. We are still prepared to go to battle for that freedom: the time has not yet come when we feel that we must accept, in the name of peace, the threatened domination of some supra-national government, whatever the cost to our liberties may be. It is by no means certain that this time is as remote as many in the West (at least affect to) believe. The terrors of war are now so frightful that the moment may not be so very distant when the wise, the only, course for men will be to accept the tyrannical rule of an alien power rather than expose themselves to the risk of universal destruction. It could be that, sooner than we think, Gandhi's doctrine of *satyagraha*, of passive resistance, will have to be accepted by all intelligent peoples as the only reasonable method of struggling against an invader who is prepared to use not only nuclear but also chemical and biological weapons. In an unlimited nuclear war it is, after all, not just the end of civilization that might come, but more precisely the end of the race, the termination of the species. It cannot be the path of good sense to bring mankind's history to a close in mass suicide: better, it may one day be argued, in the face of such a contingency to accept the iron rule, perhaps of Communism, and trust to the long passage of time, to the infinitely subtle and complex processes of history, to the manifold possibilities of the human future, for an ultimate restoration of those values of truth and freedom which we hold so dear.

It is fervently to be hoped that this day will never come; that so fearful a decision as that to abandon all our noblest aspirations may never fall to our lot. Certain it is that the time for such a resolve is not now come; we are not yet so convinced, either of the inevitable outbreak of war if we firmly stand our ground, or of the use of the ultimate weapons if it should come, that we are not still prepared to fight, even unto death, for the free institutions under which we live. But the liberties of Englishmen may be threatened from other quarters than international Communism, as they have been by three different powers seeking on separate occasions in the course of the last four centuries to dominate Europe by armed force. Nor do threats to human liberty come only in the accoutrements of war; they may be quite as grave in the insidious panoply of peace. If Britain is still prepared to go to war to preserve her liberties, she must equally be on her guard against their peaceful and gradual subversion. If she is to enter a European political union she is vitally, profoundly, interested in the kind of political society it will be. She must, in brief and blunt terms, be assured before she does so that the union will have a very good chance of being a stable, working democracy.

England was, after all, the most important single source of that constitutional freedom and self-rule which is the supreme political contribution of the West to the progress of mankind. The system of political self-government which she slowly and painfully evolved, in the Middle Ages and in the sixteenth and seventeenth centuries, was the principal model and inspiration for the development of modern democracy throughout the world. The rights that the American people so properly extracted from a temporarily decadent British government in the War of American Independence they had learned to cherish because they were derived from the British people; the political thinkers who prepared the way for the

French Revolution owed much of their inspiration to the English example. Britain herself in the nineteenth century was slower to adopt full democracy than the United States, but by the twentieth she had come to stand side by side with her great sister nation across the Atlantic in her dedication to the cause of free and democratic self-government. Despite many vicissitudes, England has enjoyed at least some rudiments of constitutional government for more than six centuries and a fairly full measure of liberty and self-rule for almost three of them; during the latter period her orderly processes of national public debate and decision have scarcely once been rudely broken by the successful illegal application of force. Whatever the many failings of her social and political system, Britain has long enjoyed a tradition of practical intellectual freedom, and of stability in self-government essentially unrivalled in the world.

Therefore, before Britain enters an irrevocable European union, her people must be as sure as is humanly possible, not merely that her new bonds will not entail the severance of other and to her more life-giving ties, but also that the essential elements of her hard-won democratic way of life will be safe in her new circumstances. But to attempt, as we here must, to lift aside, even for a dim moment, the veil of the future is a task of sisyphean difficulty: one can but clumsily calculate on certain lines of probable development. Nothing in the pages which follow can be more than a groping effort to guess what threats certain facts may imply to the British people's mode of living should they definitely pledge themselves to European unity. On the other hand, just because it is so difficult to discern even the main trends of the future with any clarity, those who attempt to do so must not surrender themselves to vague and Delphic warnings, nor hesitate, from fear of making mistakes, to examine the issues in as concrete a way as possible. Up to now far too much discussion of the implications of European political unity has been theoretical and evasive.

Let us, therefore, look for a moment at the actual size of the European national populations with which the British people would be so intimately associated in the processes of self-government. (These figures are very nearly as good for our purpose as the figures of national political electorates, which are much more difficult to obtain and even more difficult to compare.) To do so does not imply that a European federation would instantly become what the spokesmen of the South in the American War Between the States called a 'government of the mass', a unicellular body politic proceeding by unified representation or plebiscites of the whole. In fact, of course, federalism can give a very great degree of protection to regional differences. But, as that same American Civil War itself illustrated at a fearful cost, on certain fundamental questions in any federal union the will of the popular majority must prevail. In any effort to create among the longstanding and deep national divisions of Europe a real and lasting union, it will be necessary from the first to make absolute and absolutely clear the ultimate control of the federal government over the constituent states of the union, and that government must be popularly elected throughout the whole. (Since the plebiscite is a frequent European device in politics, it might even be that a union might have to be ratified by a Europe-wide popular referendum.) It would be far too dangerous in a united Europe to encourage loose talk such as is still possible in the United States about the 'sovereign states of the union', lest it relapse once more into an anarchy of sovereign nations.

In such circumstances, we cannot afford to neglect, as has largely been done in discussion of European unity heretofore, the facts and figures concerning the peoples who would compose the body politic of a European union. First, then, let us consider the position if Britain entered a union composed of the present six countries of the European Economic Community. Their populations are as follows: [1]

West Germany	51,469,000
The United Kingdom	51,455,000
Italy	48,483,000
France	44,091,000
The Netherlands	11,021,000
Belgium	8,989,000
Luxemburg	316,000

This is the population of such a union, grouped by nationalities, but there is, of course, no certainty by any means that voting on great issues within such supra-national organizations as we are now considering would follow strictly national lines: it would be greatly to be hoped that it would not, but rather that, as happened after the inauguration of the Constitution of the United States in 1789, great federal political parties would come into existence, binding the whole political super-structure together in an increasing unity. But, as European commentators have long noted, national divisions in Europe are far more ancient and far more fundamental than, in most respects, those between the American states ever were. There would be a good chance that for many years the national groups within a European union would vote together with some solidarity on major issues.

The significance of an analysis by national populations, however, goes further than this, for, despite obviously wide infra-national variations, the mass of the people of a given nation, long nurtured in the same society and under the same government, will be at much the same level of political experience and education, and hence of practical political capacity. A nation with an unhappy record of government arbitrariness or incompetence, or with little experience of democratic procedures, may, very crudely, be assessed as a unit in the matter of political competence. It is in this light that Britain must consider the figures just quoted. This process of consideration, which here follows, will not be a painless one, for candour is essential to it; here, in a consideration of the political abilities of the peoples of Europe, of their probable capacity to perform successfully the formidable and complex task of creating and operating a new stable and democratic body politic, we have reached the very kernel of those largely unspoken fears of the British people and their leaders, those fears which have at bottom inhibited them from unreservedly adhering to the common institutions of a Europe pledged to the creation of a political union. It is understandable that diplomatic discretion should on this issue have restrained the tongues of those in Britain bearing political responsibility; it might not be wise for her statesmen to speak their minds freely and publicly on the political competence of her neighbour nations. But the individual Briton must not withhold his comments, provided only that they are sincere and not malicious; he has indeed, if he has given any mature consideration to the matter, a positive duty to speak out, arrogant and pharisaical though his conclusions may at first sight seem.

The union which we have envisaged would have a total population of 215,824,000. Of this total just under a quarter only would be British, so that on any issue about which the continental nations were united against her Britain would be hopelessly outnumbered. Even if she found herself in alignment with the small Benelux powers, they would not between them muster even one-third of the whole population. It is true that protection might be given to member states through representation by nations as units in an Upper House, similar to the Senate of the United States, while a Lower House alone had representation in proportion to population — in which case Britain and the three small powers might outvote the other three provided they stuck together — but it is hard, in view of the depth of Europe's national divisions, to envisage a genuinely representative European union which did not give effective power to a numerical majority of the whole. On many issues no doubt Britain would not be at odds with all three great continental states: she might frequently find herself, for example, at one with France. But in national terms the power in the last resort would be in the hands of Germany, Italy and France, great continental powers with which in many respects Britain has less in common than they have with one another, even despite the historic gulf between France and Germany.

But the crux of the matter is not the interests of the nations so much as the political capacity of their inhabitants, and how can we better judge this than by looking at their political records? We must consider impartially for a moment the histories of these European states, and then frankly ask ourselves whether they are such as to make us confident of the ability of their peoples to maintain stable democratic governments capable of wise and even altruistic decisions. Certainly we cannot condemn a people solely on the basis of their history. Nations, like individuals, undergo great changes with the passage of time: revolutions occur, reforms are made, interests alter. But, also like individuals, it is hard for nations to change: they, like us, are to a remarkable degree the heirs

F

and victims of their past. It is difficult for the leopard to change his spots, and the best guide we have to the capacity of a nation is its *curriculum vitae*. Plainly there is no place here for a detailed analysis of the history of the European nations, but we may very briefly ask ourselves — Britons indeed must do so in a matter as vital as this to the whole future of their country — to what extent the record of Britain's three great European associates inspires confidence in their capacity to maintain a just and democratic government. While doing so we must bear in mind always that self-government is a task of great difficulty in which probably the most important factor is long political habit, for really stable constitutional rule comes only with the aid of protracted use.

Germany became a national state in 1871 as the result of three deliberately contrived wars in seven years. The German Empire, which was thus created, less than ninety years ago, 'by blood and iron', did not immediately run riot. But, through its unprecedented armaments, particularly at sea, through its fears of 'encirclement' (so oddly combined, or so it seemed to the superficial glance, with its political arrogance and ambition), through the excessive power of its military autocracy, and through the unhealthy emotional influence wielded by its last Emperor, William II, Germany became the most important agent in that growing armaments race and that increasing international tension which resulted in the First World War. The Weimar Republic which was shakily erected on the foundations of the German Empire's defeat gave dramatic evidence of the weakness and instability of German democracy by falling beneath the feet of the Nazi movement. There followed a personal tyranny, based on the crudest of barbaric political doctrines, never exceeded, in the extremity of its intolerant power and the scale of the disasters it precipitated, in the whole history of Europe: the horrors perpetrated by the Nazis, indeed, were, as Churchill said, unsurpassed in the 'dark, lamentable catalogue of human crime'. In the Second World War the entire basis of German political life was destroyed, partly as a result of the hostilities themselves and partly as a result of the deliberate designs of the victors. On this basis of destruction and despair the Allied

Occupation powers encouraged in West Germany the growth of democratic institutions, beginning at the very bottom with local government. Their efforts were rewarded by one of the most remarkable national rebirths of modern times, with the emergence of a co-operative and democratic and apparently stable West German Federal Republic in 1949. In the ten years which have followed Germany has, under a great leader, Chancellor Konrad Adenauer, prospered economically to a remarkable degree, has remained a loyal adherent of the free world, has maintained her democratic processes, and has even made honourable and public amends for past sins, such as the fearful Hitlerian persecution of the Jews. But we must still ask how much ten years mean. How deep are the roots of democracy in Germany even now? Has any adverse wind yet blown strongly enough to test their strength? Britons must, and do, wish the German democratic experiment well, but they would be foolhardy indeed to count on the German electorate in a European union as a guarantee of stability, justice and freedom.

The case of Italy is less grave, though not lacking its affinities to that of Germany. Guiltless of the extreme anti-democratic excesses of which the Germans under Hitler showed themselves capable, the Italians also lack Germany's energy, seriousness and weight. The actual unity of Italy, which had been sought by patriotic Italians since the fifteenth century, only began to be realized under Piedmontese leadership in 1859, but was finally accomplished with the establishment of the royal government in Rome in 1870. Under the House of Savoy Parliamentary government was established firmly enough to last for half a century; there was great freedom of thought and speech; and the franchise was progressively widened as the years went by. But there was growing corruption in politics, an unhealthy proliferation of parties, and an excessive fluidity in political groupings which made stable government very difficult, even though there were fundamental cleavages of outlook between extremists of Right and Left in the country which might have seemed to provide a basis for effective two-party government. Italy, despite some economic expansion, remained a very poor nation, and the strain and disillusionment resulting from her

participation in World War I led to great Communist activity
and increasing civil disorder. Mussolini and his Blackshirts,
the first of the uniformed thug bands of Fascism, took advantage of this situation to seize absolute power in 1922, though
they retained the monarchy in a nominal role. The Italian
people acquiesced in this state of things for twenty years.
Representative government disappeared, and with it freedom
of speech and of the press, to be replaced by the strong rule
of a tyrant. Under his leadership the Italian people were
involved in a war to conquer Abyssinia in 1935, and
eventually, as an ally of Hitler, in World War II. By over-
throwing Mussolini and making peace with the Allied
invaders in 1943, Italy avoided the worst consequences of
defeat, as exemplified in Germany, but she emerged from the
war impoverished and disordered, and with the largest Communist party in free Europe. Under another great post-war
leader, Alcide de Gasperi, the Italian Republic restored
representative institutions and freedom of thought, and
established seemingly stable government under the moderate
influence of a great central coalition. But the economic and
educational problems of Italy remained formidable; it seemed
almost more the power of the Church than of the State which
kept the government in power; and there still remained, to
Left and to Right, ominous numbers of Italians hostile to
democracy. The Italian electorate can hardly be much more
completely relied on for solid, reasonable and wise political
actions in a European union than the German.

But what, it will be said, of France, for four centuries the
leading state in Europe, giver of law, culture and institutions
to so many of her neighbours? What of that France whose
people made the French Revolution — one of the greatest
national revolts in the history of mankind — and who were
so conscious of its importance to free government that they
abolished their calendar and called the first year of the
Republic Year One of the era of liberty? The unquestioned
greatness of France is so dominant in our minds that we are
inclined to avert our eyes from the realities of French political
life, for they constitute the great tragedy of a brilliant people.
The influence which France had in the nineteenth century
in spreading far and wide ideas of free and equal government

(by force of arms for a substantial period) was very potent — so much so indeed that the reaction against the ideas, which in due course followed, was often violent enough to sweep them back into limbo. As, with the penetrating gaze of genius, the great Edmund Burke had from the beginning prophesied, the French passion for innovation broke all the bonds of political tradition and subverted the order of civil society; the result, as he also prophesied, was the tyranny of Napoleon, which brought law, efficiency and order, but no liberty and hence no true stability.

The origins of France's internal instability lie deep in her history; in many respects the most rational and efficient people in Europe, the French have been no more able than others to evade their heritage, in this case of violent political extremes. The anarchy and chaos of the religious wars in the sixteenth century was so destructive and universal that in the era of Richelieu and Louis XIV the great monarchy went to the opposite extreme of absolutism in its determination to ensure order. Then, largely because of the genius of the French themselves in making such a success of it, the system became so immovable and unchangeable that it needed the profound cataclysm of the Revolution, which began in 1789, to alter it, and as a result there followed a short but intense period of violence, of political licence alternating with arbitrary rule. The eventual outcome was the Napoleonic Empire and ten years of warfare of an unprecedented bloodiness. With the overthrow of Napoleon the pendulum swung in the direction of a quieter life under the Restored Monarchy and Louis-Philippe, but by 1848 it had swung violently back to Republicanism, followed by the Second Empire. When the Third Napoleon in his turn (and with much less difficulty than his uncle) went down to defeat, the establishment of the Third Republic was heralded by the passionate disorders of the Commune. This republican régime, despite the instability of its early years, was to survive, even through the terrible strain of World War I, longer than any French system of government since 1789, but in its last twenty years it seemed hardly capable of decisive political action; beneath the constant ripples of changing governments, its depths remained motionless.

It was not the fault of the Third Republic, or at least not of it alone, that France fell before the onslaught of Germany in 1940, but nations have to grapple with the circumstances which fate thrusts upon them, and it was now the unhappy lot of France to have to bear the searing shame of national defeat and division. Not that the defeat itself is shameful — this is a common fate of nations — but the failure at first to redeem herself by fighting on in her overseas empire left a deep trauma on the soul of France, one which the nature of the Vichy regime, and of such leaders of it as Pierre Laval, was not calculated to cure. But almost at once her process of redemption began under the proud inspiration of General de Gaulle, who, literally alone in the beginning, led her back to nationhood, only to be in effect rejected when the war was over by the politicians of his country, who re-established, under the guise of the Fourth Republic, the spirit, and many of the institutions, of the Third. Even more than its predecessor it seemed to demonstrate that France could only obtain domestic quiet, which would pass for stability, at the price of virtually total inaction, of a sort of political *accidia*. And in Algeria she was faced with a problem so grave and so charged with emotion that only the most vigorous action could hope to solve it.

France sought, and perhaps found, the answer to her dilemmas by turning once more to the greatest of contemporary Frenchmen, de Gaulle, who was established in power with huge popular support in 1958. For the success of his policies almost all observers abroad most ardently pray; for the grandeur of his conception of the destiny of France, Englishmen are compelled to admiration. It may even be that in his régime — popularly supported, dynamic and capable of noble decisions — the French people have at last found a stable and effective form of government. We fervently hope that it may be so. But the outsider cannot but observe that de Gaulle, careful as he might be over the formalities, came to power through the threat, indeed in a sense the use, of force, and not by regular constitutional processes; that the Executive is now so strong that it can hardly be challenged; that the representative legislature is left with singularly little power; that this is essentially a personal form of government, sanctified by popular plebiscite, not dissimilar to Napoleonic rule; and that no one can foresee how it will function if the master hand should be removed or lose its cunning.

With the best will in the world, when Britons contemplate the prospect of entering a political union with their allies, the French people, for whom so many of them have so much respect, they cannot but recollect that in the one hundred and sixty years since 1789 the French form of government has been altered by violence, domestic or foreign, at least ten times, and perhaps more. In these circumstances they must wonder how much more to be relied upon the French electorate might be than the Italian or the German in providing that indispensable element of stability, without which a functioning democratic European union would be an impossibility.

There are, it is true, other peoples in Europe who have a more promising history of constitutional self-government; foreign invasions apart, the people of The Netherlands have long conducted their own affairs with order, good sense and efficiency. Belgium has had a more difficult and briefer career, but has not been without success; tiny Luxemburg, too, might be counted for virtue. But in a union of the Six with Britain, even the combined weight of the British, Dutch, Belgian and Luxemburg populations (totalling 71,781,000) would not suffice, as we have seen, to counteract that of the three powerful continental nations with their 144,043,000.

If, on the other hand, we think in terms of that wider European union which might have been, or might even still be, possible if the United Kingdom should decide to take the plunge with Europe, is the position greatly altered? Suppose for the sake of argument that we postulate a union consisting of the Seven countries of the Little Free Trade Area and the Six of the Common Market. Let us remember that this will be the most favourable community from which to set out towards a democratic European union with some hope of success, for the next two most likely adherents after the Seven and the Six would probably be Greece and Turkey, with their 8,096,000 and their 25,500,000 inhabitants respectively — and neither of these populations could be regarded as an asset, as far as stable self-government is concerned. Nor indeed could the 29,431,000 Spaniards, who might well be next on the list. The total population of the Seven, excluding the United Kingdom, is 36,384,000. This is made up as follows:

Portugal	8,909,000
Sweden	7,367,000
Austria	6,997,000
Switzerland	5,117,000
Denmark	4,500,000
Norway	3,494,000

Of these powers Norway and Denmark would be democratic assets, and Switzerland and Sweden most definitely so; but Portugal has never really managed to operate a successful democratic government and has now been a dictatorship for a long time, while the democratic career of Austria has been a chequered one.

Thus what might be described as the politically reliable national elements in a European union of the Seven and the Six (Britain, The Netherlands, Belgium, Luxemburg, Sweden, Switzerland, Denmark and Norway) could be reckoned as totalling 92,259,000. On the other hand, those upon whom less pressure could safely be put without inviting the possibility of a resort to very unwise or even unconstitutional measures (West Germany, Italy, France, Portugal and Austria) total 159,949,000.

Britons contemplating this profoundly difficult question, so vital to their future and to the future of free government in the world, must reluctantly come to the conclusion that even here there is not a sufficient margin for safety. The numerical control of any European union would lie in the hands of peoples whose history does not give a sufficient assurance of success, in organizing stable self-government, for the people of the United Kingdom to take the risk of joining it. If it is argued that in a federal union, within limits, the form of government of the constituent states does not matter, one must point to the vital clause in the Constitution of the United States which lays down that 'The United States shall guarantee to every State in this Union a Republican Form of Government . . .'—and the Americans of that era included as an essential part of the meaning of the word 'republican' the idea of self-government. Whether or not peace in the world is indivisible, democracy in a state — federal or otherwise — certainly is: the poison which destroys the processes of self-government must be fought at once wherever it enters the body politic. In a European union the guarantee of democracy to its constituent elements by the federal government would be as indispensable as the clear supremacy of the civil over the military arm within that federal government itself would be. But against a majority which is not indissolubly wedded to, and long and successfully experienced in, the difficult art of democratic self-government, no written constitutional guarantees will avail. Whatever the constitution of the union said on paper, its immensely strong and powerful central government, to which the member states had irrevocably surrendered not merely their titular sovereignty but their actual ability to save themselves, would be, given the historical background of its largest peoples, in constant danger of relapsing into tyranny. The general will for freedom would not be unquestionably strong enough to preserve democratic liberties. It is just for this reason that Britain should refuse to enter a European political union.

But it is not the only reason. Democracy is, in the view of those who believe in it, the only permanent way of ensuring good government; it must be based on the dual premise, first that in the long run the people as a whole are the wisest judges in their own affairs (as Burke characteristically put it, ' I am not one of those who think that the people are never in the wrong. . . . But I do say that in all disputes between them and their rulers, the presumption is at least upon a par in favour of the people '),[2] and second that it is by freedom of speech and thought alone that truth, the only safe basis for political action, can be ascertained. But, indispensable though it is, democracy is only a means to good government; given human nature, it is perfectly possible for the majority to be wrong. And Britain, before entering a European union, needs to be reasonably confident not merely that democracy would be preserved within it, but also that the decisions of the majority of its people, on matters of fundamental concern to her, would be just and wise. Britain has certain valuable political and economic ties, as we have already observed, with the outside world, particularly with the Commonwealth and with the United States; as I wrote in 1952,

> 'The truth is that Britain's interests are by no means exclusively, or even primarily, European. She has been historically, and still is, subject to three main political, social and economic attractions, that of the British Empire and Commonwealth, that of the United States, and that of Europe. Geographically she is closer to Europe; politically and emotionally she is much closer to the Commonwealth, and, in some respects, to America; economically, she is closest to the Commonwealth, next closest to Europe, and least close to the United States.'[3]

The people of the United Kingdom must be confident, before joining it, that a European union would never compel her to surrender, or sacrifice, any of her vital overseas links.

If she were to enter the union without this certainty, she would become grafted on to Europe, would acquire new and powerful bonds with the continent, while still preserving those with the Commonwealth and the United States. Then, one unhappy day, the majority of that union might force upon her the most fearful of choices, to break either the new ligaments that made her one with Europe or those older but still vital ones that knit her indissolubly to her kin overseas. This would be an agonizing reappraisal indeed, for whatever decision she made she would have no choice but — the phrase is not too strong — to tear herself apart. Without feeling real assurance that this dreadful dilemma would never face her, Britain cannot enter a European union.

And how can she feel that assurance? How can she ever be confident that the European majority's sense of its own interest will not force such decisions upon her? How can she know that the vast imports of food and raw materials by which alone she lives and maintains her standard of living will not be one day imperilled by the actions of the European government by which she would be ruled? Already, as a result of the economic commitments she would need to make even if she merely joined the Common Market, she would have to sever a number of her special links with the Commonwealth, a process which would infallibly continue. And are we to suppose, in the ultimate political sphere, that even more galling problems might not arise for a Britain which had surrendered her freedom of choice to a European majority? What might be, for instance, the attitude of that majority if some day Britain felt impelled—as she certainly would, one hopes—to go to the assistance of an Australasia attacked by an increasingly mighty and aggressive China? What would Britain do if, more immediately likely prospect, the European majority—led perhaps by a France misled into a phase of arrogant chauvinism and abetted by a West Germany seeking unity with her *alter ego* in the east—decided, on a wave of resurgent anti-Americanism, to cut their ties with the United States and adopt a policy of neutralism? The answer to all these questions is that Britain can never be reasonably sure, as far as she can now judge, that the continental majority will never imperil her vital overseas connections; and therefore—if those connections are really so important that she truly cannot live, in any real sense of the word, without them —Britain should never enter a European union.

Whether those ties, first with the Commonwealth and then with the United States, really are so vital to her, we must consider in the next two chapters.

NOTES

[1] These and subsequent figures are from the *United Nations Demographic Year Book 1958*, Table 4, Estimates of Population (1957 figures unless otherwise stated).

[2] Ross J. Hoffman and Paul Levack (Eds.), *Burke's Politics: Selected Writings and Speeches of Edmund Burke on Reform, Revolution and War*, New York 1949, p. 7.

[3] *Great Britain and the United States, A History of Anglo-American Relations, 1783-1952*, New York 1955, p. 940.

CHAPTER V

Britain and the Commonwealth

WITH the economic ties between the United Kingdom and the outside world, and particularly the Commonwealth, we have dealt at sufficient length in earlier chapters to make it unnecessary to do more here than to re-assert their importance. The unique reliance of the British Isles on overseas commerce and their special dependence on extra-European trade tie them indissolubly in an economic sense to the wider world, and particularly to the Commonwealth. Even though their reliance on the Commonwealth may be reduced with the years, particularly if other channels of trade are deliberately cultivated, their dependence on other continents beside Europe hardly can; and for the present the Commonwealth, with which so much of Britain's foreign trade still takes place, is bound to the United Kingdom by a life-giving cord which might be imperilled by entry into a European union.

Economically, the Commonwealth is important to Britain in the same way as — though, through long habit and imperial preferential arrangements, to a greater degree than — the rest of the non-European world, but politically the bonds which tie her to the Commonwealth are peculiar and in many senses unique. They are, too, of the utmost consequence to the people of the United Kingdom, and also to many of the peoples of the Commonwealth, although the extraordinarily nebulous nature of the constitutional relationship may tend to blind outsiders to this fact. This free association of independent member states, having no symbol of their association except a Crown which is theoretically powerless (and actually powerless in a number of the states such as India), is indeed in many ways a political phenomenon quite without parallel. So complete is the autonomy of all the members that they are not even bound to make peace and go to war together, and can actually, as in the case of India and Pakistan over Kashmir, be in a state of armed truce one towards another. Member nations can of course leave the Commonwealth at any time if they please, and it is always possible that South Africa, for example, will do so. The Commonwealth is in reality held together, to a greater or less degree, by a sense of common history, and, above all, by a sense of the practical value of such a voluntary association in a troubled world.

But important though this sentiment between the members of the full Commonwealth may be, it is far transcended in intensity by the feelings, and facts, which bind together what may be regarded as a kind of inner Commonwealth circle, consisting of the older colonies of Britain which came earliest to self-government and independence, and which were predominantly British in language and in stock — Canada, Australia and New Zealand. The bonds of feeling between these four powers are peculiarly strong and have been of the greatest importance in sustaining the position of Britain in the world at large.

It is not necessary to dwell upon these facts at great length, but some note must be taken of them. The existence (with the important exception of French Canada) of a common tongue is a factor of immense importance, not only because it makes understanding on great issues easier (or, perhaps one should say, misunderstanding less easy) and because it facilitates innumerable practical contacts, but also because it provides in the joint literature a common source of spiritual and emotional experience and belief. There is no more important bond than this in the affairs of men. We struggle hard to be rational in our political judgements, but in the end it tends to be emotion that controls our actions; and if those emotions have been nurtured to a considerable degree on the same food, united action is very much more easily attained.

Closely associated with the common language, and also of the greatest importance, was the fact that these colonies drew so much of their stock from the United Kingdom. This is not for any 'racialist' reason (although it would be surprising if people of the same racial stock did not have certain

advantages, in their association with one another, over outsiders of a different heredity), but because immigrants in these
circumstances bring with them a whole complex of social
experiences which they share, not merely with one another,
but also with the inhabitants of the country they have left.
In many cases, particularly in Australia and New Zealand,
they remained belligerently 'British', vividly describing
themselves as 'Independent Australian Britons'; here are
mutual ties of sympathy making common action between new
and mother nation very much easier than it would be without
them. And those racial ties are quantitatively very important
also.

If we take the inner core of the Commonwealth, the first
Dominions, the strength of these bonds of kinship is clearly
illustrated. In Canada, where they are weakest, out of a
population of 14,009,429 in 1951, it is estimated that
4,319,167 were of French origin, whereas 6,709,685 were
British, so that almost 48 per cent of Canadians are of British
extraction. In Australasia the phenomenon is far more striking; apart from the 137,151 Maoris, in New Zealand in 1956
the overwhelming mass of the population of 2,174,042 was of
British stock, while in Australia in 1947 — there was a considerable increase in non-British immigration after this date
— some 90 per cent of the people were of British origin and
about 99 per cent had actually been born in the British
Commonwealth. Looked at from the other point of view,
between 1821 and 1910 3,419,667 Britons emigrated to
British North America and 2,044,398 to Australia and New
Zealand.

If there be added to these, and many other, cultural and
social connections, the political affinities between the inner
members of the Commonwealth, one begins to have some
sense of the strength of their cohesion, even after they have
enjoyed almost a century of autonomous development. At first
this autonomy was limited in some respects, since for many
years there was central supervision from London in foreign
affairs and defence, which kept alive the common political
tradition which they had each inherited. (The Commonwealth
Relations Office in Westminster now forms a permanent
agency to aid co-operation.) That tradition, too, though it

responded gradually to differences in national environment, remained very potent, even outside the inner circle. All of these original, and many other, members of the Commonwealth, are constitutional democracies, having an executive arm responsible to a parliament which is elected on a basis of adult suffrage by secret ballot. With certain exceptions, such as that of Quebec (and Scotland), they have similar legal systems based on the English Common Law and its accompanying rights, such as trial by jury. The Judicial Committee of the Privy Council in London long served as an ultimate Commonwealth court of appeal in certain cases. Finally, the monarchy, which is the only actual constitutional link between these four nations, remains on the whole remarkably popular, and the constant traffic of royal visits in this air age serves to keep the sense of unity very much alive, even when it is subjected to severe political pressures.

It would be unwise to exaggerate the strength of the bonds of sentiment, even between the old Dominions, but their attitude in two World Wars is still a very remarkable tribute to it. These feelings are fully reciprocal, and the people of the United Kingdom can still be deeply moved towards the parts of what was once their Empire. If the sceptic wishes to see the reality of this, let him compare the feelings which the average Englishman has towards, for example, Australia with those which he feels towards a great European neighbour such as France, with whom Britain has not fought for nearly a century and a half and whose avowed ally she has been for the last third of that time. Towards France he may have a rational amiability, and even a warm affection: towards the former he is capable of profound political emotion. Your Briton, even setting aside the language difficulty, is a visitor in Paris, but he can feel at home in Melbourne.

Thus the purely economic claims of the Commonwealth on the United Kingdom might well be capable of adjustment if she were to enter a European organization, but the political risks which would be implied in a constitutional union would be quite another thing. The emotional effects upon Britain of any differences with the Commonwealth nations which might be forced upon her by her European colleagues would be severe indeed. She should not irrevocably enter any body politic in which her economic, social and political ties with, at the very least, Canada, Australia and New Zealand are not fully and finally protected. She must not sacrifice her special relationship with her kith and kin throughout the world for participation in a union with continental Europe.

CHAPTER VI

Britain and the United States

T HE shock of a rupture with the United States, if one were to be forced upon them by membership of a European union, would be less emotionally disturbing for Englishmen than a breach with a member or members of the Commonwealth (though in fact, in these days, a rupture with the United States would almost certainly produce a breach with Canada, and probably in the long run with Australia and New Zealand). But it would none the less be severe, for during the last seventy-five years of the long period of Anglo-American peace (which has lasted since 1814 — a few months longer than the Anglo-French peace) the people of Britain and the United States have tended to move together once more politically and socially. This is a complex question in itself, and vexed by the 'hands-across-the-sea' clichés about blood being thicker than water, but it is clear that in mutual comprehension and good feeling towards one another the two nations are far closer than they were a century ago.

The whole history of Anglo-American relations is bedevilled by a very natural ambivalence; springing as the two peoples did from common seed, and familiarly associated as they were through the long colonial childhood of America, they never quite lost their sense of social kinship, even after the violent dissolution of their relationship in the American Revolution; nor were they able at first to live economically remote from one another, even when they had become politically independent. Thus it was in the political sphere that the estrangement was most nearly absolute, and particularly, of course, in foreign affairs, where they not only fought a second war in 1812 but remained resentful and suspicious of one another throughout most of the nineteenth century. But with the re-entry of the United States into world affairs which resulted from the contraction of the globe in the twentieth century, they found themselves with a common interest in protecting the freedom of the West; thus they were 'associated' in the First World War and allied more closely in the years between 1941 and 1945 than perhaps any two nation states had ever been before in the history of the West. Even in the peace, or rather the 'cold war', which followed World War II — with the exception of the Suez catastrophe — their co-operation was on the whole maintained, and in 1959 the newly returned British Conservative government based its foreign policy firmly on what Prime Minister Macmillan called the 'interdependence' of Britain and the United States. Their international relationship had certainly never, since before 1776, been closer in time of peace than in the years after 1945.

In their domestic political life they have shown the same tendency to symbiosis in the present century. The fundamental legal and political rights enjoyed by their citizens had in many respects remained a joint heritage even during the years of estrangement. *Habeas corpus*, trial by jury, the British tradition of the supremacy of law, these were as much an Anglo-American as a Commonwealth bond. Furthermore, as the United Kingdom ceased in the nineteenth century to be an oligarchy and became, like America before her, an avowed democracy, so was one of the main differences with the United States removed. Similarly, as Britain, beginning with America's neighbour Canada, began to transmute her Empire into a free Commonwealth, so also did the most persistent emotional discord between the United States and the United Kingdom — that over 'imperialism' — begin to resolve itself, albeit of necessity very slowly. During the first half of the nineteenth century humanitarian and political reform movements in the two countries — anti-slavery, temperance, peace — had been peculiarly close, had been indeed in the full sense *Anglo-American* movements. In the twentieth century other agencies of co-operation — the English-Speaking Union, many varieties of exchange scholarships and fellowships, the Pilgrims — came to take their place; and mutual political fertilization of ideas, as of the New Deal by English social legislation of earlier years, was increasingly effective. The internal political life of the two countries, like their international attitude, had never been closer since the eighteenth century.

Their economic relations were more complex. At first, after the American Revolution, their trade was hampered by the French Revolutionary and Napoleonic Wars, but with the return of peace in 1815 their mutual commerce increased far beyond even its magnitude in the days when America had been a part of the British imperial system of trade protection. Indeed, as far as their commerce was concerned, the mutual dependence of the countries was at its height between 1825 and 1890, after which, with the growth of American economic maturity, a decline in the importance of the connection set in. Thus it was, happily, during the years of maximum estrangement in the international sphere that commercial contacts were most close; and it was in these same years that vast sums of British finance capital were invested in the development of the United States. But so steady thenceforward was the shrinkage of their mutual trade that British imports from the United States, which had constituted 23·7 per cent of her total imports in the 1880-4, had sunk to 8·8 per cent of the whole by 1948, while her exports to the United States had dwindled from 12·2 per cent to 4·3 per cent of all her exports in the same period. Even more striking, the percentage of America's total imports which came from the United Kingdom dropped from 40·6 in 1846-50 to 4·1 in 1948, and the percentage of all her exports thereto from 50·71 to 5·1 in the same period.

But these figures are deceptive, for during the years of World War II the enormous scale of Lend-Lease to Britain reflected a heavy British dependence on the economic resources of the United States for the waging of war, while during the post-war years the United Kingdom was for a period almost equally dependent on American financial aid. (Even at the time of the Suez crisis of 1956 it seems that one of the chief reasons for Britain's acceptance of a cease-fire was her realization that, without it or American assistance, the collapse of the pound would be inevitable.) With the economic recovery of Britain, however, and as a result of intense British efforts to narrow the 'dollar gap', Anglo-

American trade began to increase strikingly once more in the nineteen-fifties. This upward trend, the first very marked one for 60 years (except in the special circumstances of war), was so well maintained that in 1959 it appeared that Britain would have a substantial surplus in its trade with the United States for the first time for nearly a century. Thus there has been in the last decade a marked regrowth of Anglo-American economic interdependence, though it is not yet restored to a scale which will match their political interdependence.

The bond between the two societies constituted by racial intermixture is also one of great, though often unrealized, importance; less clear and decisive than that with parts of the Commonwealth, it has nevertheless been persistent and powerful. Seen from the British end this is unquestionable, for whereas between 1815 and 1940 18 per cent of British emigrants to English-speaking societies went to Canada, 10·5 per cent to Australasia, and about 13 per cent to all other regions, no less than 58 per cent went to the United States. And even at the American end, swamped as they increasingly were by other stocks, the British had one immense advantage — they were there first, and thus were able to leave a much more marked, indeed indelible, imprint on American society, for at the end of the colonial era the population of the United States was probably about 90 per cent English-speaking in origin. Nor did the British lose ground very quickly, for between 1820 and 1945, out of 38,461,395 immigrants to the United States 11,978,614 were from the English-speaking world.[1] This constitutes a vital, and vitally important, connection.

Finally, Britain and the United States also share (though less completely, naturally, than Britain and the Commonwealth) common social attitudes and even emotional responses, which arise naturally from a common cultural inheritance. They, too, share — all the witty aphorisms to the contrary notwithstanding — the inestimable boon of a common language possessing a literature of great antiquity and continuing richness; it is characteristic that it was one of the first great American literary figures, Nathaniel Hawthorne, who wrote, ' I never stood in an English crowd without being conscious of hereditary sympathies.' Though the correspondent of the

New York Observer exaggerated when he declared in 1831, 'England to an American is not foreign',[2] there was more than a modicum of truth in his statement. Similarly, when *Whitaker's Almanack* long ago began to list the United States not among 'Foreign Countries' but in a special unnamed category of its own immediately after 'The British Empire', it was giving expression to a real British sentiment. To a somewhat less degree perhaps than in the case of the Commonwealth countries, but noticeably none the less, the Englishman feels somehow more at home in the United States than in Europe. These fundamental sympathies have, particularly in recent years, been strenuously, and on the whole very successfully, cultivated, despite the real differences which still exist between the two peoples. Certainly, as I wrote in 1952, 'greater efforts have never been made by two sovereign and independent nations to create the conditions in which such differences can be prevented from doing harm. And these positive efforts are supported by the long traditions of Anglo-American history, by the common language, by a kindred democracy, and by the strong emotional bonds of mutual friendship and dependence forged in the one hundred and forty years of Anglo-American peace'.[3]

The increasing closeness of the United States and Britain has of late years been hastened by, and largely taken the form of, a heavier American impact on the United Kingdom, which has resulted naturally from the remarkable increase in American power. Britain has become steadily more conscious of this gravitational pull from the United States ever since American population and productive capacity surpassed hers in the middle years of the nineteenth century. Acceptance of this fact, that the political and economic leadership of the world was passing from her hands into those of the United States, was not always easy for Britain; there were periodic upsurges of resentment among the British people which checked for a little the tide running so strongly towards closer Anglo-American association. These sprang mostly in mid-twentieth century from a feeling that the power of Britain in the world was ebbing as that of America flowed; and the last and in some senses most violent of these waves of emotion came at the time of the Suez crisis in 1956, when American power was directly used, for the first time for many years, to frustrate British policy. But, sensitive as Britons are to what they feel is a decrease in their influence, what is, in fact, the power of Britain today?

The answer is that her power has never been greater. Her population is more numerous, her agricultural output is larger, her industrial production is greater, her normal over-all standard of living is higher, than at any time in her history —and she has, for the moment with France, Russia and the United States, the nuclear weapons. British power is absolutely greater than it has ever been before. But *relatively* she is weaker than she has been for perhaps two hundred and fifty years. In 1700 she was probably the second power in Europe and the world, though the fact may not yet have been apparent to other nations; at the beginning of 1959 she is still in a sense the third military power in the world, but the gap between her strength and that of the two giants, the United States and Russia, is widening rather than contracting, and she may not easily be able to maintain herself in third place against a resurgent Germany or a China coming swiftly to military strength. The consciousness that Britain has not ceased to go forward; the proud sense that she has never yet been defeated in war (except by the United States in the American War of Independence); the wide extent—even yet —of her Empire, and the great strength of her Common-wealth partners; and her possession of the nuclear weapons— none of these things has made the fact of her relatively decreased power in the world any easier for many of her proud and patriotic people to bear. From this consciousness arose the deep passions which shook many Britons at the time of the Suez crisis, and which resulted in a vigorous outburst of anti-Americanism.

But adjustment to the irreducible brute facts of environ-ment is the inexorable, perhaps the fundamental, law of life, and never could it have been more truly said by a great people of their declining greatness,

> ' The fault, dear Brutus, is not in ourselves,
> But in our stars, that we are underlings.'

There were notable signs by 1959 that the British people had really begun to come to terms in their hearts and minds with the realities of their international position and in particular of their relationship with the United States. This is not altogether surprising, for Great Britain grew to her particular grandeur in the long years of her national development, not only through an island position which had great advantages political and economic, and through a spirit of patriotism and naval skill and valour which kept her free for nearly a millennium from foreign invasion, but also through a degree of political ability in some respects unequalled. The well-spring, the origin, of that combination of political principle with political pragmatism, that delicate adjustment of proper means to realistic ends which has characterized the democracy that is the greatest gift of the English-speaking world to the political development of man, was Britain. The ingredients of English historical greatness have not only been devotion to principle and great energy, but a political acumen sometimes amounting to genius. In 1959, it is to be hoped, the British people have allowed a true perception of reality to control their emotions and have adjusted their course to the presence on the international scene of two political Leviathans which put her to a considerable extent in the shade.

Most happily for her, the greatest of these is the United States. Happily, for two reasons; first and foremost, that she has been able in the main to pursue with great success a policy of friendship with America. The increasing association of the two peoples has not been merely the result of the impersonal pressure of forces and events, nor even of the many individuals and organizations on both sides of the Atlantic actively striving to promote it, but of a policy pursued, on the whole with remarkable constancy, by British governments since the beginning of this century. The nature of that policy was vividly apparent to all by the Second World War, with Churchill's masterly fostering of the Anglo-American alliance, but even acute observers have not always realized that it was at the time of the Spanish-American war at the turn of the century that Britain veritably began to lay siege to the citadel of American confidence and that Britons deliberately, persistently,

energetically, and even with a sense of urgency, set out to win
that friendship with the United States on which her foreign
policy has ever since been fundamentally based. But it takes
two to make a friendship, just as much as a quarrel, and for-
tunate indeed was it for Britain that the American people had
no enduring urge to seek colonial acquisitions, no political
desire to govern other people even in the Americas, no overweening ambition to dominate, let alone conquer, the world.
How different would her history, and that of the world, have
been if the souls of Germany and the United States had been
transposed! How blessed a thing it has been for all men
everywhere in this century that America has never had the
furious arrogance of Nazism nor the compelling drive of
Communism towards world power.

The belief in democratic self-government for every people,
which Britain and the United States share, made it easier than
it would perhaps have been in any other circumstances for
the former to concede, without any overt struggle, the leadership of the free world to the latter; and this is the process
which in fact the twentieth century has witnessed. Indeed, it
is hard to find a parallel in history to this transference of
international pre-eminence from one great power to another
without any resort to arms. This dispensation, happy for all
nations, but particularly for Britain, was what that great
American, A. T. Mahan, had hoped for when he wrote in
1897:

> 'How shall two walk together except they be agreed? How
> shall there be true sympathy between a nation whose political
> activities are world-wide, and one that eats out its heart in
> merely internal political strife? When we begin really to look
> abroad, and to busy ourselves with our duties to the world at
> large in our generation—and not before—we shall stretch out
> our hands to Great Britain, realizing that in unity of heart
> among the English-speaking races lies the best hope of humanity
> in the doubtful days ahead.'[4]

This process was made much easier by the fact that both
Britain and the United States were industrial, commercial,
maritime powers.

Such was indeed the second reason for Britain to be happy
that it was the United States with which she had to deal.

Though they might in commerce sometimes be rivals, they had a common interest in keeping open the maritime channels of trade. Britain had, from the early eighteenth century to the 1920s, led the world in the quantity of her foreign trade; in mid-nineteenth century she controlled 25 per cent of the world's international trade and in 1914 the figure still stood at 18 per cent. During most of the nineteenth century France had ranked second, followed by the United States, but in the 1890s Germany moved into second place. In 1913 the value of the foreign trade (exports *plus* imports) of the leading nations (in millions of U.S. dollars) was as follows: [5]

Great Britain	6,837
Germany	4,970
United States	4,392
France	2,953
Netherlands	2,814
Belgium-Luxemburg	1,612
Russia	1,491
British India	1,383
Austria-Hungary	1,319
Italy	1,170
Canada	1,026
Argentina	1,007
Australia	755
China	710
Japan	679
Brazil	643
Switzerland	614
South Africa	520

World War I gave a severe check to the trade of Germany, and during most of the twenties Britain and America were running neck and neck in the quantity of their commerce, the United States leading the world in exports, the United Kingdom in imports. The Great Depression was a particularly severe blow to the American economy, and as a result Britain forged ahead, being followed by the United States, Germany and France in that order. During World War II the United States moved rapidly to the top of the list. The trade of selected leading countries in 1948 (in millions of U.S. dollars) was as follows: [6]

	Exports	Imports
U.S.	12,545	7,163
U.K.	6,379	8,114
Canada	3,110	2,637
France	2,011	3,443
Belgium	1,690	1,986
Netherlands	1,024	1,872
W. Germany	592	1,400

The ascendancy of the United States in international trade was thus already decisive, and this trend continued.

The figures for 1952, 1956 and 1957 (provisional) are as follows for the leading powers (in millions of U.S. dollars):

	1952[7]		1956[8]		1957[8]	
	Exports	Imports	Exports	Imports	Exports	Imports
U.S.	15,164	11,632	18,947	12,645	20,642	13,079
U.K.	7,540	9,733	8,880	10,471	9,310	11,038
Canada	4,729	4,458	4,946	5,799	5,146	5,867
W. Germany	3,990	3,818	7,358	6,617	8,575	7,499
France	3,896	4,431	4,541	5,558	5,065	6,110

For purposes of comparison, though based on a different and much less reliable assessment, the figures for the U.S.S.R. for 1956 and 1957 (in millions of U.S. dollars) were:

1956		1957	
Exports	Imports	Exports	Imports
3,669	3,613	4,381	3,938

Thus the West still retains a commanding lead in international trade. But perhaps the most striking fact from our point of view, after the American pre-eminence, is that between them the United States and the United Kingdom, whom Woytinsky calls 'the two giants of the world market', together control approximately 30 per cent of the world's trade. The United States has made inroads on British markets since the war, and she now needs to import more of certain metals, minerals and tropical products than heretofore, but she could still pay for these with some two or three per cent of her production: essentially America's great overseas commerce is a by-product of her enormous economic strength. This is in glaring contrast to the absolute dependence of the United Kingdom on maritime trade for her life.

Nowhere is the huge actual power of America in overseas

trade, and yet her relative lack of dependence on it compared with Britain, better shown than in the strength of her merchant navy. The British Isles cannot survive without ships: America could continue to live, in all probability quite well, without any merchant navy at all. In 1939 the merchant shipping fleet of Great Britain substantially exceeded that of the United States, but, largely owing to the prodigious war-time shipbuilding efforts of the American yards, in 1947 the British total of shipping was about the same as before the war, 17,848,000 gross tons, whereas that of the United States had grown almost threefold in eight years, to 32,423,000 tons. By 1954 the British merchant fleet had risen to 19,014,000 tons, while that of America had sunk to 27,344,000, including her large reserve, or 'mothball', fleet. Nevertheless, her supremacy was still substantial.

In this way, at every turn in mid-twentieth century, Britain, like the rest of mankind, is faced with the fact of American economic dominance. Russia is making very swift strides and appears confident of her ability to overtake her rival, but on any present assessment America is still far ahead. By one reckoning, the *per capita* income of the United States in 1952 was $1,823, which is so high that only her nearest rival, Canada, attained more than two-thirds of that figure; the *per capita* income of the United Kingdom for that same year was $751. The national income of the United States in 1948 was $223,500,000,000, well over five times that of her nearest recorded rival, Britain.[9] The population of the United States is roughly 6 per cent of the total population of the world, but certain estimates made in the 1950s have claimed that she produces something of the order of one-third of all the world's goods and one half of all the world's manufactured goods. Woytinsky calculates that the share of the United States in world income increased from 26 per cent in 1938 to a fabulous 40·7 per cent in 1948.

This economic strength is the foundation for great political and military power. Thus in 1953 the expenditure of the central government of the United States (which was only about two-thirds of total government expenditure) was $74,607,000,000, compared with $14,020,000,000 for the

United Kingdom. Of this American total, 65·9 per cent was for defence.[10] In 1954-5 the Budget accounts of the United States carried an expenditure on the Army of $9,427,000,000, which was something like six times the British figure; her expenditure on the Air Force in the same period was $16,647,000,000, which was about thirteen times the British. All the world is now well aware — most of it with grave disquiet — of the fact that the Soviet Union has drawn very close to, if not equalled, the United States in military nuclear capacity, at least as far as the major atomic weapons are concerned, and that she is almost certainly substantially ahead in the use of ballistic missiles, which her supremacy in space exploration demonstrates; but this merely illuminates even more brightly for the free world their absolute dependence on the great military power of the United States for their safety.

It is well indeed for them that the power of the United States is so huge — and huge it is. Comparisons with the U.S.S.R. are difficult, not merely for statistical reasons; much of Russia's great success in certain fields, such as nuclear ballistic missiles, for instance, is the result of tremendous concentration therein. Her armed forces have long been unquestionably the largest by far in the world (numbering probably 3,900,000 in 1959, compared with approximately $2\frac{3}{4}$ million for the United States in 1958), and, though very well equipped, they are remarkably cheap, because of low rates of pay and standards of living; but the Soviet industrial machine is being used to absolutely full capacity to achieve these results, having nothing like the American reserves of power, the economic 'slack' which is so vital in case of war. It can be argued that the United States remains, taking everything into consideration, the best balanced and most powerful military force in the world; her nuclear retaliatory capacity is still annihilating, and, despite all reservations, the fact that she spends, as it seems, much more on defence than Russia ($38,000,000,000, excluding foreign aid, in 1957, as compared with an estimated $24,000,000,000 in 1956 for Russia, though this is a figure which must be treated with extreme caution)[11] still means something.[12]

Certainly the British dependence on American might is very heavy, despite the fact that she herself has, and can deliver, the hydrogen bomb, for Britain is so small and so densely populated that she is peculiarly vulnerable to nuclear destruction, indeed annihilation. But granted the vital importance of nuclear missiles and nuclear, as well as other, air power, it is still control of the seas which would count for Britain in any war which did not end after a short nuclear Armageddon. But how likely is it that a large-scale world war will not begin with, or very shortly develop into, a fission-bomb holocaust which would certainly set civilization back unnumbered years and might even bring the species to extinction?

It is plain that the military thinkers of the West, in their first flush of enthusiasm for — it might be fairer to say horror of — the atomic bomb, thought that nuclear weapons would certainly be utilized, as they were in World War II; it is very probably true that America's possession of the atom bomb alone prevented the collapse of Western Europe in the face of Communist pressure in the immediate post-war years. Even when the appalling power of the hydrogen bomb became known and when the Soviet Union exploded an atomic bomb in 1949 (followed by Britain in 1952), there was a marked tendency in both Britain and the United States to rely more and more exclusively on nuclear weapons for Western defence — that is to say, since Soviet strength was so great on the ground in Europe, on 'massive retaliation'. But when Russia also exploded a hydrogen bomb in 1953 (followed by Britain in 1957) and when the continuation of three sets of atomic tests directed the attention of the world increasingly to the hazards of nuclear radiation, statesmen began to think again.

At first, American thought increasingly moved towards the production of smaller, 'tactical', atomic weapons (and American practice had already gone some way in that direction), and hence to the idea of 'graduated' retaliation — the use of minor nuclear weapons in minor and limited wars. But, so far, the fear that this might place the opposing forces on a slippery slope of increasingly strong reprisals, leading in the end to full-scale nuclear warfare, has acted as a check on this school of thought, and in 1959 there was a tendency in the United States (and Britain) to reassess the need for stronger conventional forces once more, in case of war without resort to nuclear weapons. This new tendency seems to be a result partly of a general revulsion against the idea of using the ultimate weapons when the enemy has not used them first, and partly of a gradual growth, after the death of Stalin, of the feeling that, desirous as they are of the triumph of Communism, the Soviet leaders are just as reluctant as those of the free world to envisage the possible extinction of the human race. These views were probably strengthened by the visit of Premier Khrushchev to the United States in 1959.

There thus seemed a real possibility that the nuclear stalemate, which Churchill, with his customary clarity of judgement, had predicted some time before, might even endure in case of a world war. There was, whatever their vices and failings, little sign of that form of megalomaniac violence which had characterized the Nazi leadership, among the men in the Kremlin; Hitler might well have launched a thermonuclear weapon, which would have destroyed Germany as well as the Allies, rather than face defeat, but it seems much less certain that Khrushchev would. There are in the case of chemical, and probably bacteriological, warfare precedents even in World War II for both sides refraining from the use of weapons which they believed would be as dangerous to themselves as to the enemy; the cases are not admittedly exactly analogous, but they are more so than has often been admitted. It is then a very real possibility that there might be a large-scale war without the use of the major nuclear weapons, or even a 'broken-backed' war following upon a short nuclear fury. In these circumstances we cannot dispense with orthodox strategic calculations: we must still take into account the traditional factors which have governed military policy in the past.

And this for the United Kingdom essentially means naval policy, supplemented in the mid-twentieth century by air policy. As we have seen, it was through her sea power that Britain developed her overseas political connections and her unique dependence upon trans-oceanic commerce. This dependence was fully appreciated in 1914, when her sense of the bonds of her Empire was closer, but when her dependence on overseas supplies of food and raw materials was probably no greater than it is now; as the *Fodo Number of The Times* declared on June 8, 1914, 'Foreign food is the foundation of our existence. . . . That, though some people are apt to forget it, is the elementary reason and justification for the precautionary policy of the Big Navy.' But the leading article of *The Times Food Number* of 1957 did not once mention the British (or any other) navy, let alone the possibility of war — though the British people could starve quite as thoroughly in a war now as they could have done in the two world wars. This curious myopia is characteristic of the attitude of many Englishmen today: in an odd way, once they have become aware that Britannia no longer rules the waves, they seem to lose all interest in their present, far more difficult and unenviable, situation. Because this question is so crucial to the continued existence of Britain, we must examine it a little further, and particularly in the light of the rise of the now supreme American navy.

During the first century after 1783 there was no comparison between the strength of the navies of the two English-speaking powers. Britain's own naval dominance was, in 1782, more seriously challenged than at any other time in the eighteenth century by the great hostile coalition which was formed against her, but her maritime supremacy was reasserted in the French wars and riveted firmly in place by Nelson's great naval victories which culminated in the complete triumph of Trafalgar in 1805. For the next fifty years Britain's absolute naval superiority was unquestioned. With the coming of the ironclad steamship in mid-century, vividly projected on a small scale in the American Civil War, there was a momentary fear in Britain lest the conservatism of the Royal Navy should imperil her nautical strength by a too slow adaptation to the new methods, but as long as Britain was not only the leading shipbuilding nation but also the leading industrial power and producer of iron and coal, this was an unreal fear, and she soon forged far ahead once more. Indeed, she continued for many years to maintain the 'two-power standard' — the traditional British superiority in capital ships over the pooled strength of the next two largest navies.

During this whole century after Independence the United States maintained a very small navy. She relied upon vast distances, and upon British control of the seas for her protection; she placed her trust in the pacific intentions of

Britain towards her, a policy which had first been formulated at the time of the enunciation of the Monroe doctrine. In a sense the situation was a stalemate; both powers had learned in the totally inconclusive War of 1812 that neither could fundamentally harm the other, and, as the power of both increased, it became clear that in any conflict Britain could not seriously hurt America by naval action, while America was powerless against Britain, although she could certainly wreak her revenge upon Canada. But the two peoples were still far from friendly, and the Americans unquestionably, if not always consciously, resented the fact that British economic and maritime ascendancy made the United States to some extent dependent upon British goodwill for her imports of manufactured goods and her exports of raw materials; it was frustrating for them to feel that they could not have challenged British naval power even if they had wished to do so. And this was a matter of strength rather than skill, for during most of this period the Americans had a most vigorous nautical tradition; in the era of the Clipper ship New England seamanship was inferior to none, and in the War of 1812, within the limits of their power, the Americans had given the British navy a number of rude, if minor, shocks.

But by the last years of the nineteenth century the whole setting of the picture of international naval power had changed. Both Germany and the United States had become highly industrialized powers, capable of constructing and maintaining large modern battle fleets, but as late as 1890 the United States, and as 1895 the German Empire, still possessed only third class navies — the United States Navy was even weaker than that. From this time forward a radical change in the balance of naval power became apparent. The American naval expansion owed much to her new-found imperialism and to her growing sense of proximity to the affairs of the rest of the world, but it also owed much to that fear of Germany which became the dominating consideration in British strategy. The great 1901 naval law of Germany proclaimed her intention of providing her Empire with a fleet inferior only to the British, and capable of meeting even that on equal terms in the North Sea. It is well known that the deadly Anglo-German naval rivalry which now arose ended all hope of an Anglo-German *entente*; that it led Britain to a *rapprochement* with France and to a specific naval alliance with Japan, which ended her isolation and allowed her to redistribute her naval resources to meet the German threat; and that it forced her to abandon the two-power standard in favour of a mere policy of maintaining an adequate lead over Germany. It is less often appreciated that fear of Germany greatly stimulated American naval expansion, and made it certain that Britain and the United States would draw so close together that within a decade Britain would tacitly adopt a strategic policy of simply not reckoning on the possibilty of the hostile use of American naval power. By 1906 *Jane's Fighting Ships* placed the United States Navy, for the first time, second to that of Britain, a position below which it was never henceforward to sink. This was a completely logical result of her meteoric rise in the hierarchy of industrial strength: it was the first step in a remorseless, inevitable process of which we now see the culmination. Certainly it was the step that counted. The acceptance of this 'axiom', as Grey expressed it, on which the British government now acted until 1914, 'that of not taking account of the American Navy in calculating the requirements of the British Empire',[13] was of the utmost consequence for the future.

The next step was, after some initial hesitation, taken in the same way, even though it was a much more dramatic one. During the First World War the United States Navy grew greatly in strength, and, despite the co-operation of the two forces after America entered the war, the tension over Freedom of the Seas between 1914 and 1917 was partly responsible for a sharp outburst of Anglo-American naval rivalry during the Peace Conference, in the course of which Lloyd George declared that, 'Great Britain would spend her last guinea to keep a navy superior to that of the United States or any other Power, and that no Cabinet official could continue in the Government in England who took a different position.'[14] Yet within three short years, in the Treaty of Washington of 1921, Great Britain had accepted the principle of Anglo-American equality in aircraft carriers and capital ships. She did so fundamentally because she knew that she had no choice. America had emerged from the war economically and

H

industrially paramount, and the plain fact, which none could evade, was that she could certainly outbuild Britain in any naval armaments race which occurred and that such a race Britain could in any case not afford. This acceptance of virtual Anglo-American naval equality was one of the most momentous decisions in English history, and it did not pass unnoticed or unopposed. Yet on the whole it was accepted by the British people with a reasonable grace; as one naval authority wrote, 'the trident of Neptune passes into the joint guardianship of the English-speaking peoples'. It is not clear how fully the ultimate implications of the deed were realized, but few actions in British history have required more painful common sense, for it was 'an act of renunciation unparalleled . . . in history . . .' 'Renunciation' is perhaps too heroic a word to describe a resigned acceptance of the inevitable, but 'unparalleled' it certainly was. It is safe to say that any power but America might have had to fight for its supremacy, and that the fight might have been long and grievous. But in terms of what American friendship was to mean in 1941 and thereafter, few British decisions have ever paid such magnificent dividends.

There was, it is true, some backing and filling by British leaders in the late twenties, but it was ended by the London Naval Treaty of 1930, which restored Anglo-American good feeling and extended naval parity to virtually all types of warship. In fact, the United States never built up to the full limits of her entitlement before the coming of World War II, by which time, of course, Britain was perfectly happy to see her construct as mighty a navy as was possible. Thus during the war years America became actually, what she had been potentially for a quarter of a century, the world's greatest naval power. Indeed, as we shall shortly see, she became a more dominant naval power even than Britain had been at the height of her maritime greatness. The implications of this superiority never have been in the post-war years, and perhaps are not now, fully grasped by all elements in British public opinion, as was clearly illustrated in 1951 by the outcry in Britain against the appointment of an American as Supreme Commander of the naval forces of N.A.T.O. in the Atlantic. The arrangement was made during the tenure of the Labour government, and when the Opposition, who bitterly criticized it, came to power shortly thereafter, the matter was taken up by Churchill in Washington. Illuminating indeed was the communiqué finally issued after the visit to her American ally of this, the greatest perhaps of war ministers in all Britain's history, on this naval issue so vital to the life of the British people:

'The President and the Prime Minister with their advisors have had several discussions relating to the arrangements about the Atlantic command. . . . As a result they agreed that His Majesty's Government and the United States Government would recommend to N.A.T.O. certain alterations in the arrangements. . . . These changes, however, do not go the full way to meet the Prime Minister's objections to the original arrangements. Nevertheless, the Prime Minister, while not withdrawing his objections, expressed his readiness to allow the appointment of . . . [an American] Supreme Commander to go forward.'[15] Never perhaps has the necessary policy of conceding gracefully what America is determined to have and has the power to take, even in affairs literally vital to Britain, been more graphically epitomized.

And America, though she desires to take very little, has the power to take very much, in every sphere of international affairs, but particularly — and here is the irony for Britain — in all those matters affecting command of the seas, which are still, as they have always been, more crucial for the existence of the British people than anything else in the world, for American naval strength, like that of Britain before her, is perhaps the supreme manifestation of her power.

Her navy in 1956-57 had seven times the personnel of the Royal Navy. As against the 5 battleships, 22 aircraft carriers, 31 cruisers and 366 destroyers, escorts and frigates of the navies of the whole British Commonwealth, the United States Navy had 15 battleships, 103 aircraft carriers, 74 cruisers, and 664 destroyers, frigates and escorts. Estimates of expenditure on the American navy for that year were almost exactly ten times those for the British navy. It is not necessary to say more than that in 1954-5 *Jane's Fighting Ships* wrote that the United States Navy was 'equal to all the major navies of the world' combined.

Nor can Britain be content, as she once was, with the neutrality, even the benevolent neutrality, of the American navy, being prepared herself to take on all other comers, for she has fallen into third place among the earth's navies. *Jane's Fighting Ships* wrote in 1956-7 of 'the rapid ascendancy of Russia to the position of a major naval power second now only to the United States'. The Soviet Union has followed her obvious strategy of planning to sever N.A.T.O. communications and cut off Britain from her ally and the rest of the world, and so has concentrated on the types of construction most damaging to Britain. A large percentage of her new construction consists of submarines, particularly long-range ones, and since the war she has built more cruisers and destroyers than all the other nations put together. Thus, though she has certain grave offensive weaknesses compared with the farther ranging British and American navies, as for instance in aircraft carriers, her navy is very well suited to its primary purpose in case of war — defending herself and attacking Britain, while not directly assaulting America except by ballistic nuclear missiles fired from submarines. Though in 1956-7 she had two less battleships than the combined British Commonwealth, she had almost exactly the same number of cruisers, more destroyers, frigates and escort vessels (450 to the British 366), and, of course, a vastly greater submarine fleet (400 to the British 72). The submarine menace in a war with Russia (whether or not she conquered the European mainland and added the weight of her air power to it, as did Hitler) would be incomparably more dangerous to the British Isles than it ever was in World War I and II with Germany, for she would start it with perhaps 600 underwater craft.

Such are the realities of power which lie for Britain beneath the conventional phrases of diplomacy today: such is the degree of British dependence upon the United States. The United Kingdom can hardly even allow herself to envisage in the future any international policy which might result in a clash with the United States: she has no option, indeed, as she has already discovered, but to concert all her major external policies with her great transatlantic neighbour. On major issues, whithersoever America will not go, she cannot go.

How then can she ever consent to enter a European union in which her independence of action would be lost along with her national sovereignty? The risk to her democratic institutions, the possible commitment to a European 'third force' alienated from the United States, which might result, would spell total disaster for her. It would threaten her bonds not merely with America, but with the Commonwealth and the whole world as well; this would be so both because the Commonwealth in such circumstances would have little option but to follow America and also because the range and scale of American sea power is so great that all Britain's communications with the outside world would be imperilled. Thus any rift, produced by the policies of a European union of which she was a member, between Britain and the United States would no doubt be less emotionally agonizing for her than a mere breach with the Commonwealth, but it would be potentially infinitely more calamitous. When the United Kingdom held back from the Common Market, clearly involving, as it did, ultimate and absolute political commitments, she was not merely giving vent to a reactionary insularity and isolationism, but was showing a profound, if instinctive, understanding of her fundamental interests. For Britain to enter a purely European political union would be for her, indeed, an act of desperate folly.

NOTES

[1] See Allen, *op. cit.*, pp. 95-108.
[2] Quoted Allen, *op. cit.*, p. 164.
[3] *Ibid.*, p. 173.
[4] A. T. Mahan, *The Interest of America in Sea Power, Present and Future*, London 1898, p. 259.
[5] Woytinsky, *World Commerce and Governments*, p. 49.
[6] *Ibid.*, p. 50.
[7] *Ibid.*, p. 58.
[8] *United Nations Yearbook of International Trade Statistics 1957*, New York 1958, Table A.
[9] Woytinsky, *World Population and Production*, pp. 392-4.
[10] Woytinsky, *World Commerce and Governments*, pp. 700-708.
[11] John Gunther, *Inside Russia Today*, New York 1957, pp. 378-9.
[12] See Chapter Eleven (A) below for a fuller treatment of this subject.
[13] Quoted Allen, *op. cit.*, p. 748.
[14] Quoted *Ibid.*, pp. 703, 742, 743.
[15] Quoted *Ibid.*, p. 902.

CHAPTER VII

The Dilemma of Britain

THIS is the dilemma of Britain. The little United Kingdom, close packed with her fifty million inhabitants, has, despite the rapid liquidation of her imperial responsibilities, unique political commitments in, and economic ramifications through, all the four quarters of the globe. This peculiarly widespread and complex pattern of economic veins and political arteries traverses all the oceans of the world. The economic ramifications, facilitating imports of vital food and raw materials and equally vital exports of manufactured goods with which to earn the money to buy the imports, are just as important now as they have ever been. The political commitments may be diminishing, as the Empire is converted into the Commonwealth, but they will be huge for many years to come, will never, in all probability, disappear entirely, and are at the present time peculiarly onerous because of the complexity and difficulty of the great programme of imperial disengagement.

This economic and political vascular system, which sustains Britain by its contacts with all parts of the earth, was created during the seventeenth, eighteenth and nineteenth centuries, when Britain was in the plenitude of her international power. But now her strength is relatively less, and she no longer has the same ability to command, by her own will and act alone, that once she had. In particular, because of her extraordinary dependence upon maritime communication, she, more perhaps than any other power, is at the mercy of America, which now controls the seas. Thus Britain which, during the boyhood of most of her leading figures, was answerable to none, is acutely conscious of the present pre-eminence of the United States, who has in the last forty years assumed the paramount power which Britain exercised in mid-nineteenth century. The emotions, which this dwindling of her imperial domain

and this relative decrease of her power induced, have not prevented her from realizing the continuing and supreme importance of her connections with the wider world, and especially
the Commonwealth and the United States.

They have, however, made it less easy for her to adjust
rapidly to the novel conditions created in the last decade by
the development of ideas of European unity and to the pressing issues posed by the actual creation of the European Common Market. And the challenge which this presents to her is
so real and serious that it is imperative she find a satisfactory
response.

On the purely economic level, the Six, unless they adopt the
most liberal international trade policy (and, though at the
moment the indications are favourable, it is as yet far from
certain that they will), could be a formidable obstacle to an
increasingly rapid rise in Britain's standard of living, because
they make inaccessible to her their own very important markets. To a people so greatly dependent on foreign commerce
as the United Kingdom this could be a grave matter. Her
economic progress might well be slower than that of her great
neighbours, who would be taking full advantage of the splendid opportunities which many students of the problem (particularly in America) believe will be created by this great new
area of free trade. That Britain's leaders have realized the
profoundly important nature of this problem is clearly evi-
denced by their proposals for a continental Free Trade Area,
and subsequently, when this proved unacceptable, for the
Little Free Trade Area — the latter being proposed partly to
make the best of a bad job, and partly to strengthen the bargaining position of its members *vis à vis* the Six when the time
comes to reopen the question of an all-embracing European
Free Trade Area or of lesser measures of trade liberalization.

Even a full-scale Western European Free Trade Area, however, could not very materially alter the fact of Britain's
dependence on the outside world for her food and raw
materials. That this was recognized by her government is
probably illustrated by her stipulation, when she originally
proposed the Free Trade Area in 1956, that agriculture should
be excluded from its scope. Britain could perhaps get more
food than she now does from Europe, but she could not get

nearly enough to meet her needs. Still less could the European area supply her with the raw materials for her industry, which are almost as vital to her as her foodstuffs. Thus participation in a European union is not going very radically to lessen Britain's economic dependence on the outside world.

In strategical terms this means that Britain can never afford to enter into commitments in Europe which would make it possible for her to be alienated from the power that controls the seas, the United States. Furthermore, the emotional effects, if a similar breach with the Commonwealth should occur, would be deeply disturbing for Britain. In this century she has fought two great European wars, in both of which not only did the Commonwealth rally remarkably to her cause, but the United States also became her associate or ally. This underlines the true risk for Britain of the political implications of European unity; she has to reckon with the possibility of political disagreement, and even conceivably war, between the United States (with whom Canada, and probably Australia and New Zealand, would be bound in the end to side, painful as the decision might be for them) and her European associates. If it is said that this nightmare is a nightmare only, with no basis in reality, Britons cannot but recall the history of the three major European powers in the century and three-quarters since the American people gained their independence.

Italy, after a long period of disunity, had a number of years of not too successful constitutional monarchy, and now, after twenty years of Mussolini, contains the largest Communist party in the free Western world; Germany, from the anarchic sovereignties of the Holy Roman Empire, has been formed by the iron will of Prussia into a nation which has twice done more than any other state to plunge Europe and the world into global wars; and even France has had in that time not only some seven revolutions or *coups d'état*, but two periods of outright Napoleonic dictatorship. It is true that for ten years past (one seventeenth of the time since 1789) all Western Europe has worn a democratic face, but he would be a bold man who maintained that self-government and peace were undoubtedly solid and secure there for the future.

Thus any close connection between Britain and Europe,

with which the United States is not irrevocably, that is to say institutionally, associated on an equal basis, might one day force upon Britain a fearful decision. She might have to choose between, on the one hand, tearing herself out of the European body of which she had by then grown to be a part economically and politically, and, on the other, brutally severing the political and economic sinews and tendons which bind her to the English-speaking world. This is not of course inevitable; many might say that it is not very probable; but it is most certainly possible, and it is a risk which Britons must weigh and judge *now*.

If she were ever faced with such desperate alternatives, either choice might well prove disastrous to her, although not necessarily to her European partners. They have, many of them, survived for limited perods in modern history virtually cut off from the wider world: Britain never has and never can. On the other hand she has survived complete if temporary separation from virtually the whole of Europe. National economies are trained by the political and economic arrangements of governments to develop in certain ways; under her benign, but in some ways over-confident, free trade policies in the last century, Britain's economy grew in such a way that she is permanently dependent upon the primary products that come to her across the great oceans. If she ever opposes in war a hostile combination which controls the seas (and any combination which includes the United States will do so as far ahead as we can see), she will inevitably go down to final defeat; even if her communications with the continent remained intact, the inevitable cutting off of her ocean lines would bring swift starvation, for she is even more dependent on them for her existence. Europe might lament this fact, but would probably be as little able to do anything about it as Britain was able to do about the fall of Europe in 1940. On the other hand, if she once allows her economy and life to become fully integrated with that of Europe, any attempt to take the opposite course and to cleave in a crisis to America would be painful, or even impossible. The consequent upheaval might well leave her maimed and powerless, and the revulsion of feeling in Europe might have grave repercussions. The more successful, in a sense, her integration with Europe had proved, the more grave any necessary separation from Europe might be for Britain and all concerned.

In either event, Britain would in effect be faced with the necessity of rending herself in two if real strain were ever thrown on relations between the United States and Europe — and most of the Commonwealth (it would have no real choice) would go with America. All this takes no account of the appalling moral effect on Britain of being faced with the possibility of opposing, in the last ditch, the members of the English-speaking family.

When such might be the ultimate consequences of Britain's entry into a European union which had political as well as economic implications, she would be ill-advised indeed to take the plunge.

CHAPTER VIII

Britain and N.A.T.O.

WHAT, then, is the answer for Britain? Must she remain indefinitely frozen in immobility, unable to enter a thriving European union where economic opportunities exist for her on an unprecedented scale? Must she sit in paralysed inaction while a new political giant is created on her very doorstep in Europe — she who has always feared the growth of any single pre-eminent and potentially aggressive European power and who has fought it consistently, by a policy which came to be called the Balance of Power? Must she, at best, continue to react to every move in Europe with counter-suggestions, which, partly because they look like reluctant second-bests and partly because they are suspected of being merely efforts to sabotage the Grand Design, prove unacceptable to the Six? Must she leave all real initiatives in this field to other powers and see her international stature, both economic and political, dwindle remorselessly away as her Empire is dissolved and the super-states of the world community of nations grow ever more powerful?

Certainly she must not. But she cannot escape from the horns of the dilemma in which she now finds herself by a policy such as she has pursued since the war — a policy of leaving every genuine and profound initiative on a matter of such vital concern to Britain in the hands of other powers. With the exception of Churchill's original affirmation of the idea of European unity, what has the fundamental policy of British governments, Labour and Tory alike, been? The original Council of Europe of 1949 Britain entered but emasculated; the Coal and Steel Community she declined even to negotiate seriously about; the European Defence Community she probably did more than any other nation to destroy when she refused to join it; and to the Common Market and Euratom she finally decided, after going some distance in negotiation, that she could not commit herself. It is true that at this juncture she began to see that her position might be seriously jeopardized if the Common Market came into existence without her, and accordingly began to do some serious thinking.

As a result she proposed the idea, complementary to the Common Market, of a wider and looser European economic grouping, starting from the broad base of the members of O.E.E.C. and the European Payments Union. When this attempt to gain acceptance for the idea of a Free Trade Area failed, she thought again, and then launched the project of the Little Free Trade Area. But neither of these interesting plans, the latter of which is now materializing, was a real and spontaneous British initiative: both were merely reactions to initiatives from elsewhere. At no time — with one exception, and that abortive on the occasion in question — has Britain really put forward a new, constructive proposal of an imaginative kind entirely off her own bat. (Her proposal at the Council of Europe in May 1957 to 'streamline the various assemblies of N.A.T.O., W.E.U., the Council of Europe, O.E.E.C. and the Coal and Steel Community, by the creation of a European-Atlantic Assembly, can hardly count, since she explicitly ruled out for the present the idea of giving the new body any executive power.) Nor has she really felt, let alone shown, a dynamic enthusiasm for any of these proposals, such as the splendid drive displayed in the last decade by the 'Europeans'.

The single exception to this seeming rule of never acting except in reaction to the actions of others, of never challenging but only responding, was the interesting proposal put forward in the autumn of 1957 by Mr. Peter Thorneycroft, then Chancellor of the Exchequer, for a Commonwealth free trade area. Unfortunately, this suggestion, revolutionary in scope though on well-worn lines of Commonwealth preference, was put forward at a Commonwealth meeting in Ottawa in a manner which suggested that it was not seriously intended. It was prompted by the newly elected Canadian Prime Minister's ebullient and perhaps precipitate demand for a 15 per cent increase in Canadian trade with Britain, and it was put forward without warning, so that it gave the

impression of being — and may well have been — merely a
way of pricking this perhaps excessively inflated Canadian
ballon d'essai. This was a great pity, because the idea did not
deserve to be shoved under the carpet in the hasty way it then
was. The proposal for a Commonwealth free trade area was
a genuine initiative, a real British effort to overcome her
dilemma by a far-reaching plan of her own: it is a dismal
commentary on her political vision, energy and ingenuity that
it has been the best spontaneous and novel proposal that
Britain has been able to manage since the issue of European
unity first came alive ten years or so ago.

Why has this been so? It is not that Britain has been
incapable of vigorous policy initiatives; far from it. She was
not only chiefly responsible for making something of the
splendidly generous Marshall idea for economic aid to
Europe, by taking the lead in setting up O.E.E.C. and
E.P.U., but she also in reality took the basic initiative that
resulted in the Brussels Pact and in N.A.T.O.; in addition
she laid claim to having salvaged the defence structure of
Europe, by her proposal for 'Western European Union',
when German re-armament was imperilled by the failure of
E.D.C. But all these initiatives resulted in organizations
which strictly limited the absolute political commitments
exacted from their sovereign members, and this in fact may
partly explain her willingness to co-operate in them. Yet in
actuality N.A.T.O. has limited the national sovereignty of
its members in practice in a way quite unprecedented in
time of peace, and it is not simply sensitivity on the subject
of her ancient political independence which has inhibited
Britain from effective international initiatives of a sweeping
and striking kind. There is another and equally profound
cause — the Englishman's incurable pragmatism.

This is now a British political characteristic of such long
standing as to be almost inbred, and has taken shape in what
Englishmen have come proudly to call the 'middle way'.
This moderation, this tendency to compromise, which has
been historically associated with her slow, protracted development of constitutional government, has deep roots in English
history and owes much to the insular geographical position
which has so long protected her from foreign intervention;

certainly it can be seen at work as early as the emergence of
the Anglican Church, characteristically vague and all-embracing in its doctrines, and even more clearly later in the rise
of the spirit of toleration in the early eighteenth century.
Not that it has always been apparent even in relatively recent
times; during the Civil War and the Cromwellian military
autocracy in the seventeenth century, her politics were the
very reverse of moderate, and foreigners regarded the English,
with their wild search for freedom, as prime examples of
instability and political licence. Even Dryden, himself an
Englishman, described his countrymen as

> . . . a headstrong, moody, murmuring race,
> As ever tried the extent and stretch of grace;
> God's pamper'd people, whom debauch'd with ease,
> No king could govern, nor no Gods could please;
> (Gods they had tried of every shape and size,
> That godsmiths could produce, or priests devise:)
> These Adam-wits, too fortunately free,
> Began to dream they wanted liberty. . . .[1]

But the very violence and turbulence of the seventeenth
century bred an overt and deeply-felt desire for political
tranquillity, and this, in the eighteenth century, slowly began
to mature.

From that time forward, as Britons boast, there has been
an unbroken tradition of constitutional government and a
remarkable degree of political continuity in the mother
country, although she proved at first unable to handle things
so well in the colonies and dismally failed at any time satis-
factorily to settle the tragic Irish imbroglio. This now
ingrained national habit of avoiding political extremes by a
steady and utilitarian pragmatism has been acquired by
displaying a high degree of conservatism and caution, and by
making all political progress piecemeal. The United Kingdom, for example, converted itself from an oligarchy to a
democracy possessing adult suffrage through no less than five
great measures of parliamentary reform spread over nearly
a century of her modern history. She has been as reluctant to
shed the obsolete as she has been slow to adopt the new, and

English life is still filled with the paraphernalia of bygone ages. There has been a great house-cleaning in the last century and a quarter (before that even Edmund Burke, in some respects the most conservative of men, was impelled to protest that 'when the reason of old establishments is gone, it is absurd to preserve nothing but the burden of them'),[2] but much still remains that is of very doubtful value, as well as much that is of real use.

This precious asset of political moderation and stability, this practical approximation to the 'golden mean' of the Greeks (who themselves perhaps talked of it so much because they were in general so unsuccessful in following it), is one which has been bought at a price. Britons now will never 'go the whole hog' politically until they are forced by some enemy to do so in order to survive: it is highly significant that the only revolutionary proposal for a foreign union ever made by Britain in modern times was that to France — in the last throes of French defeat in 1940. (Even union between Malta and the United Kingdom seems to have gone by the board.) Having chosen evolution instead of revolution, Englishmen have developed an excessive fear of thorough-going measures; they are notoriously mistrustful not only of any wholehearted and far-reaching political programme, but also, for the most part, even of any abstract idea. They call moderate, pragmatic and 'sensible' what is sometimes piecemeal, hesitant and haphazard: what they regard as the wisdom of experience is sometimes fantastic good luck in muddling through. Similarly they mistrust exact formulas, crying with Burke 'Do not talk to me of metaphysical distinctions; I hate the very sound of them', and even mysteriously suspect their inventors of being 'too clever by a half': hear Macaulay declare that nothing is so useless as a general maxim and Englishmen echo that there is no tyranny so dangerous as that of a general idea. They believe in unwritten constitutions, the 'law' of precedent, and 'crossing your rivers when you come to them'. For practical illustrations of this, it is not necessary to look farther than the governmental system of Britain herself, topped by a constitutional monarch whose power is nowhere authoritatively laid down; it is a state running very largely by mere habit and convention, and very little indeed by specific legislation. This spirit is embodied above all in the constitutional 'system' of the Commonwealth, which is headed by a Crown to whom the vast majority of its citizens do not owe allegiance but which they recognize as the symbol of their association; it is a political entity having real vitality and usefulness but virtually no precise or written constitutional bonds.

This 'gradatim' policy, this spirit of step by step, has not served Britain badly in the past, in ages when she was in the van of the nations in strength and natural advantages — when, in other words, she had great margins of strength. But now her circumstances are very different: she is outclassed by the red giants and supernovae of the international firmament and has very little space for manoeuvre. In these circumstances, a refusal to contemplate the long and decisive stride of abandoning national sovereignty might prove to be the worst mistake of Britain's history, for her people might have cause to rue the day when, partly from their instinctive mistrust of the specific, rigid, and sometimes vastly detailed written constitutions which new federal states must necessarily have, they turned their backs on opportunities of entering new supra-national unions. Other nations do not all by any means share this mistrust of political absolutes. The French are always wiping large sections of their political slate clean, and there are very few peoples in Europe who have not had, for reasons external or internal, to do the same at some time in their history. Other states, which may be better examples to follow, have successfully performed the feat of starting constitutionally almost from scratch; Canada, with her difficult inbuilt national cleavage, was able to form the Canadian confederation; even South Africa created a Union which has endured for fifty years. But it is to the example of the making in 1789 of the United States Constitution that Britain must primarily look to give her courage. Here, in one prodigious leap into the light, a document (now a century and three quarters old) was drawn up which, with splendid elegance and astonishing brevity, laid down the political system under which the most powerful nation in the world has grown to greatness. It is the classical example of the 'all or nothing', as opposed to the 'little by little', pattern of political life. If

Britain is to solve her present dilemma she must needs be readier to follow that example.

There will be plenty of scope for the gradualist instinctiveness of the British political genius in helping to make the system work once it has been established. The Americans, too, are a pragmatic people, and they showed their remarkable political abilities in the way they clothed the bare bones of the written constitution with flesh in the years after it was inaugurated. But it was the first step that counted: only after that had been taken was a political development possible so utterly and happily different from that, for example, which went on at the same time in Latin America. The Constitutional Convention of 1787 and the ratification of the Constitution were the supreme triumph of that remarkable generation of statesmen whom Americans call the Founding Fathers. Only by a dramatic gesture of this nature, a whole-hearted commitment to a new and larger body politic, can Britain break out of the vicious circle she is now in, with its imminent risks of steadily diminishing political and economic returns. Let the British electorate for once remind themselves that,

> ' He either fears his fate too much,
>   Or his deserts are small
>   That puts it not unto the touch,
>   To win or lose it all.'

But once the people of Britain have made up their minds that this policy of drift, which is not too unkind a word to apply to what has been accomplished by her leaders in this field, where are they to address themselves if their interests forbid them to enter a purely European union? The answer is that they must turn their eyes once more outwards, as Churchill said they would when he declared in 1944, according to General de Gaulle, ' This is something you ought to know: each time we must choose between Europe and the open sea, we shall always choose the open sea.'[3] But they must not look to the Commonwealth alone. If all else were to fail Britain might strive to strengthen her exclusive bonds with those parts of the Commonwealth which desired such a development, but in the first place she must set her sights

I

much higher than that: nothing else should content her but the institutional cohesion of all three of her essential circles of association, Europe, the Commonwealth and also the United States. Britain is, or could be made, the natural link between Europe and the English-speaking world, just as she really is geographically the pivotal point of N.A.T.O.; and it is on this basis that she should first organize her ideas about a new and greater union. As I wrote in 1952: 'Only within such a broad organization as is the North Atlantic Treaty Organization can Britain find a full and happy life for her people. This must remain her level of co-operation; nothing less will satisfy her needs . . .'[4]

Of late the air around us has been filled with lamentations about the inadequacy of N.A.T.O., both militarily and administratively, but, though there has been much talk of reform, no national government has come forward to press consistently, energetically and seriously for the gradual transformation of N.A.T.O. into an Atlantic Union. Yet this is the only satisfactory solution of Britain's increasingly acute dilemma about European unity: it is a goal towards which the British government should have been pressing for a decade, ever since N.A.T.O. was formed. But in fact, it appears, they have never considered it seriously, and the initial momentum of the developing alliance, which might have been sustained, has been lost. Now, however, Britain's leaders have little choice, for only by unremitting zeal for Atlantic Union can Britain avoid, not only the just blame for preventing full European unity, but also the disadvantages of finding herself outside the great new political grouping or the even greater disadvantage of tying herself exclusively to Europe. There is no evidence that they have grasped the fact even now, but grasp it they must, and the sooner the better, for every month that passes sees the division of Europe becoming more complete and more irrevocable. If Britain is to strive to convince her partners of the free West that such an Atlantic Union is necessary and feasible, there is no time to lose.

At the time of writing, the apparent policy of the British government is to press on with the inauguration of the Little Free Trade Area while assuaging continental fears by repeating that she wishes no ill to the Common Market; and when

this has been accomplished, to reopen, from this slightly
stronger bargaining position, negotiations for a presumably
modified form of the Free Trade Area for the whole of
Western Europe, the preservation of whose basic economic
unity, as expressed in O.E.E.C. and E.P.U., Britain has always
claimed to be her primary concern. Thus Mr. Macmillan, on
the eve of Dr. Adenauer's London visit in November 1959,
declared that Britain welcomed the Common Market and that
her aim was 'the widest and most fruitful association of
European countries', but that she could not shut her eyes to
'the dangers of economic division in Western Europe'.
Britain looked forward to the launching of the Free
Trade Association of the Seven, but regarded it 'as a step
in the direction of a closer economic association in all
Europe'.

But Mr. Macmillan's assurance that Britain had 'no subtle
or obscure policies' seemed to miss the point, for his speech
contained no single word on Britain's attitude to political
unity in Europe — in which alone in his heart the German
Chancellor is really interested, whatever may be in the heart
of General de Gaulle. The British government is presumably
opposed to Britain's entry into the Common Market because
it has clear political implications; and in this they are correct
and wise. They presumably favour a European Free Trade
Area because they believe it has not, or at least that those
implications can be sufficiently controlled as to render them
innocuous, and in this it is to be hoped that they are right.
But Britain can never face this question without embarrass-
ment, and can scarcely discuss it without causing suspicion in
other lands, until she decisively and resolutely espouses the
greater cause of an Atlantic Union, economic and political
both.

What is meant by the term 'Atlantic Union'? What is
envisaged in the idea? Let it first be said that over-precision
at this stage would be a great error and a waste of time. This
is no place to produce blue prints for a new society (some of
which, such as Clarence E. Streit's *Union Now*, have long
existed) but rather to argue the necessity of a certain course
of action — a federal Union of the West — and to suggest a

very small number of possible and extremely flexible ideas as to its extent and nature. First its nature.

Here, so successfully has it progressed to date, we may learn from the experience of the Common Market. Wisely, given the depth of national feelings in Europe, the Six did not try to emulate the American Convention of 1787 by creating a federal constitution at one blow; rather *they have envisaged a long period of progressive construction, but they have insisted from the beginning on a firm commitment to the idea of ultimate union.* This was the commitment at which Britain rightly baulked, not rightly because it was a commitment, but rightly because it was exclusively European. It would seem wisest that an Atlantic Union should also be built by deliberate stages, but from the beginning a firm commitment to 'a more perfect union' should be demanded from its members. From the time the very first steps are taken, the ultimate goal of a permanent federal association should be recognized. This term itself is large and comprehensive, and there are many degrees of federalism, but one thing is clear — each stage must from the beginning be regarded as irrevocable: to this extent must national sovereignty be at once submerged.

It would also seem desirable that the ultimate aims for the central authority should include three minimum essentials of power. First, that it should in due course gain complete control of all policy concerning tariffs and external trade, as well as currency, and of such powers over the financial and economic life of the federation as are deemed necessary to make the customs union work (it might for example be wise for the union government itself to be able to take measures to cushion the more drastic effects of the first steps towards unity on certain sectors of the nations' economy); these aims would clearly require the right to tax. Second, that it should ultimately have indisputable paramount control over matters of defence, which would obviously also necessitate the power to tax. Third, that it should have exclusive control over foreign policy. Finally, it would be necessary in all these branches of government to accept the fundamental premise that it would enforce its will by the direct application of its laws to the individual citizens of which the federation as a whole was composed and not to its member states. More

powers it might well acquire in time: less would not ensure
its survival or its usefulness. These minimum aims should be
be accepted from the outset.

As to the order in which the progressive steps towards unity
might be taken, we can learn once again from the example
of the Six. The 'Europeans' tried the economic tack first,
and then turned to the political, but returned once more to
the economic when the political failed; a similar flexibility
is essential in moving towards Atlantic Union. In some senses,
since N.A.T.O. already exists, it might seem good to start with
the political aspect first, perhaps defence matters or matters
of foreign policy. On the other hand, as the issue of the
Common Market and the Free Trade Area has already been
raised in an acute form, and as economic matters are sometimes less politically sensitive, it might be better to begin
with the idea of an Atlantic free trade area or customs union.
It conceivably might even be thought wise, in view of the
vested interests of leaders of national governments, to disregard the European experience altogether and to set the ball
rolling by summoning a fully fledged constituent assembly,
or constitutional convention, to consider the whole question
ab initio. But if one approach should fail, we should not be
discouraged from trying again, and if necessary again and
again, on another line.

And what of the composition of the new Union? Once
more, great flexibility would be desirable when negotiations
began, but we should think perhaps, in the first instance, of
two main groups, the larger, North Atlantic, group, and the
Commonwealth group. It might well be thought wisest to
begin with a solid basis consisting of the original twelve nations
of N.A.T.O. (Belgium, Canada, Denmark, France, Iceland,
Italy, Luxemburg, The Netherlands, Norway, Portugal, the
United Kingdom and the United States), *plus* West Germany,
plus the other two long-established members of the Commonwealth, Australia and New Zealand. The three neutral
nations, Sweden, Switzerland and Austria, might also wish to
be included. It might possibly be thought justifiable to
include the remaining members of N.A.T.O. (Greece and
Turkey), and perhaps others, such as Eire or Spain or Finland. But while the detailed plan should be left flexible, the

initial and essential core of the Union must obviously be found among the countries of Western Europe, North America and Australasia. The obstacles of distance, so long advanced as arguments against widely scattered political groupings, are hardly very formidable, even in the case of Australasia, in the era of the jet plane.

This is the grand object for which Britain should be striving. For once she must bring herself to stake everything on a struggle for this bold, revolutionary plan. Otherwise this time she may muddle through only to disaster — or at least to a future in which it will become increasingly difficult for her to keep pace with political, economic and social progress in other lands. Positive steps *vis à vis* Europe are urgently necessary for Britain: she may yet find herself unable to effect even the loosest unity of the whole of Europe on the economic plane, and the Little Free Trade Area is not enough alone. To enter the Common Market, or even a United States of all Europe, has too many political dangers and disadvantages for her: to stay out may have almost as many. Closer bonds with Europe are not enough: even closer bonds with the Commonwealth or the United States are not a complete answer. There is for Britain no fully satisfactory alternative to Atlantic Union.

NOTES

[1] John Dryden, *Poetical Works*, London 1832, ' Absalom and Achitophel ', p. 126.

[2] Burke, *op. cit.*, p. 190.

[3] *The War Memoirs of Charles de Gaulle: Unity, 1942-1944*, New York 1959, p. 253.

[4] *Great Britain and the United States*, pp. 942-3.

CHAPTER IX

Great Britain and Atlantic Union

WE observed two main dangers for Britain in entering a European union. The first — that it would conflict with her prior economic and political ties with the Commonwealth and the United States — would, as we have just seen, be removed almost entirely by Atlantic Union. The second danger is that Britain's democratic institutions might be seriously imperilled in a union the majority of whose electorate had given so little proof in the past of political ability or stability. Atlantic Union would solve this problem also, for it would contain a majority of voters from lands with long-established and successful democratic systems of self-government. This would be true whether one reckoned by counting heads or by counting nations; both in the Senate and the House of Representatives, if we may borrow terms from American constitutional practice, power in the last resort would be in the hands of men and women representing experienced democratic electorates.

If we assume in the first instance a basic Atlantic Union such as we envisaged earlier, consisting of the original twelve N.A.T.O. powers, *plus* West Germany, *plus* Australia and New Zealand, we have the populations shown below: [1]

Belgium	8,989,000
Canada	16,589,000
Denmark	4,500,000
France	44,091,000
Iceland	165,000
Italy	48,483,000
Luxemburg	316,000
The Netherlands	11,021,000
Norway	3,494,000
Portugal	8,909,000
United Kingdom	51,455,000
United States	171,196,000
	369,208,000

West Germany	51,469,000

	420,677,000
Australia	9,643,000
New Zealand	2,229,000

	432,549,000

If for good measure we also assume the participation of Sweden, Switzerland and Austria, we reach a figure which we will call Total A.

Carried Forward	432,549,000
Sweden	7,367,000
Switzerland	5,117,000
Austria	6,997,000
Total A	452,030,000

If we think it justifiable to add the two other members of N.A.T.O., Greece and Turkey, the figure is:

Carried Forward	452,030,000
Greece	8,096,000
Turkey	25,500,000
	485,626,000

If we add virtually all the states which might possibly adhere in the near future, we reach a grand total, which we will call B:

Carried Forward	485,626,000
Eire	2,885,000
Finland	4,336,000
Spain	29,431,000
Total B	522,278,000

How may we assess the political competence of these peoples? It must be stressed again that it is greatly to be hoped that, once such a Union was formed, the body politic would divide — as did the United States after 1789 — on other than purely state lines; and there are many wise and sensible political beings in nations whose overall record in democracy is bad, just as there are plenty of political incompetents and villains in those countries whose history of self-government is better. But, speaking generally, we may once more — we have no real alternative — judge in broad terms on the basis of past national experience.

When estimating European union we considered as the reliable elements, Britain, The Netherlands, Belgium, Luxemburg, Sweden, Switzerland, Denmark, and Norway, a total population of 92,259,000. We put in the other scale West Germany, Italy, France, Portugal and Austria, totalling 159,949,000. If we now look at the countries comprising Total A above we see that the states added are Canada, Iceland, the United States, Australia and New Zealand, whose populations total 199,822,000. *All of these peoples have had long and on the whole remarkably successful experience of democratic self-government, and when we add them to the reliable 92,259,000 we already have, we find a very large, stable and competent majority indeed — 292,081,000 in 452,030,000 — in our basic Atlantic Union.* The minority would be 159,949,000. If we take a larger basic group, the majority is still substantial, for, even with Greece, Turkey and Spain put among those with as yet insufficient democratic experience and Eire and Finland among the others, the figures are; overall total 522,278,000; reliable majority 299,302,000, minority 222,976,000. It should be possible, also, if the day should ever come, to absorb the 16,401,000 inhabitants of East Germany without excessive strain.

But at this juncture some European critics may very probably wish to call a halt: Frenchmen, Germans and Italians will certainly have done so long ago. Even many Britons may be surprised at one item — and it is the most important one — in this classification. They would accept Canada, Australia, and New Zealand without question. Some of them will perhaps raise an eyebrow over Eire, but their real query will be about the United States. We have here, without shilly-shallying, to face the fact that Englishmen are still by habit of mind excessively Eurocentric and astoundingly, alarmingly, ignorant about the great American republic. Many of them regard the United States as a young and inexperienced nation, with an outmoded, incomprehensible and inefficient constitution; they consider that Americans boast much about their democracy, but that it is vitiated in practice by materialism and corruption; but they readily admit that the American people have come, through good fortune as well as hard work, to possess enormous international power. These British critics will point out, quite rightly, that it is on the great population of the United States that all our calculations — indeed this whole hypothesis — depend; to what extent can we fairly say that the United States is more to be relied upon in a democratic Union than, for instance, France?

The United States can, with the exception (as more sophisticated Europeans will not fail to point out) of the Civil War, reasonably claim to have the oldest continuous tradition of democratic self-government in the world. The Civil War, it is true, did rip the whole fabric of American life apart, and its consequences are still very much with the American people, but it was, as Lincoln said it was, essentially a war to preserve democracy — a war precipitated by a problem, that of Negro slavery, far exceeding in difficulty almost any internal problem with which the United Kingdom has ever had to deal. Indeed, in the whole of Europe perhaps only the present problem of France in Algeria in a very small way resembles it. It was a war to test whether any nation conceived in liberty and dedicated to the proposition that all men are created equal could long endure — but endure it did. What is more, it endured without any lasting interruption of the democratic constitutional processes of the United States which were at once regular and indispensable; *habeas corpus* was, it is true, suspended and the President assumed very far-reaching war powers, but a regular full-scale Presidential election was held in the North at the height of the war, with a very popular Northern general standing against Lincoln on a platform not far removed from outright opposition to the continuation of the struggle. This in the throes of a Civil War which was the bloodiest conflict of any kind which had taken place in the world up to that date. By contrast, the uninvaded United Kingdom did not think it wise to hold an election at all in the course of either of the last two world wars.

The Constitution which brought the United States into being in 1789, called by Gladstone 'the most wonderful work ever struck off at a given time by the brain and purpose of man',[2] was the artifact of a generation of political masters. The degree of its democracy must not be over-emphasized, for a number of what we now consider its essential hallmarks were lacking. Female suffrage was, of course, unheard of, and, even though modern historical research has tended to emphasize the extent to which many states then approached manhood suffrage, some of their constitutions (in the Deep South, for example) were highly oligarchical. The first great national party which held office, the Federalist, was in many respects aristocratic in flavour, and it was not until the spate of reforms in the state governments carried through in the era of Jacksonian Democracy that full manhood suffrage actually became the order of the day in many parts of the Union, while even after the Civil War — and indeed up to the present day — the South continued to deny the franchise to its large Negro minority. Nevertheless, for all that the Constitution itself was the product of reaction against the extreme radicalism of the Revolutionary era, it did on the whole from the beginning effectively secure, as it proclaimed that it set out to do, 'the Blessings of Liberty to ourselves and our Posterity'.

In 1789 there were, of course, other states in the world with a history, in some degree at least, of self-rule. The United Kingdom had a far older system of representative government (from which, needless to say, the American derived), but it was, and was to remain for more than forty years, exceedingly debased as a form of popular representation; so great was the corruption, by money and by 'influence', that only at times of great crisis was the sovereign Parliament powerfully and directly moved by popular feeling. At the end of the eighteenth century, too, Switzerland had an ancient federal system with a vigorous representative element in it, but she was in the future to undergo foreign occupation and internal revolution (and incidentally has not even now adopted female suffrage), as also were such venerable, and, in some senses, constitutional states as The Netherlands and Sweden. France, too, was shortly to set out upon her at times highly influential, though exceedingly chequered, democratic career. But for the development of popular government in the nineteenth century, the American Revolution, and the Constitution which finally emerged from it, in fact set the tone, even though in a fashion which owed much to America's British origins: though liberalism may have been in the air in the later eighteenth century, the birth of the United States imparted to it perhaps the most important impetus it was from that time forward to acquire. Englishmen, for example, have not yet fully appreciated the influence of American democracy on the movement for Parliamentary reform in Britain in the nineteenth century, especially in precipitating the Reform Bill of 1867.

The American tradition, which the American people began to build in 1776, has never strayed far from the fundamental democratic principles enunciated in that year, and has never forgotten that the governments instituted among men derive 'their just powers from the consent of the governed . . .' Nor has American democracy stood still in these years; rather has it been a kind of constitutional and administrative laboratory of the democratic process, devising and testing such institutions for the strengthening of popular government as the referendum and the recall, and carrying out such political experiments as the unicameral legislature and the election of judges. It has so jealously guarded the freedom of the press that many believe that 'the fourth estate' has acquired excessive power, not of comment but of interview and question. The European observer of the American scene can hardly fail to be impressed with the directness, scope and detailed application of American self-government at all levels of political society, from a township floating a bond issue for its own schools to the President's regular press conference.

This tradition of democracy has been preserved, and indeed deepened, in circumstances of such difficulty in some respects as to be almost unimaginable in much of Europe. Her foreign wars between 1814 and 1914 were, it is true, minor, but so were those of certain European states, including Britain. On the other hand, during the first two-thirds of her independent existence she subjugated a continental wilderness with astonishing speed and success, and at the same time became the greatest commercial and industrial power in the world. In the most recent third of her existence, she has been the chief agent of victory in the two world wars. These things she accomplished while absorbing into her growing body a fabulous total of well over 40,000,000 immigrants from other lands, most of them utterly devoid of political experience, so that for long periods of American history more than 10 per cent of American citizens were foreign born. These things were not, of course, without their effect upon American democracy, and they go far to explain the gap which there is between theory and practice in the governmental processes of the United States. But there can be no serious question of the reality and stability of American democratic self-government. Because it would have her weight in the scales, there is a far, far better chance that democracy would flourish in an Atlantic than in a European Union. Within this wider unity not only would Britain's extra-European ties be automatically safeguarded, but her long tradition of self-government would also be preserved.

If the only reasons for Britain to seek Atlantic Union were negative ones, it could hardly be expected that she would undertake the quest with too much energy, let alone enthusiasm: the perils of inaction on this issue are not yet sufficiently imminent or formidable to arouse her instinct of self-preservation, though they are in fact real enough. But there are also positive advantages for Britain, especially in the economic sphere, in becoming a member of an Atlantic Union.

Until the marked improvement which took place, with a return to something closer to what used to be called financial orthodoxy, under the Tory government between 1957 and 1959, Britain's steps ever since World War II had been dogged by a recurrent series of balance of payments crises, by a chronic weakness of sterling. This economic recovery, which was so striking as to be almost dramatic, was only in part the result of stricter government financial policies and owed much to favourable alterations in the terms of Britain's trade, a factor over which she has, of course, very little control. To

some extent, too, this is true of the general improvement in
the economic position of Europe *vis à vis* America in recent
years (which was so considerable as to produce in 1959 a substantial deficit in the actual balance of payments of the United
States and a consequent weakening of the dollar), although
it was also the result of the splendid increase in European
productivity which had taken place since the inauguration of
the Marshall Plan twelve years before. But in the event of
bad international economic weather, Britain may some day
very well find herself once more facing, willy nilly, the
unpleasant alternatives of persistent balance of payments
crises on the one hand, or economic depression, with its
accompanying unemployment or austerity, on the other.

The fundamental reason for this balance of payments situation, complex as it is in its particular symptoms, is the fact of
which we are already so aware — the unique dependence of
the United Kingdom on world-wide foreign trade, much of
it with the Empire. When during World War II Britain was
forced both to dispose of great quantities of her overseas
investments and also to lose a very large proportion of her
established international markets, she surrendered — in the
good cause of victory — the economic defences which she had
built up over the years against the peculiar dangers of her
international economic position. How big that surrender was
and how serious those dangers were was indicated by the
prodigious increase in her exports (estimated at the time as
175 per cent) needed to prevent a serious drop in her standard
of living — needed, that is to say, merely in order to mark
time. In fact, of course, Britain has done very much better
than this and has advanced a good deal. But the war alone
did not create the situation, it did but bring its underlying
perils to the surface.

Those perils are perhaps best understood by comparing the
realities of Britain's economic position with those of, for
example, the United States. For all the bulk and the relatively
increasing importance to America of her foreign commerce,
this great continental nation is remarkably self-sufficient: she
is indeed — and this is the crux of the matter — an international market in herself. Her thriving cities are fed very
largely from her own vast farmlands: her industrial raw

materials, likewise, are largely the product of her own fields and mines. She is not independent of international trade and unaffected by its terms, but she is remarkably cushioned against its shocks. *Above all, she has political control over the great majority of the markets in which she buys and sells her food and raw materials and her manufactured goods.*

This does not remove, as if by magic, the stresses and strains of commercial life, so many of which tend to show themselves in Britain as balance of payments crises; the extraordinary history of the bimetallist movement in the United States in the late nineteenth century (about which so little is known in Britain) is a vivid illustration of this fact, for they here assumed the shape of a prolonged struggle between the industrial 'East' and the rural 'West' over the desirability of going over to an inflated and inflationary silver-cum-gold currency — in terms of international trade, 'going off gold' and 'devaluing the dollar'. But the essence of this very close domestic parallel to Britain's international problem is that it became a political battle, that is to say, one in which the American authorities could act to exert some measure of economic control. Similarly, the Great Depression shows clearly enough that the American economy has had desperate problems of its own, not unconnected, in their beginnings at any rate, with foreign trade. At the outset the difficulty in 1929, as it had also been in the case of the depression of 1893, was that American political authorities had, or were thought to have, inadequate powers to take sufficiently vigorous economic remedial measures. (It is also true that in the pre-Keynesian era orthodox economics was literally flummoxed by what was happening, in America as well as Europe.) But there are at least some grounds for hoping that the American government now has both the power and the understanding to take effective action of this kind, and that this is part at least of the reason for the virtually uninterrupted rise in the American standard of living in recent years.

How different is the position of the United Kingdom! Her trade is to an extraordinary degree scattered broadcast among numerous countries of the earth, and when economic storms blow there is no single captain who can give the orders. However inefficient and reluctant an agent of economic control the federal government of the United States may have been at times, it was infinitely better than 'the usual diplomatic channels' or even an international conference: meetings in the fo'c's'le are no substitute for a single authority at any time, let alone in a gale. The great practical weakness of Britain's economic position is that it is essentially an international one, so that her government has a minimum of control over its conditioning circumstances.

It is true that she has contrived some measures to alleviate these difficulties, particularly the association known as the Sterling Area. Because, as we have seen, a very high proportion of her trade is with the Commonwealth, and because, although she no longer has any political control over its members, she has habit and a great willingness to co-operate on her side, she has been able to maintain this system, by which a number of countries, mostly of the Commonwealth but not including Canada, to some extent pool their dollar resources in London and agree to use them only for essential purposes. That the Sterling Area is a powerful instrument is illustrated by the fact that it accounted in 1949 for 14·1 per cent of the world's exports, as compared with a figure of 14·9 per cent for the 'dollar area'.[3] (If the so-called 'transferable account' nations are also included the figure was very much higher.) But even the Sterling Area is only a volutary agreement between sovereign states, and because London is the sterling banker it in fact brought its own special difficulties to Britain, by involving her seriously in some economic disturbances among member states which might not otherwise have affected her very closely. As long as Britain depends so much on foreign trade with many and diverse sovereign nations, in a world with very little economic or social uniformity and co-operation, her situation will always remain peculiarly uneasy, subject to fluctuations beyond her control, and not without real risks.

One particular difficulty of Britain illustrates all the rest. It has recently been pointed out that the secret of American productivity is not only the extent of the domestic market and the richness of the resources of the United States, combined with American skill, energy and enterprise, but also the existence there of a unique depth of uniform consumer demand, which is a vital requisite for taking full advantage of modern techniques of industrial mass production.[4] This demand is facilitated greatly by American advertising and market research, but the heart of the matter is the presence of a large, stable purchasing public whose ideas, needs and wishes are remarkably homogeneous. (The American public rarely rebels, as it has recently done in its desire for the small car, against the dictates of the industrial giants which are soothingly communicated to it by Madison Avenue.) Detroit, for example, produces for a market uniquely large, uniquely prosperous, and uniquely uniform, and this confers on it a tremendous technical advantage over automobile industries in other lands.

British industry, on the other hand, to an important extent produces for independent markets so various and so numerous that her technical problems sometimes seem almost insuperable. Different sectors of her international market are not only at different levels of wealth, but are totally different in population, climate and terrain — to say nothing of economic habit and desire. The American automobile has to suit great differences of environment, but none so diverse as the British exported car, which may equally go to Canada, New Zealand, Europe, or Africa; not merely to countries mountainous or flat, hot or cold, but to roads paved and unpaved, splendid and non-existent. And the aids to this commerce, to the discovery of these requirements, are immensely more complex than in the case of America : market research must be carried out in dribs and drabs in differing societies demanding different methods of approach. Nor do the great mass media of advertisement exist as a single whole; television in some places may be in its infancy, there are thousands of different radio networks, written advertisements may have to be in a hundred different tongues and jargons. And even when the product leaves the factory, it has to overcome formidable obstacles in transport, currency, tariffs, trade quotas and all the rest before it reaches its destination. The achievements of British industry under such circumstances are remarkable, but its difficulties are illustrative of most of those which flow from her peculiar international economic position.

But if she became a part of an Atlantic Union she would

K

have taken, by the act of membership alone, a real step towards a new economic solidity and progress. Her balance of payments problem would become, for the Union government, a domestic trade and currency problem; this mere fact would do something to cure it, and the government would have effective power to do more. The Union, too, would contain within its own borders a remarkably large percentage of both the food and raw materials and also the industrial resources that she, or any other member, needed. As the peoples of the Union grew gradually closer to one another, a greater degree of uniformity in material demands (not, it would be hoped, in cultural life, where diversity is precious) would make possible the highest rationalization of industry. This area, under a stable representative government, would exceed enormously in size and resources the United States sub-continent, unrestricted trade throughout which made the modern American economic achievement possible: it would indeed be a modern version of the great world area of free trade through which Britain prospered in so unprecedented a way in the nineteenth century—but with the supreme advantage that it would be a single political unit for essential purposes. This would constitute a gain for all nations in it, but a particularly great one for Britain.

There is a second positive economic advantage for Britain in Atlantic Union which deserves attention. The economic object of all societies, in so far as they are aiming at material objectives, is to increase their wealth; in this democratic era there is an accompanying aim that this wealth shall be, at least to some extent, fairly distributed among the people. On the Left of British politics for the last half century, the second aim has been dominant; the rise of Labour (and the last years of Lib-Lab before it) have been indissolubly associated with the desire greatly to equalize the distribution of national wealth, a fact which is demonstrated by the essential role of the trade unions in the movement. Because this was a political movement for economic ends and because of the prevalence, during that whole era, of socialist ideas, it was through the state—and particularly in theory by the nationalization of the means of production—that this redistribution of national income was to be, and has largely been, effected.

The achievements of this character in Britain (accomplished directly by Labour or Liberal governments, and indirectly by their pressure on Conservative governments) were by the middle of this century far reaching and in many respects good. But Labour then showed itself largely incapable of grasping the fundamental fact that there was going to be no more wealth to distribute until more wealth was produced. Other nations had more firmly apprehended this truth: that the only foundation for increasing national income is increasing national productivity. More than any other single factor it may well have been Conservative understanding of this truth which has led to its series of electoral victories, three in as many general elections. Labour failed to appreciate this fact largely because it was wedded to doctrines of state control and because the influence of the trade unions, ever mindful of the Great Depression, was very conservative. The Soviet Union was showing, it is true, what productivity was possible for a totally state-controlled economy, but this was achieved at a cost in human suffering and liberty which almost no one in Britain, even in the Labour Party, was prepared to contemplate for a moment. On the other hand, in a United States which still liked to think of itself — with a degree of truth, despite the great growth of state influence over economic life in the previous decades — as a free enterprise society, there was a living, unparalleled example of what even a modified *laissez-faire* system could do in the way of producing riches. But to Labour, because of its socialist colouring, the great stronghold of capitalism must be, by definition, economically obsolete and dangerous, so that the achievements of American industry sometimes seemed to become little less than abhorrent.

A majority of the British electorate, however, appeared convinced by 1959 that it was not through a Labour government, with its restrictive policies of state control, that national wealth was going to be most rapidly increased. They rightly saw that a greater measure of economic freedom and scope for enterprise, even if it sometimes seemed to bear heavily on a few members of society, was the only way to ensure continuing increases in national productivity. An economic society reasonably free from controls and restraints, and rewarding hard work and initiative, they deemed essential to a rise in the general standard of living. They also began to gain a dim perception of the fact that a highly flexible, highly efficient and highly productive economy was peculiarly necessary for Britain, which is so vulnerable to the often unpredictable gusts and eddies of international trade. But they were not, even yet, sufficiently aware of the vital necessity for her to be able to adjust herself rapidly and effectively to the sudden changes in the economic climate of the world, which she must inevitably expect.

But even under a Tory government this aim of flexibility will not be easy to attain. The British are a conservative people, and do not always take readily to rapid alterations in their way of life; nor are they so mobile in their habits as their American cousins. Furthermore, there are in the United Kingdom powerful vested interests which are suspicious of economic change; the British trades union movement, partly because it is one of the oldest in the world, is one of the most conservative and tradition-bound, and with Labour in Opposition it tends to be the practical centre of labour's power. This conservatism has often great political advantages, and it enables the labour movement to avoid the grim corruption which has done so much to mar American trade unions. On the other hand, it is probably the most serious single obstacle to the quickest possible growth of British productivity, and hence to the most rapid and greatest rise in the standard of living of the British working man. In this respect Britain's labour leaders could learn a very great deal from the ready and swift adaptability to technological progress — which has been greater of late than ever before, and will continue to accelerate at an unprecedented rate — of their counterparts in the United States. The hide-bound traditionalism of, for example, labour in shipbuilding yards (to say nothing of its fantastic inter-union jurisdictional disputes) is a deadly and deadening frustration to Britain's efforts at rapid economic development. Britain, like America, though for different reasons, will have in the near future to take a long hard look at the place which trade unions now occupy in her national life.

It is not, however, labour alone in Britain which is conservative, for British industry, though it has made remarkable progress in the last few years, has a tendency to traditionalism, even immobilism, which is sometimes as great. The United Kingdom is here suffering from the fact that she was the first industrial nation in the world; she acquired many of her habits and much even of her industrial plant when industrialism was young and relatively inefficient. Human nature being what it is, at least—so it seems—in Britain, there is a reluctance to change to new and better ideas and equipment if one is doing reasonably well already with those one has— even though one would do very much better if one did change. A great renovation of British industry would in any event have been necessary in the interests of economic expansion if there had been no Second World War. As it is, in the cotton industry for example, the government is having, by a mixture of the stick and carrot, to facilitate, indeed to enforce, this process of renewal and reinvigoration. Elsewhere, such as shipbuilding again (where Britain has recently lost, both in quantity and, in a sense, quality, the lead among the nations which she so long enjoyed) new brooms are urgently needed, but are not really in sight. Britain has her young and highly efficient industries—I.C.I. and Unilever for example—but, all in all, there are huge areas of British industry and its labour which need a stimulus to change far more sweeping than any British government alone can easily give.

The truth is that in the search for economic efficiency there is no substitute for competition. Out-of-date machines, traditional markets and outmoded methods are partly the result of circumstances and partly of fixity of habits of mind and the rigidity of long-established patterns of behaviour: old societies, like old people, stiffen mentally as well as physically, and only the stimulus of deliberate and vigorous activity can keep them flexible. Happily, too, societies do not age according to the relatively unchangeable laws of individual life, of birth, growth, decay and death, and are in any event capable of standing up to, and indeed profiting hugely from, shock treatments that would slay the average individual. Britain, if she is to improve her standard of living at a rate comparable with that of many other countries at the present time, must still vastly increase her productivity; this can most swiftly and

efficiently be accomplished by a powerful dose of competition
for both labour and industry. Total immersion in an Atlantic
Union would serve this purpose admirably, for the competition would not be from the uncertainties of an uncontrollable
international market, but from an area which would then be
stable and domestic. The shock of the cold water would be
considerable, and would be painful to some, but it would
produce, to change the metaphor abruptly, a winnowing-out
of the chaff of inefficiency in British commerce and industry
such as the country has seldom if ever experienced. Nothing
could better promote Britain's most necessary economic objective — increased productivity and flexibility.

Not that in fact, in these days, the medicine need be, or
would be, as unpleasant as all that. There would be no
question of diving naked into the icy pool in the expectation
that it would miraculously transform itself into a warm lake
by recreating the economic conditions of free trade and free
enterprise envisaged by the classical economists, in which
unrestricted play was given to the law of comparative advantage and the highest expectations entertained as to the
mobility of capital and labour. The Common Market has
shown the way for a step-by-step approach over a period of
years to a goal already accepted. Furthermore, the clock of
modern habits of state intervention cannot suddenly be put
right back, even if this were desirable, and agencies of
government would be able very substantially to cushion at
first the worst effects of sudden change, by all the fiscal
instruments of the modern state, taxation, tax exemption,
subsidy and so on. Above all, our society (and by this I mean
the Atlantic area) is now quite wealthy enough to protect
those who, by reason of age or genuine incapacity, are pushed
to the wall during the process of drastic change.

In the long run, however, the effects of recreating within
the borders of Atlantic Union an area of free trade, of
uninhibited capital movement, and of increasing mobility of
labour, exceeding by far, in area and in quantity and variety
of resources, the continental United States, and approaching
in size Adam Smith's 'great mercantile republic' of international free trade, would be, as far as the fallible human
mind can foresee, extraordinarily beneficial to its member

peoples, and above all to Britain. Not only would it resolve her economic, as well as her political, dilemma, but it would offer her, with her sister nations, possibilities of material betterment not merely far greater than Common Market or Free Trade Area, but unprecedented in the history of man.

Thus Atlantic Union alone has the power to solve the baffling problems which confront the United Kingdom. If she earnestly and ardently pursues this aim, she removes from her shoulders the blame — in a sense the rightful blame — for being the principal power which has prevented the full and thorough-going unity of Europe. She can no longer be accused of 'dragging her feet' when she proclaims her desire to substitute for it a Union more 'fundamental and astounding'. By ensuring that the new body politic (to which she, and her companions, will in due time surrender their national sovereignty) includes all those nations or groups of nations — the inner Commonwealth, the United States and Europe — with which she has vital life-giving ties, she avoids the fearful necessity of ever having to tear herself apart by choosing between them. More than that, she renders it as sure as it could ever be that orderly and free democratic self-government will continue to prevail within the Union. She can, on the economic plane, ease at one stroke, by participating in the creation of Atlantic Union, the difficulties financial and economic, as well as strategic, which arise from her precarious international position, uniquely dependent as it is upon a vast, yet scattered and world-wide, commerce. Finally, she can by this bold and imaginative act make possible for herself, as well as her colleague nations, a standard of living such as she could never hope to attain in conditions of national sovereignty.

But she alone can really take the initiative, because, though it is in the interest of all, it is peculiarly in her interest. The countries of the Common Market feel that they have made their contribution; the other nations of Europe and the Commonwealth look naturally to Britain, the only great power in their midst, for leadership; the United States is distant and remote. Geographically as well as politically and

emotionally, the British Isles forms the natural and indispensable link between Europe and America, and a passive link
will serve no longer. Britain must bestir herself in this cause
as never before; she alone can make a start in suggesting,
planning, cajoling and increasingly pressing upon the nations
of the North Atlantic the imperative necessity of Atlantic
'Union Now'.

NOTES

[1] *United Nations Demographic Year Book* 1958, as above in Chapter IV.
[2] Quoted *Allen, op. cit.*, p. 116.
[3] Woytinsky, *World Commerce and Governments*, p. 92.
[4] See Chapter XIII below.

PART II

The Challenge to America

'But if we fail, then the whole world, including the United States, including all that we have known and cared for, will sink into the abyss of a new dark age made more sinister, and perhaps more protracted, by the lights of perverted science.'

Winston Churchill, 1940

CHAPTER X

The United States and World Leadership

BRITONS, to whom Part I of this book is in the first instance addressed, may at this juncture feel irresistibly impelled to ask — with no little irritation, and borrowing therefore the pungent phraseology of their American friends — ' So what? Where do we go from here? ' They may indignantly point out that, even if they were persuaded by all the arguments in favour of Britain's participation in Atlantic Union, this would not have got them very far, because the main foundation-stone of such a political entity would necessarily be the United States, which on past showing would be much more likely to play the part of the principal stumbling block. And it must be confessed that at first sight it may well appear that the edifice of Atlantic unity, which I have been describing, is very much less a practical proposition than a castle in the air.

Barbara Ward wrote in 1951:

'. . . there are strong arguments for the view that a close Atlantic union, with a federal constitution and government, a pooling of power and a single electorate cannot be an immediate or overriding aim of Western policy. The first and obvious reason is that American public opinion is not prepared for it. . . . So long as the United States feels, deep in its bones, that no permanent external relations are necessary, just so long will Britain's preference for a partnership including America seem tiresome and unreasonable. One of the great attractions of the " European Solution " in American eyes must be that it involves no permanent American commitment. An Atlantic solution does and, so far, the evidence does not suggest that the United States is yet prepared to accept the idea of a full federal Atlantic union.'[1]

If in fact we were to ask the very large majority of Americans today whether they were prepared to accept an Atlantic Union their answer would almost unquestionably be

in the negative. The long history of America's actual geographical isolation from the other hemisphere, her persistent
tradition of isolationism in international affairs, her deep
sense of political 'apartness' from the old world, and her real
feeling of new world superiority to the moral decadence,
corruption and inequity of Europe still make the idea of a real
and permanent re-integration of the United States with
Western Europe initially repugnant to American sensibilities.
This attitude of America, often reinforced though it was by
the immigrants who had delighted to shake the dust of Europe
off their feet, has changed much since its first efflorescence
at the time of the Revolution, but the bitter words spoken by
Franklin then are still capable of a response in American
hearts; he talked of 'the extreme corruption prevalent among
all orders of men in this rotten old state. . . . I wish all the
friends of liberty and of man would quit that sink of corruption and leave it to its fate.' To some Americans a proposition
for Atlantic Union would appear at first blush to be like —
the words again are Franklin's — 'coupling and binding
together the dead and the living': [2] to many Americans it
would certainly seem as if in some way they were being asked
— the metaphor is of a different dimension — once more to
pull Europe's, and particularly Britain's, chestnuts out of the
fire for her.

Yet remarkable changes *have* occurred since 1951. When
those words were written by Barbara Ward the Truman
Doctrine was hardly four, and N.A.T.O. hardly two, years
old. The vast scale of the cold war was perhaps scarcely
grasped fully; long-term competitive co-existence had never
been heard of; the cloud of Chinese power was not much
bigger than a man's hand; above all, the alarming economic
progress of Soviet Communism, the terrifying growth of
Russian military power, had barely — in those pre-Sputnik
days — been glimpsed. And in deeper perspective, against a
longer background of American history, the whole-hearted
assumption by the United States after World War II of the
thankless role of free world leadership was, to those at least
who had grown up in the blindest heyday of American isolationism, an astonishing revolution. Facts have no equal as
teachers, and these facts may well serve to convince Ameri-

cans, in the way which Barbara Ward had in mind when she wrote eight years ago, that 'It takes arguments at once fuller, deeper and more intangible to suggest that America's need of its allies is not much less acute than their need of America.'

American public opinion is highly amenable to argument, both theoretical and practical; it is far more readily responsive to theoretical argument than the British, with their instinctive suspicion of the clever, and far more openly receptive to practical suggestion than the French, with their unreasonable obsession with rationality. The American people must be presented with, indeed subjected to, persuasive and intensive argument on the great theme of Atlantic unity, for the time may now be riper than it was eight years ago; it may in truth be overripe, for it is not for political argument to wait upon events, but to precede and shape them. That public opinion is not ready may inhibit political action by statesmen: it is no reason whatever why writers or thinkers should hold back, for the forming of public opinion is their aim and function. And not only is the public mind of the United States open to conviction (as is the mind of every healthy democratic society on all but a few basic axioms of conduct), but it is also capable of extraordinarily rapid change. So much in American life is the result of the tension of opposite opinions that from time to time thought and action seem incapable of motion, but occasionally it happens that all the forces of American opinion are stimulated, or can be induced, to pull in the same direction. The result is a speed and suddenness and strength of change which confounds her enemies and even sometimes dumbfounds her friends.

Let us then, having in Part I argued our case before the British public, turn our attention in Part II to presenting argument before American opinion: let us see what the stake of the United States in Atlantic Union is.

The first and fundamental fact is one of which the United States has already shown herself aware: her geographical isolation is at an end. This is the age of the I.C.B.M., the Inter-Continental Ballistic Missile, the multi-stage rocket with the nuclear warhead, and the layman, if he once had doubts of the capacity of the Soviet Union to launch and guide a hydrogen weapon with accuracy from Russian soil to American targets, is unlikely to have them any longer since Russia's strikingly successful space exploits. In these days, when the world's greatest cities may be annihilated in a matter of minutes and when overt military thought and preparation declares that the only effective defence against hydrogen weapons is the threat of devastating retaliation, it is hardly necessary to emphasize or underline the statement that the United States is isolated no longer.

Full ostensible recognition has, of course, been accorded to this fact by American policy ever since World War II — ever since the American bi-partisan lead in the formation of the United Nations and, perhaps more particularly, since the foundation of N.A.T.O in 1949 and the clear American assumption of her responsibilities in Asia with the defence of South Korea in 1950. It was recognized, by the existence of the strategic nuclear bomber force of the United States, well before Russia established the primacy, among instruments of mass destruction, of the long-distance rocket. Set against the background of American diplomatic history, this *volte-face* in the international outlook of the United States was remarkably swift and complete. Hitler and Stalin between them, with assistance from Japan and Red China, very effectively gave the final blow to the long tradition of American isolationism in foreign policy. This tradition, having its origins in an early American revulsion from the affairs of the outside world, was reinforced by the actual isolation of the U.S.A. in the nineteenth century and by her absorption in the conquest of her continental domain. By the end of that century, however, the great and unprecedented scientific and technological cataclysm of the Industrial Revolution had begun to narrow the confines of the earth at a remarkable and accelerating pace, so that by progressive, if sometimes reluctant, stages — first the outburst of American imperialism at the turn of the century, and then the participation of the United States in World War I and World War II — the American people became convinced that they were in world affairs to stay.

For the United States, however, it was not simply a matter

of participating in international affairs: she was forced to assume the active leadership of the free world. With the increasing, and increasingly unrivalled, stature of the two super-powers, the U.S.A. and the U.S.S.R., there was no alternative to disorder in the ranks of the liberty-loving nations, and perhaps chaos and defeat, except American leadership. Britain, which had in the eighteenth and nineteenth centuries led the forces of constitutional government and national freedom in a sporadic kind of way, was still powerful as the possessor of nuclear weapons, but she was now outclassed by the giant powers and could no longer do much more than support and assist the leadership of the United States. Because of the continuation of the cold war, that leadership, magnificently inaugurated as it was with the Truman Doctrine and the Marshall Plan, had to be constantly maintained in the years that followed. Its achievements during that time, in the Berlin air lift, in Korea, and in the Middle East, were truly remarkable.

But no one could pretend that it was an easy task. International leadership is never easy, simply because it is international. Behind the Iron Curtain under Stalin Russia's leadership of the Communist nations was not international: as events in Hungary were to show beyond all cavil in 1956, the leaders of the Soviet Union even after his death did not permit any real or practical expressions of national sovereignty on the part of any state in their grip. The fundamental aim of all America's leadership, on the other hand, was to preserve freedom, and she could exact nothing from her allies except by their consent and co-operation. By this she meant, and they meant, their consent as independent sovereign nations.

Liberty in the history of the modern world had always gone hand in hand with the independence and sovereignty of nations. America, ever since she had dissolved the political bands which tied her to the British Empire and assumed, 'among the powers of the earth, the separate and equal station to which the laws of nature and of nature's God' entitled her, had thought of 'free and independent states' as the only effective guarantee of 'the blessings of liberty'. Thus when the United States entered upon the world stage more than a century later Woodrow Wilson declared that peace after World War I could only be made on the basis of 'an evident principle. . . . It is the principle of justice to all peoples and nationalities, and their right to live on equal terms of liberty and safety with one another, whether they be strong or weak.'[3]

The fate of the League of Nations, which enshrined this principle of national freedom and equality, was not such as to fortify the liberal nationalist view of international society, and the United Nations, with its concentration of strength in the hands of the great powers, was designed to take a more 'realistic' stand. But in fact the American belief in the equality of all nations, great as well as small, and in national sovereignty as an essential bulwark of liberty, remained strong, while the total failure of the Security Council, owing to Russian intransigence, to operate as it was intended, meant that the real power of the United Nations had in practice to be vested in the General Assembly, which contained no less than 82 sovereign nations at the end of 1958. It was in fact the perfect embodiment of the idea of national equality, for the vote of the newest member in 1959, Guinea, was theoretically equal to that of the greatest member, the United States. Only in circumstances of extreme crisis did it prove possible for the Assembly, and hence the United Nations, to take the barest minimum of effective action; and even that action tended to depend in fact, as it had done even in Korea in 1950 (when by a Russian miscalculation the Security Council was able to operate for a brief spell), upon the independent resolve of the United States.

But fortunately, the peace and freedom of the world does not depend in practice primarily, or even in any great degree, upon the present effectiveness of the United Nations, but upon the network of regional alliances and special defence agreements built within it by the United States. It depends particularly upon N.A.T.O., for S.E.A.T.O. (the South-East Asia Treaty Organization) does not compare with N.A.T.O. in power and cohesion. Yet, although it is probably stronger and more unified than any previous alliance of sovereign powers in time of peace, N.A.T.O. remains an unruly team which is far from easy to handle. Even Britain, America's staunchest and most reliable ally, showed herself capable, with France, of the extraordinarily stupid and extremely dangerous independent armed invasion of Egypt during the Suez Canal crisis of 1956. Only by the most intense diplomatic and economic pressure and the active mobilization of an outraged international opinion was the United States able to induce Britain to cease her fire. But this fearful split in the ranks of the free nations, at the moment when the Soviet Union was smashing by military might the indigenous forces of freedom in Hungary, might have imperilled the future of liberty for all mankind. There could be no better illustration of the immense difficulties inherent for the United States in her leadership of the free nations — so long as they each and all retain their arbitrary national sovereignty.

Even when no crisis comparable in violence with this one arises, the anarchic effect of their national sovereignties upon the co-operation of the free nations is none the less — though it may be less obviously — marked. The task of mustering the votes and the good will even of friendly governments for any particular course of action, either through the cumbersome channels of normal diplomacy or in the crowded corridors of the United Nations, is a herculean one, and often enough it is frankly impossible. Thus over and over again the allies in fact have lost the initiative to the Communist world because they were incapable of formulating a common policy, and they were incapable of doing so fundamentally because of their insistence on the unreal and outmoded fetish of national sovereignty. No international machinery which is constructed to preserve the supposedly absolute freedom of action of its member nations can ever again meet the full needs of the free peoples. Yet frequently in international crises in the past the United States has had to bear the blame which should properly lie at the door of each and every sovereign state in her camp. Thus the seeming paralysis into which American foreign policy has all too often tended of late years to sink has not been due only to defects in her own will and foresight, but also to the almost insuperable problem of exercising any effective leadership at all in conditions of unbridled sovereignty.

For the principle of national independence has become the

principle of international unanimity: virtually any positive action of N.A.T.O. as a whole, except in the extreme crisis, can be vetoed by its smallest and least powerful member. The effect, on the affairs of the free nations, of the absolute, the *liberum* veto — the final exemplar of extreme, anarchic individualism — may not be so glaring as its effect in the Security Council of the United Nations, but it is no less grave and far-reaching. Yet because liberty once thrived under the protection of the nation-state, it certainly does not mean that it can only remain safe in conditions of unrestricted national sovereignty. Indeed the very reverse is now the case, for that sovereignty has become an actual obstacle in the path of progress, one which positively imperils rather than protects and fosters freedom. It has become urgently necessary to submerge the national sovereignties of at least certain of the nations of the free world in a larger Union if that world is to triumph over the world of Marxist Communism.

Of this fact the United States should be peculiarly aware, for she was the first effective exponent — the inventor indeed — of modern federalism. That 'more perfect union' formed by the Constitution of the United States was seen by its proponents as the only alternative to the anarchy of sovereignty for each of the thirteen states, even though they were bound together in an alliance which they called a Confederation. As Hamilton put it, 'this would bring us to a simple alliance offensive and defensive and would place us in a situation to be alternately friends and enemies of each other, as our material jealousies and rivalships, nourished by the intrigues of foreign nations, should prescribe to us'. Such a solution to these problems the Founding Fathers rejected, and formed instead a stronger federal union: this constituted one of the most remarkable acts of political wisdom and foresight of which we have record. On it the whole modern greatness of the United States has depended.

Just such a choice now faces the nations of the Western world. Their liberties will be as safe in the hands of a new representative Atlantic Union as those of the American people have been under the Constitution of the United States, and far safer than they are likely to be under sovereign nationalism, in much the same way that the freedoms of the United

States have been solid as a rock compared with those of the Latin-American republics. There have of late been many voices raised in criticism of the meagre institutions of N.A.T.O., prophesying disaster if they are not strengthened for action outside the narrow European sphere and fortified economically and politically. These voices echo the words of Hamilton: 'In our case, the concurrence of thirteen distinct sovereign wills is requisite, under the Confederation, to the complete execution of every important measure that proceeds from the Union. It has happened as was to have been foreseen. The measures of the Union have not been executed. . . . Each state, yielding to the persuasive voice of immediate interest or convenience, has successively withdrawn its support, till the frail and tottering edifice seems ready to fall upon our heads and crush us beneath its ruins.'

In this way the fact of national sovereignty has come to make well nigh impossible effective American leadership of the free world, and for that world the only effective alternative to the real danger of an international Communist triumph is a sharp diminution of the sovereignty of its member nations. 'But if we are unwilling to be placed in this perilous situation, if we still will adhere to the design . . . of a superintending power, under the direction of a common council, we must resolve to incorporate into our plan those ingredients which may be considered as forming the characteristic difference between a league and a government . . .'[4] We must, under the leadership of the United States, which was never more needed or more fitting than here, form a more perfect Union among the nations of the West: we must form an Atlantic Union.

That the United States has not been unaware of the disadvantages of national sovereignty is demonstrated by the extent to which in the years of her leadership she has pressed upon the nations of Europe the desirability of a European union. We have already noted the existence of this pressure, but we have not remarked upon its intensity. So great was this that until, somewhere about the beginning of the first Eisenhower Administration, the American government came to accept the at first unpalatable fact that Britain was not going to join a purely European union, it produced from American leaders many protests that the United Kingdom, by 'dragging her feet', was imperilling not only nascent European unity but even cordial Anglo-American relations. The strength of America's conviction that Europe's ills could only be permanently cured by the application of the same remedy as America had applied to hers in 1789 was one of the principal reasons for the eventual emergence of the Common Market, the foundation for what is intended ultimately to be a comprehensive and complete union of the Six. This Common Market, with its 168 million inhabitants, producing in 1958 some 237 billion kilowatt hours of electricity and some 60 million metric tons of steel,[5] would, if it developed a genuine political unity, be a rival to both the Soviet Union and the United States.

Indeed, one cannot but wonder whether the United States was not excessively sanguine, even perhaps naïve, in the almost gay abandon with which she pressed forward the birth of this new Leviathan, without any prolonged and serious consideration of what its effects upon her own position might be. It may prove that this open-heartedness and open-handedness of the American people, this expression of a deep and abiding faith in the wisdom and amity of a sovereign Europe, is the course of a higher wisdom than timid calculations of American national interest: it may well be that the apothegm of Emerson, once echoed by Franklin D. Roosevelt, that the only way to have a friend is to be one, is the true path to success in America's relations with continental Europe. It is perhaps a grotesque exaggeration to envision the United States as a new Frankenstein, who has created a monster on the mainland of Europe which may one day get out of control. Certainly, excessive doubts and fears on this score will be suspect to many, Americans as well as Europeans, when they emanate from insular Britain — suspect because they may be regarded as a clumsy British attempt to refurbish the old and much misunderstood doctrine of the Balance of Power, the policy by which Britain always attempted to check the rise of any nation which threatened to dominate by force the continent of Europe.

These British fears do not result from mistrust of a

European union of the Six *per se*. To a constitutional democratic power in Europe, which raises its vast bulk by consent
of all its peoples, there can be no possible objection. Nor does
the doctrine of the Balance of Power have real meaning any
longer within the narrow confines of Europe. But the people
of the United States would be unwise to harbour too many
illusions about European politics. God forbid that the Americans should lose the idealism which is so splendid a feature
of their polity, but let them recollect that they have been
most successful when they have exercised it within a realistic
framework. Their greatest international triumphs have come
when they have recognized unpleasant facts — facts after the
downfall of France in 1940, facts after Pearl Harbour, facts
above all when Yalta was forgotten and the existence of the
cold war recognized. The present fact simply is that the
United States has now assumed on the world stage *vis à vis*
Communism the role that Britain so long played on the
European — the preservation of the Balance of Power, the
prevention of the conquest of the free world by force or subversion. And it is in this context that the new European union
must be judged.

It may well prove that Europe will remain the close and
permanent, independent and sovereign, ally of the United
States: such has certainly been one of the pillars of the policy
of Dr. Adenauer's Germany. But on the very morning when
these words were written *The New York Times* carried a
headline 'Bonn and Paris Seek World Role: Third Force
Position Seen for Europe'. Under that headline a correspondent, Sydney Gruson, writes:

> 'Each man [de Gaulle and Adenauer] has certainly a national
> interest in what is becoming an increasingly close alliance
> within the greater alliance of the Atlantic community. And
> each has apparently decided that, in a world dominated by two
> super-powers, the United States and the Soviet Union, his
> national interests are best served by the creation of a power that
> might approach that of the Big Two — a European power. . . .
> 'General de Gaulle and Dr. Adenauer conceive the West
> Europe of the future as the third world force, not yet as power-
> ful or decisive as the United States or the Soviet Union, but with
> the potentialities — the people, the resources, the dynamism —
> for strength.'

At the moment this new power is content within the Atlantic community, but it would be folly for Americans to shut their eyes to the fact that a 'dynamic' 'third force' almost by definition sees itself as an independent arbiter between the United States and Russia. The notion of a 'third force' first arose indeed—quite separately from the idea of European unity—in a post-war European atmosphere of neutralism and anti-Americanism.

As *The New York Times* goes on: 'In a news conference last March, General de Gaulle spoke of the possibilities confronting France and of the thought that France might have to withdraw from the quarrels of the greater powers.' The General's relations with the United States have not always been of the happiest, he has a real belief in the special destiny of France, and he has always—with a sometimes overweening arrogance of Europe's place in the world—resented the decisive role which America was able to play in the affairs of Europe after the war. In this interview he firmly repudiated the idea of French withdrawal from the competition of international life, and insisted more strongly than ever on the need for France, and hence Western Europe, to possess nuclear weapons and the means of delivering them. The Atlantic community may be safe in the hands of de Gaulle and Adenauer, but how long will life, and power, be vouchsafed to them? Already, in *l'affaire Mitterand*, there may be signs of yet another recurrence of violence and instability in the life of France, despite the great strength of de Gaulle's Executive, and for the present popular, position.

Of Germany Gruson writes: 'But one thing is sure. Both in the greater alliance and in the complex relationship he has established with France, the Chancellor saw the safety of West Germany, not only safety from outside aggression but safety from the inner convulsions of the German people themselves. Perhaps this was the decisive motivation for Dr. Adenauer.'[6] If these are the innermost sentiments of Germany's great leader himself, would not the United States do well to cherish some healthy doubts about the future stability and policies of what the Germans are coming to call 'Frankenreich'?

For the new Europe will not exist in a vacuum, but subject

to intensely powerful pressure from without. Italy, as we have already pointed out, has probably the largest Communist party outside the Iron Curtain; France probably still has the second largest. An independent third force can theoretically throw its might as well to the second power in the East as to the first power in the West. The glittering prize of German unity, of reunion between East and West Germany, is the great, ever-present attraction for the German people of a European-Russian *rapprochement*. Who can deny the possibility of internal convulsions in the Six, or of a great economic slump in the free world, followed by a powerful resurgence of European anti-Americanism? If these things are possible, so, with the continuing increase of Soviet power, is a defection of Europe to that Communist world which already possesses so great a proportion of the central Eurasian land mass. These things may not be probabilities: they are certainly possibilities. America would be wise not to disregard them. European neutralism, at least, is a potential development of which the United States should always be acutely aware.

The remedy for this situation lies ready to her hand. By promoting and joining a true Atlantic Union, by creating a new federal structure for the West, she can ensure, as far as is humanly possible, the preservation of the unity of the Atlantic nations, which constitute the central and vital body of the free world. She is not without historical experience of this process of merging existing sovereignties in a wider and more powerful one, and of doing so perhaps predominantly for reasons of foreign policy: she knows through that experience that nothing less than a true Union will suffice. And she may reflect with satisfaction that no single problem, not even that of nationality, which will face an Atlantic Union will exceed in its disruptive and explosive power the American Union's problem of Negro slavery; an Atlantic Union once formed is far less likely than was the American to face in a few years the threat of a bloody civil war.

By creating a new body politic she will solve, in a sense automatically, the almost insoluble problem of leading a group of national states, for all will participate in the processes of policy making. No longer will there be a periodic clamour from the smaller countries that their voices cannot be heard, for they and their peoples will be represented in the federal government, and the whole body will be bound by the decisions of its duly elected representatives. Nor should it prove unduly difficult to ensure the maintenance of democratic procedures and of orderly constitutional government, for, as we have seen earlier, there would be a very substantial majority of electors in the Union with long experience, within their own nations, of successful self-government.

The objects which the American people wish to achieve in international affairs will in this way be a great deal easier to attain. Furthermore, the preservation of Atlantic unity, the creation of a real Union, will give to the West a far greater influence for good in the United Nations, and in the affairs of the world. The United Nations has proved a difficult and cumbersome instrument through which to work; Atlantic Union will be a highly effective lever for the attainment of Western aims, within that body as well as outside it. It will greatly strengthen the hand of the free nations in the world forum. It will prove a far more potent means of attaining the West's objectives than an unwieldy alliance of sovereign and independent nation states.

NOTES

[1] Barbara Ward, *Policy for the West*, New York 1951, pp. 283-4.
[2] Quoted Allen, *op. cit.*, p. 217.
[3] James Brown Scott (Ed.), *President Wilson's Foreign Policy: Messages, Addresses, Papers*, New York 1918, p. 363.
[4] *The Federalist, No. 15.*
[5] *The New York Times,* Sunday 8 November 1959.
[6] *The New York Times,* 8 November 1959.

CHAPTER XI

The United States and the Sino-Soviet Bloc

A. Soviet Russia

THE gigantic strength of Atlantic Union will, of course, be supremely valuable in the cold war with Russia: it is perhaps the strongest argument for bringing it into existence.

We have already observed in an earlier chapter the great power of the United States standing alone, but this American strength must be more clearly compared with that of the Soviet Union. Figures for this kind of comparison are apt to be highly misleading, but it seems most likely that America's absolute expenditure on defence (though not necessarily what she gets for her money) very substantially exceeds that of Russia, and that she spends a higher proportion of her national budget on arms. Thus the proportion spent on defence in 1952 was 71·6 per cent compared with an ostensible 23·9 per cent for the U.S.S.R., though this latter figure may be more than usually deceptive.[1] In 1959 the United States still has much the largest navy in the world; she is able to deliver crushing nuclear retaliatory blows to virtually any target in the Soviet Union; and she is probably ahead in the quality of her aircraft and in the quantity and variety of her atomic weapons, particularly at the tactical level. There is thus no occasion for immediate alarm, but there may be plenty of need for immediate and vigorous action. For can this American shield of the free world be considered strong, or anything like strong, enough?

The Soviet Union has had the most powerful army in the world since World War II; in 1959 it appeared to number 2,350,000, compared with less than 1,000,000 for the United States. This army in all probability is not only approaching full mechanization but is also the only major force in the world adequately equipped with post-war weapons and ready to fight a nuclear or non-nuclear war in any kind of climate or terrain. (Even in the last three years of World War II the U.S.S.R. produced more tanks than the U.S., one and a half times as many automatic weapons, twice as many cannon, and more than four times as many mortars.)[2] Already by 1956 the Soviet Union had the largest submarine fleet in the world as well as the second navy, and also an air force numerically superior to that of the United States. Above all, of course, Russia is now almost, if not quite, equal to America in her military control of nuclear energy (she actually exploded, it seems, a hydrogen 'bomb', as opposed to a thermo-nuclear 'device', before the United States), and she has considerably surpassed her in the development of ballistic missiles, having 100 principal missile bases and a missile arm of 200,000 men in 1959. It seems highly probable that the U.S.S.R has an accurate and reliable inter-continental ballistic missile with a hydrogen warhead—and that the U.S.A., as yet, has not.

America is, of course, far from defenceless, for she has not only her long-range strategic bomber force, but also her allies, from whose territories around the Russian heartland medium-range missiles can effectively and accurately be fired in large numbers at short notice. In view of the no doubt increasing efficiency of anti-aircraft projectiles in the Soviet Union, it must very shortly be upon these medium-range missiles that the free world will principally depend for its defence—that is to say for its power of retaliation—against Russia; this will remain the situation until such time as the American I.C.B.M. is perfected. In other words the United States has already discovered—in effect she did so as long ago as the formation of N.A.T.O. in 1949—that strategically her own efforts do not suffice to render her secure against the enemy: she has realized her essential military and political dependence upon her allies. But, such is her admirable faith in herself and in her national capability, that she has continued, and still continues, to rely on her own almost exclusive efforts to enable her to keep abreast of the Soviet Union in the technical developments of war. It is sometimes hard to draw the line between a splendid self-assurance and a dangerous over-confidence, but it must be said that America's unaided capacities, or at least her solitary will, have not so far appeared equal to the task. Sober judges of Russia's space achievements have opined that even in a decade the United States will be unlikely to overtake them. It may perhaps be that, as far as space travel as such is concerned, America might not wish to do so (and in this she could conceivably be wise, for we do not know what the genuine opinion of Russia's poverty-stricken masses about her vast expenditures on the unproductive exploration of empty space really is) but the crucial fact remains that space-rocket efficiency is a very reasonable gauge of military-rocket efficiency, and indeed of technical efficiency generally, while control of outer space might have over-whelming military advantages for any power that possessed it.

Ought not the American people frankly to face the fact that by pursuing an isolated, one-nation, programme of technical and scientific military research, and by failing to integrate politically and militarily the forces of the Atlantic states, they may be imperilling the success of the West in its race with Soviet Communism? Is it not possible that even America has bitten off more than she can chew? This will not be for her — bred in the bone as is her conviction that there is no problem which she cannot lick — an easy admission to make, but recognition of the limitations of the power of one's country never is agreeable. Britain, who has been undergoing the process in the last fifty years, has found it far from painless, and she has perhaps had an easier passage than the United States may have. Nations seldom remain for long at the supreme pinnacle of power; such seems to be the remorseless progression of political change and decay. Britain, although long accustomed to a leading role in world affairs, was not confident of her European pre-eminence until, say, 1815: by 1890 she was already dimly conscious that she was rapidly being outclassed, though this only became indisputably clear to her some years later. The United States was obviously moving into a position of dominance by the First World War, but such was her inbuilt resistance to unreserved participation in international affairs that she only came to a full realization of her para-mountcy in World War II. Yet less than fifteen years after the end of that war it was plain, for all to see, that American leadership was being formidably challenged by Russia. And the issue of this contest was vastly more important in many respects than that, let us say, of the eighteenth-century struggle between France and Britain; it was no simple matter of the exchange of one master for another, for the Russian challenge was also the challenge of Marxist Communism. This was a moral and intellectual, indeed a spiritual, war *à outrance*, on the issue of which the most valuable and unique gifts of Western civilization to humanity may depend — a belief in individual rights and the capacity to understand objective truth.

Americans will readily admit the gravity of the Communist challenge, and may well accept the reality of the threat of Russian military might, but at the same time they may beg leave to doubt the fundamental strength and staying-power of the Soviet Union. How strong, then, is the social and economic framework of the Russian Communist society? This is a question of great complexity and difficulty, and he who tries to answer it needs the rare gift of prophecy. Nevertheless, we must attempt a reply, for on some such answer the West must base its future course of action.

Everyone is aware, even in the Soviet Union, that at present the United States is still far in the lead both in total agricultural and industrial output and in the production of certain fundamental industrial commodities. One estimate is that in 1956 the gross national output of Russia was 42 per cent of that of the United States. Figures for the production of certain key items were as follows:

	Russia	U.S.A.
Million metric tons	1956	1955
Petroleum	84	340
Coal	430	420
Steel	49	107
Billion kilowatt-hours		
Electric Power	192	535

Only in the production of coal does the Soviet Union approach America at the present time (the American figure in the table is for an earlier year than the Russian; the figures for 1957 were, U.S.S.R. 510 million short tons, U.S.A. 530 million short tons), and this is amply compensated for by

American superiority in the production of oil and electricity. In agricultural production, although Russia is a far larger country, with 208 compared with some 176 million people, the United States is also far superior:

	Russia	U.S.A.
Millions of farm livestock	1955	1955
Cattle	67	95
Hogs	52	55
Production (million metric tons)		
Sugar	3·4	5·7
Meat	2·5	13·4
Grain	120·0	162·0

But it is not of the present we must think, but of the future; and here the Communists are immensely confident, predicting that the Soviet Union will overtake the United States within fifteen years. On past showing it might well seem that this boast can be made good. Thus comparative industrial production 27 years earlier was as follows: [3]

	Russia	U.S.A.
Million metric tons	1928	1928
Petroleum	12	129
Coal	35	549
Steel	4	52
Billion kilowatt-hours		
Electric Power	5	83

Although the great American increases in production between 1928 and 1955, particularly of electric power (partly representing in fact a switch from coal to other power sources), demonstrate American strength and flexibility, the Russian record is most remarkable for its rapid growth. It is the *rate* of increase in productivity which is the crucial fact, and one estimate holds that the rate of Russian production increase in 1957 was about 7 per cent, compared with 3 per cent for the United States. A similar estimate was that in 1957 this rate was three times that for Western Europe as a whole. On 13 November 1959 the Director of the Central Intelligence Agency of the United States, Allen W. Dulles, told a Congressional Committee, as reported in *The New York Times* next day: 'If the Soviet industrial growth rate persists at 8 or 9 per cent per annum over the next decade, as is forecast, the gap between our two economies by 1970 will be dangerously narrowed unless our own industrial growth rate is substantially increased from the present pace.'

The chief Russian weakness in the past has been in agriculture, but strenuous efforts are being made to increase production; Premier Khrushchev's own reputation is particularly engaged with this programme, but it is too early to know how rapid an improvement is being effected. There is, with modern techniques, probably ample space in Russia for great increases in agricultural production if the system can be made to operate more efficiently than in the past, so that the U.S.S.R can for a long time continue to feed a rapidly increasing population. That increase has been swift for some time past; the death rate is said to have been cut by 75 per cent since the Revolution and life expectancy raised from 32 to 64 years during the same period. The population at present appears to be increasing by approximately 3 millions a year, which would seem to be about the same increase as the American.[4] Prophecies as to the growth of populations are peculiarly difficult, and have, in particular, consistently underrated the rise in the population of the United States since 1945. Woytinsky estimated in 1953 that the population of Canada and the United States combined might be 190 millions in 1960 (it had already reached approximately 190 millions in 1958, 174 million *plus* 16 million), and at least 220 millions by the year 2000. The population of the U.S.S.R. he then projected as 241 millions in 1970 and 260 millions thirty years later.[5] This would mean much the same rate of increase in Russia as in the United States, but a rise in the Russian standard of living, which now seems very likely, may well produce a considerable acceleration in population growth.

At bottom, however, the contest may depend on the basic resources of the two lands, and here it is very difficult to strike a balance, for their resources are in many respects comparable in scale and variety, but whereas Russia is larger the United States is climatically superior. Certainly they are neither of them really rivalled in potentialities by any other single national power. The U.S.S.R. has an area exceeding 8,500,000 square miles, more than twice that of the continental United States (including Alaska), which has approximately 3,500,000 square miles. This very great discrepancy is, however, counter-balanced by the fact that many of the Soviet Union's best agricultural areas are located in regions of variable rainfall and drought, and above all by the fact that so much of the country is so far to the north, which is responsible for the Russian problem of great cold. Moscow is a little north of Hopedale, Labrador, and far north of Edmonton, Alberta, while a considerable proportion of Russia is within the Arctic Circle. Although extraordinary developments are under way in the utilization of frozen territories, this must remain a handicap. On the other hand, the Soviet Union contains the largest black soil area in the world (247 million acres). In any event the gigantic size of the country obviously confers great advantages on it.

While it is probable on balance that the United States is superior in natural resources, despite the fierce speed at which they have been and are being consumed (as, for example, the history of her forests shows), those of Russia are in 'exceptional abundance'.[6] Soviet geographers claim that the U.S.S.R. occupies first place in the world for its peat, manganese, platinum, and above all iron and oil resources; in particular they claim that she has approximately one half of the world's known oil reserves. It is generally recognized that Russia is second only to the United States in coal resources and that she has vast deposits of precious metals, as well as of nickel, zinc, tin, potassium salts and phosphates. She has a third of all the world's forest land and almost illimitable hydro-electric possibilities. She has acquired the second largest gold reserve in the world and leads all other nations in the actual production of peat, platinum, and manganese; she is second to the United States in the production of coal and iron.

Although the United States retains her lead in the production of such vital items as steel, oil, electricity and coal, the U.S.S.R. is coming up fast and has the resources to continue to do so. Not, of course, that Russia is without her weaknesses, inherent and acquired. Quite apart from the major disadvantage of her northerly latitude, she is not totally self-sufficient (no modern nation is); she has certain deficiencies, such as natural rubber and industrial diamonds — though in fact these two can increasingly be made good by synthetic substitutes. Her development of the means of utilizing her basic resources, too, has had great failings despite the very remarkable success of the Soviet governments in the expansion of heavy industry throughout their vast country, their transport system still has grave defects. They have developed a jet airliner which is said to be of the highest quality, and their planes and pilots have a good reputation, though their navigational and other facilities are apparently rudimentary. But their bulk transportation is still inadequate; in this country, which is twice as large as the U.S.A., there were in 1955 75,000 miles of technically backward railways and 129,000 miles of relatively inferior roads, compared with 222,000 miles of modern railroads and 1,300,000 miles of unsurpassed highways in America. Nor can a highly self-sufficient, even autarkic, system in any country, however large, match, on purely economic grounds, the performance of economies which have access by extensive foreign trade to the resources of all the continents, with all that this means in cheapness and efficiency.

It is, however, in the human aspects of her economic system that the chief Russian weaknesses lie. The excessively centralized planning of the Soviet economy, despite its achievements, has been in many respects grossly inefficient. It is not merely that planners — and there is in the U.S.S.R. a bureaucracy of unimagined size and density — are all too human and capable of error, and that the overall planning of an organization as vast and as heterogeneous as the Soviet Union is a superhuman task, but simply that, for the provision of what the consumer wants, there is nothing remotely as efficient as what Adam Smith called the higgling of a free market. It should, however, be noted here that the sweeping 1957 programme for the decentralization of industrial management, the second of Khrushchev's great economic reforms, was a vital, revolutionary step in this direction. Now, too, more and more is heard of the Russian consumer, although it was ostensibly for paying him too much attention that Malenkov lost the leadership of Russia so soon after the death of Stalin; and this also is revolutionary. In the past the Soviet programme of development has paid the consumer scant attention indeed, except in an ultimate and hypothetical sense; in fact the object of the programme was not the provision of consumer wants but the strengthening of the Soviet system, in order that it might be able one day to usher in the Socialist Utopia of a classless society, in which the wants of all would be fully and automatically satisfied. It is, of course, this ruthless sacrifice of every human right in the present on the altar of posterity's economy which is in one sense the fundamental issue between West and East.

For forty years the Soviet Union has grown economically by the pitiless exploitation of the Russian people; by the liquidation in the 1920s of millions of peasants (along with half of all the livestock of the country); by the merciless utilization of millions of slave labourers; by ruthlessly driving the ordinary worker, both male and female, with a harshness inconceivable in Western society since the first years of the Industrial Revolution, and above all by deliberately maintaining the lowest possible standard of living for the normal citizen. The housing shortage throughout the Soviet Union has been perpetual and crippling — and what is more fundamental in any society than the home, except food and clothing? Food, that is to say agriculture, as we have already seen, has been in a sense the greatest past failure of Communism; it has been the sphere in which most concessions have had to be made to the 'capitalist' sentiments of the country folk who still make up most of Russia's population. It is perhaps Communism's most critical testing ground in the future. As to clothing, it is possibly here, in the realm of consumer goods, that the suppression of the ordinary citizen has been most painful for him and has at bottom aroused the most resentment. The demand for basic clothing in any society is fairly inelastic, but in 1955, for a population 22 millions smaller, the United States produced more than twice as many pairs of leather shoes and nearly $2\frac{1}{2}$ times as many pairs of socks and stockings as Russia. Needless to say, in the more sophisticated consumer goods, the figures are far more striking; thus in the same year the United States produced 4 times as many radio and television sets (although wireless production is an area of successful Soviet performance, partly because of its desirability from the point of view of propaganda), 14 times as much paper, and 80 times more passenger auto-mobiles.

With the general loosening-up which has followed the death of Stalin and which has been made possible by the actual achievements of the Soviet economy, the unhappy present-day consumer in Russia is beginning to receive some more atten-tion, and indeed some more goods. Once this process has begun, no one can say where it will end. It is in reality one of the two great hopes of the West, for as the appetite for con-sumer goods on the part of ordinary Russians (and there are 200 millions of them) grows by what it feeds on, the effect on the centralized and belligerent Communist system of govern-ment may be profound, for it may fundamentally weaken the Soviet desire to impose the Communist system everywhere in the world even at the cost of tension, hostility and war. Comfort and pleasure are far more effective opiates of the people than religion; well-fed and contented populations do not long remain aggressively martial. There are some signs that the great ' thaw ' since the death of Stalin may be the first fruits of this process, of which, we may hope, the West will continue to reap the harvest in increasing abundance for many years to come.

There is a second great hope for the West in Russia. Modern life in peace or war, in Russia or the outside world, is increasingly complex, particularly in science and technology. A defence system and standards of living competitive with those of the West can only be ensured, as the Russians are very well aware, by scientific and technical skills of the highest order, and this involves education, not merely for the few but for the many. The one overriding necessity in science is truth, and once large segments of the Russian people can recognize a scientific truth, how long will it be possible to keep them believing political and social falsehoods? A lie is a lie in any branch of life, and Marxist Communism has been to an astonishing extent nurtured on lies; and indeed on the very doctrine that objective truth hardly exists. It must be admitted that the West's experience of the extent to which able, and even eminent, scientists are able to recognize the true from the false in politics — the extent, to put it bluntly, of the naïve gullibility of some scientists when they move outside the scientific realm — has not been entirely happy, but it is hardly conceivable that in the long run the spread of education in Russia will not steadily erode the palpably false supports of Communist ideology. Once the lies begin to disappear from Soviet propaganda and policy, once there are evidences that a capacity to distinguish truth from falsehood in politics is making its appearance, the free world will be much nearer to its goal of international peace, if not yet of universal concord.

Of none of these things, however, can we be sure. It looks as if there is a crucial race going on between Soviet progress in educating and raising the standard of living of her people on the one hand, and the hold exerted over the Russian people by Communist ambitions and lies on the other. Can education and a rising standard of living check the lies and ambitions before irreparable damage is done to civilization? We cannot be *certain* of the outcome of this contest, and all the time the strength of the Soviet Union grows with alarming rapidity. Therefore we dare not yet relax our military guard very much, and above all we dare not continue to underestimate the Soviet challenge to our way of life, as we have shown a consistent tendency to do ever since 1917. Every Russian achievement has come as a surprise to most of the West, because voices have so long prophesied disaster for Soviet Communism. The Russians, they said, were not 'naturally good with machines', Russia would be wrecked by the resistance of the kulaks to the collectivization of agriculture, Russia would not hold out for more than two months against Hitler, Russia would not have the 'know-how' to develop jet and rocket propulsion rapidly, Russia would take ten years to master the fission, let alone the fusion, bomb. The worst enemy of the West has been its own illusions, and above all the illusion that by some inevitable and natural alchemy freedom must triumph — quite regardless of the wisdom and energy of the free. Never has there been so grievous an error.

America must face the fact that a democratic consumer-dominated society such as hers, in which any need of that society must be 'sold' to a majority of its members, is in some respects at a serious and positive disadvantage compared with Communism, because it can only ask for sacrifices in the cause of liberty; it cannot enforce and exact them in the cause of tyranny as Russia can. Soviet triumphs in the central fields of heavy industry, jet aircraft, rocket propulsion, and nuclear armaments have been achieved precisely because the Russian government took them so seriously that it was prepared to provide virtually unlimited resources for their development: little it cared about balancing the budget, necessary though that may seem, and indeed be, in a free economy. Nowhere is this more dramatically demonstrated than in the sphere of Soviet scientific and technical education, upon which, more than any other single factor, the outcome of this protracted and fatal struggle between Russia and the United States in this electronic age may perhaps depend. While American education is still in many ways bogged down in a ' progressive' concern for the individual personalities of the children, and almost never exacts from any child the stern, and indispensable, mental toil of which it is capable, Russian education is uncompromisingly directed to the strengthening of the Soviet Union, whether in peace or war. On it colossal sums are being spent, and to it the highest prestige attaches. The results of this tremendous concentration of energy and resources are just beginning to show themselves.

In 1917 nearly half of the Russian people were illiterate. By 1957 the Soviet Union had 1,800,000 teachers, compared with 1,300,000 in the United States, and their numbers were still increasing fast. Russia provides a college or university education free to any one who can show himself intellectually worthy of it, whereas it is still true that some able Americans cannot afford to go through college, although the universities in fact contain a number of undergraduates who are capable of deriving little benefit from their presence there. In some ways the key figures in a modern industrial society are the engineers; in 1956 the United States graduated 30,000 engineers, the Soviet Union 70,000. One estimate claimed that in the same year the U.S.S.R. was training more young people in applied science than the United States and Western Europe put together. Even in a sphere, medicine, where the consumer will naturally pay the very top prices, which ought to make the Western economic system work if anything will, the Soviet Union has the highest doctor-patient ratio in the world, having in 1957 some 344,000 doctors compared with 218,522 in the United States.[7]

In the struggle between the United States and Russia there is, it must be repeated, no guarantee whatever of the victory of democracy; indeed, if democracy does not arouse itself as it has perhaps never done before, there is an increasing likelihood of defeat. As former Secretary of State Dean Acheson warned, as reported in *The New York Times* on 19 November 1959, not only have we seen 'the beginnings of new power in China', but we may very possibly, if we let things slide, find that the decade which is about to open will be 'the decade of the beginning of Soviet power'. It is true that it would run counter to all previous experience if the rate of increase of Russian economic development did not in due time slacken (though it is far from certain when this may take place — whether before or after she has surpassed the United States in strength), but our experience here is based almost exclusively on the behaviour in history of capitalist economies, and we cannot be quite certain that this may not be misleading in the case of Communist Russia. The leaders of the Soviet Union certainly have a 'profound conviction that socialism will win the economic competition between the two systems',[8] and it is their proclaimed intention to surpass the United States in strength in the early 1970s. We simply dare not run the risk of believing that by then Communist Russia will no longer constitute a serious threat to the West.

B. Communist China

And it is not Russia alone that the West may find itself facing ten or fifteen years from now, for behind her vast bulk there looms the in some respects even more ominous shape of Communist China. As a Russian leader saw it in 1956:

'Before the Second World War the socialist system accounted for 17 per cent of the world's territory, about 9 per cent of its population, and only 7 per cent of its industrial production. Today the countries of the socialist camp occupy more than 25 per cent of the world's territory, comprise up-wards of 35 per cent of its total population, and account for roughly 30 per cent of its industrial production.'[8]

Here again, of course, the imponderables enter in to make judgement difficult. No one can know that the Sino-Soviet bloc will endure as a Communist entity. At first after the downfall of Nationalist China, some Western observers har-boured expectations of weaning China away from Russia, partly because Mao Tse-tung's Communism began as an agricultural rather than an industrial movement of the ortho-dox Soviet type. It now begins to seem much more likely that we shall be trying to wean Russia away from China; and certainly there are positive signs of a growing Russian fear of what General de Gaulle has called the 'masses of China, numberless and impoverished, indestructible and ambitious, building through trial and hardship a power which cannot be measured and casting her eyes about her on the open spaces over which she must one day spread'.[9] But on the surface the Communist third of the world is still united, and we cannot be sure that it will not still be united in a decade or so. This prospect, although we cannot tell that it may not be alleviated, for example, by the positive adhesion of the swarming multitudes of India to the Western camp, is a prospect to make the stoutest heart look to its defences, for what might not the billion and more creatures of the Communist world accomplish when they have at their command the industry and resources, not only of a Russia perhaps absolutely the equal of the United States, but of an industrializing China also?

The resources of China are to some extent still unexplored; never a fully exploited 'colonial' country, nor a modern industrial nation until very recently, there is more than the usual uncertainty about her wealth in untapped raw materials. It appears, however, that, though they are not comparable in richness with those of Russia and the United States, they are far from inconsiderable. Her population is so huge that every-thing in a sense depends upon agricultural development combined with population control, and for the same reason the possibilities of agricultural increase may be more limited than in the open lands of other great nations, but, even despite the excessive claims recently made by Pekin in this respect, cultural production of a growth of ten per cent or more in the the most conservative estimates admit the likelihood in agri- next quinquennium.

Because she is underdeveloped industrially, there is no such limitation on the increasing exploitation of her mineral resources. China is rich in coal; in 1950 the Fifth World Power Conference put her reserves at 1,114 billion[10] short tons (U.S., 2,006 billion, U.S.S.R., 1,323 billion), but her actual production in 1954 was only 73·9 million short tons, compared with 419·1 million for the United States and 382·5 million for the Soviet Union. Her reserves of iron ore were estimated at 6 billion short tons compared with 90 billion for the United States; her production of iron in 1954 was 7·0 million short tons (U.S., 87·2 million, U.S.S.R., 72·0 million). Her production of petroleum, as well as her proved reserves of oil, are negligible at present, but she has very considerable hydro-electrical potentialities which are being swiftly developed; her production in 1954 was 10·9 billion kilowatt hours compared with a pre-1949 peak of 6 billion. China leads the world in tungsten production, is a leading producer of antimony, has a large output of tin and molybdenum, and has very substantial bauxite resources; but she is deficient in supplies of lead, zinc, and copper, of all of which she has a very small production.

Once firmly established in power the Chinese Communists began to expand industrial production to the utmost of their ability, like the Soviets before them; like the Soviets, too, they are concentrating first on heavy industry, and like them, they have run into difficulties. But, also like them, they have already exceeded the pace which all too many Western experts thought to be the maximum possible; thus in 1954 one prediction was that 'the Chinese Communist economy may be expected to grow at an average rate of three per cent a year over the decade' (1952-62),[11] whereas it seems that from 1952-1957 'calculated from official data the net national product had increased at an average rate of 8·9 per cent. . . .'[12] It is true that the official data may be seriously misleading, but it seems doubtful if they exaggerate China's achievement nearly three times over. Eckstein, who is quoted above, points out that Meiji Japan raised its gross national product tenfold in the sixty years between 1880 and 1940, and the Soviet Union threefold in its first twenty-five years, a higher rate of growth. He observes that the weak industrial and economic base of present-day China is more like that of nineteenth century Japan than that of Russia in 1917, and draws comfort from his predictions in view of Russia's more rapid achievement; but, with the advantage of hindsight, we can no longer do so, because his own predictions have already been very largely exceeded in the last quinquennium. There seem some grounds for believing that each new industrial nation — and China is the most recent — may find it possible to industrialize more swiftly than its predecessors. Certainly there is nothing fanciful about the claim of Pekin that it will build up 'within about fifteen years a complete heavy-industry complex capable of producing virtually all machinery and equipment needed by industry and national defence',[13] nor about its boast that by the end of this century it will 'achieve a high degree of industrialization and transform China into a world economic power'.[14]

This process will be all the more rapid if co-operation should continue between China and the Soviet Union, for Russian resources backing Chinese man power (*plus* the very considerable Russian numbers and the increasingly considerable Chinese industrial strength) make a formidable combination indeed. Chinese numbers can, of course, prove a Malthusian handicap, but if they are reasonably controlled, so that *per capita* production can increase, they become a Chinese weapon of awesome strength. One scholar in 1954 estimated an aggregate Chinese population growth of 1 per cent a year for the next ten years, but, if the figures claimed by one authority for 1959 (680 millions) are to be believed, the rate *reached 3·5 per cent in 1958*. The Chinese Communists are the only world leaders who are reputed to have declared that their country would be the residual beneficiary of a nuclear holocaust because, even if a high proportion of their people were destroyed, they would still have far more left than anyone else. Once China attains a certain industrial level, her pullulating millions may enable her to drag the Sino-Soviet alliance strongly her way, and we must not harbour any illusions that her way is likely to be pleasant for the West.

China, an independent civilization with a continuous history more than three thousand years old, long ruled by an Imperial Son of Heaven who was regarded by his people as being the supreme earthly authority and who exacted material tribute and moral submission by the ceremony of the kowtow from all barbarian foreigners including the first Europeans, traditionally had a feeling of overwhelming and innate superiority to the rest of mankind. When that superiority was in fact rudely shattered by Europeans, and particularly Britons, accomplished through the aid of Western science not merely in industrial power but in the arts of war, and by the subsequent imposition of the unequal treaties and the pseudo-colonization of China, the Chinese sense of bitter grievance and resentment became a violent fact upon which the assumptions of the West must be based for many years to come. Red China is not merely, like Russia, under the sway of the rigid Marxist creed and impelled by a deep human urge to economic improvement through industrialization, but she is also in the grip of a profound and vengeful mistrust, even hatred, of Western European 'civilization'. In the decade since 1949 America has had ample evidence of the intransigence of which the new China is capable. General de Gaulle may not be so wide of the mark when he revives in 1959 talk, which was so common at the turn of the century, about what was then described as the 'yellow peril'. Let not even the great United States, inhibited as she may be by moral scruples and her sense of self-interest from the reckless use of the ultimate weapons, underestimate the threat to her way of life constituted by the ominous growth of an industrialized Chinese giant, which already contains a quarter of the human race and could be a billion strong by 1990.

And let not the West as a whole, led as it must be by the United States, underestimate the threat to it constituted by the Communist third of the world, controlling as it does so vast a proportion of the great central Eurasian land mass — Sir Halford Mackinder's 'Great Continent' or 'World-Island', dominated by the 'Heartland' which stretches from Eastern Europe to Western China across the illimitable

Russian plain. As he himself wrote as early as 1919, after the First World War:

'A victorious Roman general, when he entered the city, amid all the head-turning splendour of a "Triumph", had behind him on the chariot a slave who whispered into his ear that he was mortal. When our statesmen are in conversation . . . some airy cherub should whisper to them from time to time this saying:

> "*Who rules East Europe commands the Heartland:*
> *Who rules the Heartland commands the World-Island:*
> *Who rules the World-Island commands the World.*"[15]

America has fully assumed by now the role of leadership of the free nations of the world against domination by a single aggressive power which controls the Heartland. She, like Britain before her, is primarily a sea power (not a land power like France and Germany and Russia and China), and her hope must lie in that immensely strong yet impalpable force, sea power, to enable her to bind together the free nations of the world and with their aid in the end to defeat even an alliance of powers controlling the World-Island.

In the past, sea power and liberty have always triumphed, because when Britain could no longer sustain the burden alone, there was always her great progeny beyond the oceans, and above all the United States, to take it up: 'in God's good time, the New World, with all its power and might, steps forth to the rescue and liberation of the Old'.[16] Geography and the history of European expansion into the open places of the earth had seen to that. It is pre-eminently, indeed almost alone, to the powers habitually referred to by General de Gaulle as 'the Anglo-Saxons', Britain and America, that the world in fact owes its present degree of freedom — a debt of which upon occasion the world seems all too little aware. So far the gods have blessed their efforts in the cause of freedom, but we do not know that they will continue to do so. As Mackinder wrote long ago:

> 'Must we not still reckon with the possibility that a large part of the Great Continent might some day be united under a single sway, and that an invincible sea-power might be based upon

it? . . . Ought we not to recognize that this is the great ultimate threat to the world's liberty so far as strategy is concerned, and to provide against it in our new political system?'[17]

Now that the challenge is much more dangerous than ever before, the old method of *ad hoc* alliances of sovereign states is adequate no longer. It is too uncertain, too disorganized, too weak a system to defeat the positive, highly centralized and powerful onslaughts of the Sino-Soviet Communist world.

In these circumstances, of the great actual and enormous potential military power of Russia and China, the West needs all the strength that it can muster. In population, an Atlantic Union could hardly hope to match the present Communist world, for Russia and China (with somewhat over 200 millions and well over 600 millions respectively), together with their satellites, already total some 900 millions, as compared with the 500 millions which is the largest probable total for an Atlantic Union in the reasonably near future. But population is not the only constituent of military power, and Atlantic Union would, it is to be hoped, in any war against aggression from the Communist camp, gather around it — in the well-established British and American tradition — other powers of the free world, Latin-American perhaps, or maybe African; it is even far from impossible that the 415 millions of India might be thrown into the scales for liberty. In any case, a nation of 500 millions, of immense wealth and great technical skill, and with no mean martial tradition, would be powerful enough to give pause to the strongest hostile power or combination of powers, when that enemy could no longer hope — as he now does — to divide, and thus to conquer, the independent sovereign nations of the West.

Atlantic Union, however, would bring other military benefits besides a great population and a much closer political unity. Centralized military control would mean a notable improvement in military efficiency; not only would this apply to the actual conduct of military operations, but also to the whole planning of, and preparation for, defence. Integrated armed forces would mean both habitual unity of command and enormous economies in defence expenditure. Centralized federal defence funds, too, would make possible absolutely greater defence expenditures if these proved necessary, for before long the Union government — such appears to be the way of federal institutions — would be far wealthier than all its sovereign member governments put together had ever been.

This would be in fact the outcome of the great increase in the fundamental wealth of the West which would result from the creation of an unrestricted Atlantic economy, and such an increase in wealth would be very swiftly reflected in military strength. This would be the consequence not merely of the existence of more money to be collected by taxes for defence expenditure, but also of the greatly augmented sums which would be going into general scientific and technological research and development, for these are the most important foundations of modern military power. More than this, far greater and more varied scientific and technological talent would be available to Atlantic Union than is available even to the greatest of her constituent members. The Russians, as we are well aware, have advantages in the 'wizard war', through a ruthless concentration on certain technical objectives, which the United States, and certainly the West as a whole, cannot easily match; but Atlantic Union would have a different but perhaps greater advantage in the unrivalled interplay of scientific experience and ideas which would be possible for it, even in fields demanding military secrecy. The talent which it could command and the resources which it would have at its disposal would give it a splendid opportunity to regain the ground which the West has lost to the Soviets in the last decade. It is in fact hard to see in what other way the lead that Russia has established over the United States in some vital activities can be overcome.

The potentialities of Atlantic Union in the scientific and technological sphere can perhaps be best illuminated — as it were in reverse — by considering for a moment the calamitous effects which national sovereignty has already had upon Western nuclear and missile development in one special region, Anglo-American-Canadian atomic co-operation. The first giant stride into the modern horror world of nuclear warfare was taken with the Anglo-American development of the atomic bomb, which completed the Allied victory over Japan in 1945 at one blow. The Manhattan Project which produced it had been the result of the merging of British and American and Canadian research efforts in nuclear physics, which was suggested by Roosevelt as early as October 1941, and it was, for all it owed to American wealth and skill, essentially a *joint* Anglo-American achievement, to which British and Canadian scientists contributed a great deal. Through these united efforts the spectral possibility that Germany might be the first power to make a nuclear weapon was banished. It seems likely that the Soviet Union had at this time made relatively little progress in this particular direction. For a brief four years, as a result of this unlimited co-operation between allies, the United States had a power over the lives of men perhaps unprecedented in human history.

Yet, to the historian unversed in the technical aspects of nuclear and rocket warfare, it appears that *at no time since the end of the War has Russia ceased to overtake the West in this field*. In other words, the Soviet Union has by prodigious efforts steadily reduced the American lead, and then in some aspects taken the lead herself. Why? Partly no doubt because of her growing strength and skill, which would inevitably have enabled her to better her position in any case, and partly also because of her single-minded and intense concentration in this field of endeavour, but partly also — who can doubt it? — through the deficiencies of the West. Prominent among these, paramount perhaps, was the jealous national sovereignty of its principal members. Partly because of the reassertion of peace-time habits of independent national action, and partly because of the deficiencies in the security system of the British (later to be paralleled by similar, if perhaps lesser, deficiencies in that of the Americans), the whole magnificent Anglo-American research apparatus — magnificent both in its spirit and in its success — was disbanded almost immediately. From that time forward the nuclear and missile researches of the two countries went forward in virtually total isolation from one another. Because America had greater resources and the advantage of the existing plant and 'know-how' this virtually meant that the burden of competition with the Soviet Union fell on her shoulders alone. The results of this isolationist development have not to date been very satisfactory.

The historian must find it very difficult to believe that this dissolution of Anglo-American nuclear co-operation did not throw away, in the name of sovereign nationalism, a most important Western chance, at the worst of retarding the rate at which it was overhauled by Russia, and at the best of staying indefinitely ahead; in other words that the separate British expenditures on nuclear and missile development did not represent just about the margin of superiority that Russia has established over the United States, and that a combined Anglo-American programme might not have prevented this calamity. The first step towards remedying this fearful error has been taken by the freeing, in 1958, of the exchange of 'classified' atomic information between British and American scientists, but when we reflect upon the appalling waste and inefficiency involved in the original act of folly, upon the consequent solemn British reconstruction of nuclear military facilities already existing in the United States, upon the lavish outpouring of public funds in Britain to produce another set of fission weapons, and another set of fusion weapons, and now another set of rocket missiles and space projectiles, the imagination boggles at the stupidity and shortsightedness of men addicted to the rigidly national point of view. And this merely as between two nations! How much more powerful does the argument become as between all the nations of the free West! There is no magic formula in military technology to cure all our difficulties, but in the stimulus which it would give and the vast resources of talent and wealth which it would make available, there is certainly a talisman of remarkable potency ready to the hand of the West in the project of Atlantic Union. (It alone, for instance, will make fully possible the joint N.A.T.O. 'effort to chart the seas of space',[18] called for by Senator Henry M. Jackson at the Washington N.A.T.O Conference in November 1959.)

It is one that we cannot afford to neglect. Russia has, as we have seen, her dilemma in the competition for world power: will the demand of the people for consumer goods, and even for the truth, overtake the power of the Communist state to impose its will upon them? We have our dilemma too. Can we equal, by voluntary self-sacrifice, the allocation of resources to projects vital to national safety, but unproductive of pleasure and comfort to our people, which ruthless Communist direction of economic development achieves? This is an open struggle: there is no guarantee of victory for freedom. But if free men choose wisely and courageously they can win, and one of the choices they must make is that for combination. 'When bad men combine, the good must associate; else they will fall, one by one, an unpitied sacrifice in a contemptible struggle.'[19] All too often has liberty perished because its bearers would not unite. By combination, by Union, the free West can swiftly and staggeringly increase its strength. It would perhaps not be going too far to say that this prescription for victory alone provides a prospect of defeating the Russians in this race without efforts so Herculean as perhaps to endanger the democratic basis of our society.

And it would be a talisman, also, in the wider political field, on which all military strength at bottom rests. Whether in these days of push-button warfare it is still true that the moral is to the material as three to one (perhaps it is even higher), it is still the case that no war can long be sustained — or even, avoided — without political determination and vigour. In his original speech at Zurich Churchill claimed that the re-creation of the European Family would 'as if by a miracle transform the whole scene', and history does seem to suggest that the successful creation of new bodies politic produces, in a seemingly miraculous fashion, an often sudden and yet sustained and intense burst of political activity. Somehow, the process of political fusion appears, as by a kind of seeming chemical reaction, to accelerate very rapidly the output of energy. It was no coincidence that the three troublemakers of the inter-war years, Italy, Japan, and Germany, were nations which had been created — by one form of political fusion or another — hardly more than half a century earlier. So too the prodigious mid-nineteenth century expansion of the United States was in no small part the direct result of the formation of the effective national Union of 1789.

Atlantic Union might well expect, in like fashion, to engender a new birth of Western political creativity: problems which now seem formidable, if not insoluble, might then find their own solutions, and spirits which were failing might flag no longer, but rally strongly. Above all, new margins of energy would be likely to become available in the struggle with Russia and China and their satellites. That fierce race for power will be to the strong, and in it the West can afford to despise no means by which decisively to augment her strength.

NOTES

[1] Woytinsky, *World Commerce and Governments*, p. 710.

[2] For these and other figures which follow I am indebted to Ellsworth Raymond, *Soviet Economic Progress: Because of or in Spite of the Government?*, New York 1957.

[3] Raymond, *op. cit.*, pp. 5, 31, and *Statesman's Year Book 1959*.

[4] Gunther, *op. cit.*, p. 396 *et seq.*

[5] *World Population and Production*, p. 258.

[6] George B. Cressey, ' The Basis of Soviet Strength ', quoted in Raymond, *op. cit.*, p. 7.

[7] Gunther, *op. cit.*, pp. 255-277.

[8] Dmitri T. Shepilov, quoted Raymond, *op. cit.*, p. 5.

[9] *The New York Times*, 11 November 1959.

[10] The term ' billion ' throughout is used in the American sense of 1,000,000,000.

[11] Alexander Eckstein, *Conditions and Prospects for Economic Growth in Communist China*, Cambridge, Mass. 1954, p. 23.

[12] Choh-Ming Li, *Economic Development of Communist China, An Appraisal of the First Five Years of Industrialization*, Berkeley 1959, p. 205.

[13] *Ibid.*, p. 217.

[14] Theodore Shabad, *China's Changing Map, A Political and Economic Geography of The Chinese People's Republic*, New York 1956, p. 49.

[15] Sir Halford J. Mackinder, *Democratic Ideals*, New York 1942, p. 150.

[16] Winston S. Churchill, *The Second World War*, Vol. II., London 1949, pp. 103-4.

[17] Mackinder, *op. cit.*, p. 70.

[18] *The New York Times*, 16 November 1959.

[19] Burke, *op. cit.*, p. 40.

CHAPTER XII

Atlantic Union and International Communism

IT may, however, be argued that this excessive concern for military strength and political power is no longer justified by the facts, because a real and visible thaw has set in after more than a decade of the seeming perma-frost of the 'cold war'. Certainly there is now powerful evidence of at least a Russian desire to avoid a direct military clash with the West, even if little similar evidence exists in the case of China. But this does not in the least mean that the Communist aim of forcing its system on mankind has been abandoned, only that overt war has become too risky in the nuclear age even for Marxism, inherently forceful and violent social doctrine though it has always been. The battle merely becomes a battle of production and ideas rather than of arms. As Mr. Khrushchev himself explained it: 'Peaceful co-existence means continuation of the struggle between the two social systems — but by peaceful means, without war, without interference by one state in the internal affairs of another. . . . We consider it to be economic, political and ideological struggle, but not military. It will be a competition of the two systems in a peaceful field.'[1]

If this metamorphosis is really taking place, free men everywhere should of course thank God with all their hearts for it, but they should not heave a sigh of relief and sink back into 'normalcy'. So long as there are great tracts of the world and huge numbers of its people, grinding out a miserable poverty-stricken existence, and as long as these nations are 'un-committed' to political democracy, or even inclining towards Communism, there can be no rest for the Atlantic nations. Competitive co-existence makes Atlantic Union, if possible, even more necessary than the cold war; if political freedom is to prevail, economic freedom must win also in the battle of standards of living. The future of India, striving as she is to rival China by developing economically through democratic methods, is of inestimable importance, but it is by the performance of the Atlantic nations themselves that the uncommitted peoples, in Asia, in Africa, in Latin America, will finally judge between the Communist and the Western way. The Atlantic states, indeed, have it in their power, by appropriate measures of aid and assistance, to ensure or at least greatly to facilitate the victory of India and other free nations in the economic race with China. But they will only be able to do so by using with single-minded energy every possible means to promote their own economic strength. The principal means they have is unity, through an economic, and ultimately political, union.

This necessity for united economic effort is in one respect made even more urgent by the prospect of an easing of international tension, for this would mean some measure of disarmament, or of 'armament control', with its accompanying drop in government defence expenditure. Nothing is more likely than such a drop to precipitate a severe economic depression in the West, and even with our modern economic knowledge it will not be an easy matter to prevent this from happening. It would be the first occasion on which there has been a drastic and sustained drop in armament expenditure, unbuttressed by a huge wartime backlog of consumer demand, since the days of the Great Depression, and it might have cataclysmic effects if we were not ready for it. Certainly the whole Western world must be on the look-out for very bad economic weather in case of disarmament, and must be prepared with energetic programmes, largely of government expenditure, to combat it. Above all it will be necessary to maintain the volume of international trade, to see that it does not become frozen into ever-dwindling bilateral channels as a result of the stiffening national economic attitudes which are so often the main result of an international recession. Against this tendency a programme for the building of an economic union of the N.A.T.O. and other states, an Atlantic common market, would be a powerful bulwark.

The need for it, however, is not confined to meeting particular economic problems which might be precipitated by disarmament, for there still remains the necessity to prove that a controlled system of capitalistic free enterprise of the Western democratic type can in fact outproduce the authoritarian Communist system. There is no ground whatever for supposing, as some seem to imagine, that it will do so *automatically*; Adam Smith's 'invisible hand' is not going to do this job for us unaided. Indeed, the Communist system has certain notable advantages in this rivalry. It has, on the surface, no labour problem, for strikes are illegal in the Soviet Union; there are, at least to the immediate glance, fewer drones in the Soviet economy than in that of the West; and the absolute and unchallenged power of the state makes directional and remedial economic control, in case of international economic difficulties, far easier than in a democratic society. Nor can we be blind to the fact that Communist drive and energy, the Communist sense of purpose and destiny, is another, and a powerful, motive which can provide fuel for an economic machine different from the basic free motive of enlightened self-interest. The West as a whole must gain a sense of urgency, must emphasize other, and in some ways nobler, motives for action than simple material self-seeking. An obvious way to do this is by bending our energies to the tremendous task of constructing in the West a broader-based international economic and political unit.

This programme, while capable of arousing energy and enthusiasm, would also in the long run hugely profit us materially as individuals: in a sense it would enable us both to have our cake and eat it. The Communists themselves are supreme materialists; the sacrifices which they extract from their unhappy peoples now they justify solely on the grounds that they will make their remote progeny rich. And fundamentally, in the free world, our altruistic and our self-regarding purposes ought to be, as they would be here, in harmony: that they are so is the underlying belief on which the whole miracle of modern capitalist productivity has been based. Do not let us, either, be mealy-mouthed in recognizing the extraordinary nature of that miracle of the Western Industrial Revolution, first in eighteenth- and nineteenth-century Britain and most magnificently in nineteenth- and twentieth-century America: it ushered in a totally unprecedented era of material plenty, at first for a few peoples, but ultimately — can it be doubted? — for all mankind. Adam Smith — of all authors least perhaps given to exaggeration — could write in 1776, in the very infancy of this development: 'it may be true, perhaps, that the accommodation of an European prince does not always so much exceed that of an industrious and frugal peasant, as the accommodation of the latter exceeds that of many an African king, the absolute master of the lives and liberties of ten thousand naked savages.' How tremendously has this process of increasing the wealth of mankind been continued by modern Western industrial society! And the process has been, with appropriate modifications, that of a free society which has believed that by allowing each man to pursue his individual economic interest the interest of society as a whole would be promoted. 'It is not from the benevolence of the butcher, the brewer, or the baker, that we expect our dinner, but from their regard to their own interest. We address ourselves, not to their humanity, but to their self-love, and never talk to them of our own necessities but of their advantages.'[2]

With certain necessary controls, we still believe fundamentally with Adam Smith that the happiest society will be that which allows men to pursue their own economic interests. We should not falter in this belief. We also believe that this system is capable, if set to work aright, of outstripping the Communist system in economic production, for we are aware of the weaknesses of the enemy as well as of ourselves; of the cumbrous nature of excessively centralized control, of the dead hand of bureaucracy, of the irreplaceable expertise of the free entrepreneur, of the invaluable fertility of individual initiative, and above all of the sovereign quality of willing labour. Even if we did not believe in the economic supremacy of our system, we in the West should probably refuse to abandon our liberties in exchange for a more productive one, to sell our political and social birthright for a mess of economic pottage, but we should be acting from a high plateau of reasonable living standards and not from the abysses of poverty in which the bulk of mankind ekes out its existence. We cannot expect the world's poor, who so largely still outnumber its rich, to act the same way; they will have to be convinced by capitalism's economic results as well as by the existence of Western liberties.

We should also be constantly aware of another conviction of Adam Smith, that the extent of division of labour (and hence the productivity of industry) depends upon the size of the market — that is to say that, in ideal conditions at any rate, absolutely the best economic system is unrestricted free trade. The proviso is important, for Britain found out that free trade would not work in a protectionist and politically divided world; it is also clear that such factors as unemployment have a serious impact on the functioning of classical economics, and that mobility of labour can be a dangerous illusion in international free trade. But, given such important qualifications as these, it still seems to remain true that the freer the rein given to the 'law of comparative advantage', the greater the area of unrestricted trade, the better. The United Kingdom itself, curiously enough, was, at the time when Adam Smith wrote, one of the largest, if not the largest, free trade area in the Western world, and it was not for reasons entirely unconnected with this that the Industrial Revolution came first in Britain. Similarly, it was in considerable part owing to the enormous free trade area of the continental United States that America became the wealthy industrial colossus that she is today. This fact is generally recognized in practice by economists and statesmen in their perennial search for 'multilateral trade': the ultimate logical development of multilateral trade, after all, is free trade. Yet in very few countries is 'free trade' accepted even as an ideal goal, for in very few countries apart from Britain has protectionism ever in practice yielded for long to full freedom of international commerce.

Yet it is plain that in the post-war world the economic strength of the West as a whole, and particularly perhaps of Europe, has steadily grown with, and largely as a result of, the continual liberalization of international commerce, the whittling away not merely of war-time regulations, but even of some restrictions which came into being, before the war began, as a result of the Great Depression. Recognition of this need to press on with the freeing of international trade is implicit not only in such organizations as G.A.T.T., but even more in the urgent European pursuit, despite internecine differences, of Common Market and Free Trade Area. At the present time, even the United States is being made aware, not without discomfort, of her increasing dependence on international trade; the outflow of gold which has resulted from the recovery of Western Europe, and hence the complete closing, at least for the present, of the dollar gap which has so long haunted the Treasuries of Europe, is a dramatic illustration of this fact. The technically adverse American balance of trade is not yet very serious, but it calls, not only for the modification of aid policies, but for further positive European steps, some of which have already been taken, for the easing of trans-Atlantic commerce. These should be followed, not by American restrictive measures, but by still further reciprocal concessions in tariffs. In this way the course towards increasing international trade can be maintained against any contrary tendency.

The fact is, not only that America is now much the largest international trader, but also that her dependence on foreign markets will continue to increase. There are a number of indications that the long process by which, ever since the beginning of the nineteenth century, the United States has become steadily less dependent, relative to her national wealth, on foreign trade is at an end. (American foreign trade, that is to say combined exports and imports, sank steadily from an average of 16·7 per cent of national income between 1800-40 to an average of 9·0 per cent between 1946-52.) For one thing, she has been using up some of her resources — as, for example, lumber — very fast. For another, she is deficient in certain raw materials; thus, in minerals, which tend to become more important the more highly developed a country is, the United States is almost entirely dependent on imports of tantalum, asbestos, mica, nickel, chromite, tin, quartz crystal and industrial diamonds, while she meets less than 20 per cent of her needs in cobalt, mercury, manganese, and platinum. She even finds it necessary — or at least advisable — to import petroleum and iron ore. (And it will be a very long time, even if it ever occurs, before modern synthetics have a decisive counter effect, on this tendency to need increasing imports of raw materials, by producing effective domestic substitutes on a large scale.) For yet another thing, she has always imported certain tropical products, such as bananas, tea and coffee. Finally, the American consumer has shown an increasing tendency of late years to seek particular goods overseas which he prefers to the domestic product; this has long been true of such things as high-quality British woollens, Scotch whisky, and French wines, but has been most recently and clearly shown in the boom in foreign cars. Thus there is every likelihood that America's need of, and desire for, foreign trade will continue to increase, while Europe's yearning for America's products is likely to persist into the foreseeable future.

The surest way to promote this trade, and the growing prosperity which would result, is by an Atlantic Union. There can be little question that a progressive lowering of tariffs in the future is urgently necessary in any event in order to maintain the expanding momentum of international trade. This process is already under way in the Common Market, and looks like being so in the Little Free Trade Area, but these groupings are not wide enough. An Atlantic Union would be very much nearer to a system of complete international free trade, and it would have a correspondingly stimulating effect on the economic life of the whole area, even including the United States. It would be possible to organize its creation by regular and planned stages so that, in a society whose standards of living were relatively so close to one another and relatively so high, the shocks of adjustment would not be too severe; with the wealth and power of modern Western governments to cushion excessively drastic economic changes, it would be a perfectly practicable operation. More than that, it would before long splendidly and greatly simplify the increasingly complex and stupefying network of international economic regulations which, insect-like, we are busy weaving, as anyone can see who reflects on the fact that Western European nations now have not only their own national trade regulations (including special agreements with colonies and erstwhile colonies), but also special relations with Common Market or Free Trade Area countries (according to which they belong to) and also prospective special relations between the Seven and the Six as entities, as well as obligations to fellow members of G.A.T.T. — to say nothing of 'normal' trade relations with non-members of G.A.T.T. Well might Mr. Maudling remark that the present European trade situation is a 'tangled problem'. Even the increasing numbers of our bureaucrats should breathe a sigh of relief at the simplifying effect which in the long run an Atlantic Union would have, in the economic, and as a matter of fact also in the political, sphere.

The great and long-standing American fear of reducing her tariff protection — the classic argument used in favour of protection by every protectionist country, that her market would be swamped and her own industry undermined by the products of low-paid foreign labour — would not apply with nearly so much force in an Atlantic Union with a common external tariff wall as in the case of a straight proposal for drastic all-round international tariff reductions in G.A.T.T. at the present time. America would not be opening her doors to the unrestricted imports of the Orient or Latin America, areas with near-subsistence standards of living in many places, but only to the products of countries with standards of living relatively high — if not, of course, as great as her own. It would be much less in accordance with the true interests of the United States, both economic and political, to join, as has been proposed, a Latin-American Free Trade Area than a North Atlantic one. America's ties of trade and her bonds of political self-interest still link her most firmly, as they have always done (despite the abortive economic Pan-Americanism of James G. Blaine and his successors), with the Atlantic nations, even though there has been a post-war increase of her trade with Latin America. Thus in 1952 32·3 per cent of the trade of the United States was with Middle and South America, but 40·8 per cent with Europe and North America.[3]

Thus in a Union of the original members of N.A.T.O. with Australia and New Zealand, only Italy and Portugal would constitute serious problems from the point of view of discrepancy in standards of living, for they have *per capita* incomes much smaller than the rest. In any event, the vast productivity and extraordinary efficiency of American industry would protect her extremely well in competition with her partners. Her fields of potential export would amply counterbalance any losses in her domestic markets. It would indeed be the outworn and inefficient industries of a number of European countries which would feel the cutting wind of competition most keenly. America's technological mastery is the most effective protection she can have.

Furthermore, the American people may find it increasingly desirable to ensure full scope for the maintenance and expansion of their present volume of commerce at this time of growing international competition in trade. So hard is it for men to foresee with clarity the consequences of their actions, that certain American officials are now surprised at one of the earliest unexpected results of the formation of the Common Market, and then of the Little Free Trade Area — namely, a situation in which the tariffs in some countries are liable to rise against the outside world, including the United States, and even in which a bitter trade war may be imminent in the West. This is only one of the many ways in which America could conceivably come to rue the day on which she did so much to establish a European union over whose actions she retained so little effective control. Such economic results as these may be serious, but they are not so potentially disastrous as the ominous political possibilities. Nevertheless, they may well give the United States cause to think again about the desirability of an Atlantic economic grouping.

Finally, the progressive construction of an Atlantic customs, and then political, Union, would add greatly to the richness, as opposed merely to the wealth of American life. Ever since the days of Adam Smith economists have argued about the meaning of the 'wealth of nations', and the most perspicacious have always realized that welfare, not money alone, is the proper aim of man in society. For a very long time this argument that man may need other objectives besides money, that he may indeed have too much money, seemed highly abstract and academic, but it has, in a country with so high a standard of living among many of its groups as America, now become very practical. There is a great deal of evidence that the spending of their ever-augmenting wealth and the employment of their ever-increasing leisure has become one of the most important and even troublesome preoccupations of a growing number of Americans. There is a general sense of dissatisfaction in certain areas of American society with the exclusive concentration in national life on making more money, regardless of the way in which it is to be spent when it is made. This shows itself in a number of ways; in the rising demand for foreign products once rare and exotic, in the spreading interest in art and music and culture, and, perhaps most strikingly, in the prodigious swelling of the numbers of travellers, particularly to Europe. In 1957, for example, 262,730 Americans visited the United Kingdom, 565,000 visited France, and 756,938 visited Italy. (This item in the American balance of payments, incidentally, is an important one, and will become more important every year; the money which is spent abroad in this way has somehow to be earned.) All these desires of Americans would be considerably facilitated by the increasing mutual intercourse, in trade, in travel and in the affairs of the mind, which would be one of the inevitable and principal results of Atlantic Union. The variety of goods available would be enormously enhanced, the growing need for leisure occupations would be much more effectively met, and the richness of cultural life would be immeasurably increased.

NOTES

[1] *The New York Times Magazine*, 15 November 1959.

[2] Adam Smith, *An Inquiry into the Nature and Causes of the Wealth of Nations*, Volume I, Oxford 1880, pp. 13-14, p. 15.

[3] Woytinsky, *World Commerce and Governments*, pp. 78-9. A Free Trade Agreement was signed between Latin-American countries in February 1960.

CHAPTER XIII

The American Spirit and Atlantic Union

I T is good that a chapter concerned with the purely
economic contest between the Communist and the
Western worlds should end on a note not purely
material, for it would be a grave error for the West to turn
upon the outside world an exclusively materialistic mask.
Yet there is a real risk that the case of the United States may
go by default because the uncommitted world is tempted to
think of America as excessively and exclusively materialistic.
It is one of the most ironical paradoxes of our time that a
Communist creed which is dogmatically — theologically —
materialist and atheist should be capable of arousing the
fanatical and passionate devotion that it sometimes does. This
is partly because it is willing — or has been in the past — to
sacrifice every present human interest and dignity to the welfare (still purely material) of future (and unspecified) generations, and because this appeals to the deep-rooted human
instinct of self-sacrifice, if not indeed of masochism. The
American dream, on the other hand, because it is a dream for
the individual human being *now*, as well as his children in
future, seems sometimes to appeal only to the baser self-seeking interests of men. For this very reason, in less exalted and
more rational mood, the world is capable of seeing the solid
reality of American well-being and of appreciating the
abundance of material things which America's pre-eminent
standard of living is providing for her people at this very time
— and not merely promising for some future and perhaps
far-off day.

Yet the American way of life is not, as Americans know
in their hearts, solely, or even excessively, materialist. But
the world may perhaps be pardoned for labouring under the
delusion that it is, for materialism has long been one of the
most perplexing and deep-rooted of American problems. This

is a question which is, with the volcano of the TV quiz scandal erupting luridly in their midst, much in the minds of Americans today, but it is one of great complexity which must be approached with considerable caution. Thus, for example, Englishmen who launch against America an accusation of materialism, or—as is more likely—mutter an almost inaudible reference to the 'almighty dollar', would do well to remember that recent Gallup polls in the two countries, which asked how many of those approached had been to church on the previous Sunday, got a figure of 12 per cent in Britain as opposed to one of 49 per cent in the United States. But it must be admitted that from America's earliest beginnings hopes of material betterment have been one of the strongest, and probably the strongest, of motives in her prodigious development. It was the lure of Spanish treasure which led to the freebooting expeditions of Drake, and El Dorado remained the fantasy, the fixation, of Raleigh and the earliest colonizing attempts of the English.

But it would be a gross perversion of the truth to see economic motives as alone important in the European population of America; Jamestown was founded by a trading company, but in New England and Pennsylvania the foundations were the outcome of the desire, principally on the part of the Puritans, for a new religious life, far removed from the persecutions and restrictions of the old world. Here in large degree there entered the American legend that vivid, persistent and often paramount idealism of which any student of the United States is acutely aware. Men, as a great Australian historian put it, emigrate not in despair but in hope: [1] for many of those who have emigrated to America, it has had the imperishable, warm attraction of a fresh life in a virgin soil—well might they have cried, 'Oh my America, my new found land.'

Yet such is humanity and such is life upon this planet, that men, and certainly men of common clay, can seldom thrive on spiritual fare alone. Even that often austere Protestantism, which was hugely predominant in the history of the United States until recent times, came, in the fashion suggested to us by historians of religion and the rise of capitalism, to be a potent agent in the spread of material wealth. The discipline of work for God's sake merged into the idea of work for work's sake, and in practice this became hard to distinguish from work for wealth's sake. Nor was this purely a domestic development, for from the time of American independence onwards it becomes increasingly plain that the overwhelming majority of immigrants came to America because it offered them a better standard of living than their country of origin; as one early nineteenth-century British emigrant put it in more homely terms, it meant three meat meals a day. And as the nineteenth century progressed and the strict and universal hold of religion weakened to some extent in America, as elsewhere in the Western world, so did material motives become, as it seemed to many, more all pervading, more powerful, more self-sufficient. It is certainly an illusion to think of the ante-bellum South, uniquely and essentially based as it was on slave labour (which is in a sense the extreme of materialism), as an unsullied home of idealism, but Southern society paid at least lip service to other values; the triumphant North in the Gilded Age, on the other hand, certainly did not embody the less material values of New England. With the rise of modern industrial capitalism, the Jeffersonian vision of an independent agrarian society was replaced by that of a business man's society which would have been nearer to the heart of Hamilton.

In many — perhaps most — respects business still sets the tone of American life, for it is to business men that the greatest material rewards are available. In this sense the making of money is not merely the necessary preoccupation of all ordinary folk, in America as elsewhere, but is the form of life which attracts those of greatest capacity in the United States; business can still be regarded as America's business, and from one point of view the essence of business is money-making.

But wise students of America have long observed that there is something odd about the American love of making money. As Henry James makes his character Newman say in *The American*, 'I cared for money-making, but I never cared so very terribly for the money. There was nothing else to do.' G. K. Chesterton likewise pointed out that the Englishman's ideal is leisure not labour, but the American's labour not dollars. (In parenthesis, let Englishmen remind themselves, at this juncture, of the acute observation of Margaret Halsey in 1938: 'The English have refined upon our naïve American way of judging people by how much money they happen to have at the moment. The subtler English criterion is how much expensive, upper-class education they have been able to afford.') But nevertheless there is still much ground for agreeing with the observation of De Tocqueville made in the days of Jackson: 'I know of no country . . . where the love of money has taken stronger hold upon the affections of men. . . .'[2]

In most cases, no doubt, the cash for which the American strives is desired for what it will buy, but it is certainly a fact (and not confined to the United States) that some men go on seeking it far beyond the point at which, even on the broadest estimate, they need more material goods to make them happy. Here the pursuit of money has plainly become, at the least a mere symbol of success, or at the most a means to power. And at all levels of American life, the simple making of money, quite apart from its use, is at times an end in itself; living up to the Joneses may result in a more comfortable material existence, but its primary object is to compete, and, if possible, to excel, in the most generally approved field of endeavour. There indeed is the crux of this problem — why is money-making in the United States the most generally approved field of endeavour? For it may, I think, be admitted that it is, and that this is very often what Europeans mean when they accuse the American people of materialism.

The answer in part, of course, is that, even if man cannot live by bread alone, he cannot live without it. We do not have to accept an economic interpretation of history — let alone a Marxist one — just because we believe, as historians, that the mass of mankind have always been very largely preoccupied with the earning of their daily bread. In the long centuries of recorded human history until very recent times only the highly select few have had the wealth or the leisure to think about much else. It was indeed to be expected that, when the common people at last gained effective control of a great government, they should have caused it in large degree to concern itself with the betterment of their material conditions; and this proved true of the United States. The principal day-to-day interest of American politics has always been economic.

This was in large part due to the lack of any alternative, universally accepted, standard for judging achievement in American life; indeed it raises the question, fundamental for all free governments, of how easily in a real democracy any other standard it truly practicable. What are the means, common to a whole nation, by which it measures social achievement? For the Greeks, at least from the philosopher's angle, all political life was at bottom moral, and in the West, since its medieval origins, ethics and morality have been essentially bound up with the Christian religion. The American people have been in some respects a profoundly religious people, and many of them are so still. Yet in the strict sense of the term the government of the United States is not a Christian government. The Constitution of 1789 is a non-religious document; the word God indeed was omitted from it, and to this day the teaching of any particular religious doctrine by the public schools is unconstitutional. To some extent the a-religious nature of the Constitution was a result of mistrust of an established church, and to some extent (perhaps less) of the Deistic, or even agnostic, views of a few of the Founding Fathers in that rational age, but most of all it was the result of the many and varied creeds present in America and to the growth, already in the eighteenth century, of the doctrine of toleration which is at the very heart of America's political being. Certainly it has been the balance, or rivalry, of competing sects which has kept the strict separation of church and state intact in a predominantly Christian country: no change would have been possible because there could have been no agreement as to what it should be. Such agreement has seemed less and less likely as, at least until very recently, the number of sects has continued to multiply so remarkably, for in no country of the world have the fissiparous tendencies of Protestantism been more startlingly exemplified. Thus in the nature of things there has never been in America any one particular, generally accepted, religious standard, let alone any single voice of religious authority, whereas religious divisions have long been powerful agents of political discord.

Nor has the United States had a social and racial unity, with its institutional manifestations, as strongly and deeply inbred as that of most European nations. The continental dimensions of the land and the resulting and fundamental phenomenon of sectionalism presented a first and most formidable obstacle to unity, one which threatened the whole fabric of the Union in the Civil War, but which had many other, if lesser, manifestations. From the beginning these divisions between the plantation South and the commercial North, and between both and the frontier West, made exceedingly difficult, if not impossible, a national social leadership such as was provided in Europe by cohesive aristocracies, with their codes of political conduct or genteel behaviour. In some respects the lack of a class of nobility, particularly a *grande noblesse*, such as that of France, may be esteemed a great advantage for America, but the lack of a real and solid equivalent in the United States to the English landed gentry, perhaps the most important and unique feature of British constitutional development, may have been less salutary. And no educational system similar to that created by the British Public Schools movement of the nineteenth century (dedicated to the provision of a class of national leaders and imperial administrators for a society now far too large, industrialized and complex to be managed by a landed élite alone) flourished in the United States, save in a kind of way in the South; the rapid development of public education, combined with American mistrust of any form of unequal social opportunity, made any such means of creating a homogeneous national leadership impossible. Not even the armed forces provided a nucleus for it, since they were both minute in size and also very generally mistrusted, as constituting a privileged class of potential Cromwells.

With no nobility of birth, no nobility of the sword, only the *noblesse de robe* remained, and it is in fact really only in the law that one finds a breeding ground for national leadership in America which is recognizable in terms of a European, and especially a British, counterpart. In the course of American history it has indeed been more from the ranks of the lawyers than from any other single source that American statesmen and politicians have been drawn, and it has on the whole been a singularly successful well-spring of talent and experience, for the American legal system, lacking the rigid British distinction between barrister and solicitor, is less liable to have the narrowing, even pettifogging, effect which the law has sometimes had upon its practitioners in England. But despite its pre-eminent position in American political life, the class of lawyers was not (as is the case in Britain, with its essentially centralized system of justice, in which the King's judiciary was indeed one of the fundamental agents of national unification) national, virtually by definition. The bulk of American litigation has necessarily been in the state courts, and there are of course as many different legal systems as there are states, so that entry to the law has always been initially through the state bar. Like the members of Congress they so often become, American lawyers frequently remain strongly tied to the interests of their state and locality, and few lawyers, simply as lawyers, ever became national figures; for that it was necessary to enter the political, or in time of war the military, stage. Thus, so long as they remained strictly lawyers, it has been less easy than it might otherwise have been for them to participate in the creation of essentially national and all pervading standards of conduct and belief.

This lack of ready-made, generally accepted religious or social standards, and of obvious instruments for their development, was exacerbated by the problem of assimilating the overwhelming influx of vastly disparate immigrant groups. And the particular aspect which interests us here, the adherence to material criteria of judgement when others are lacking, is especially illuminated by this. How does the first generation immigrant prove his worth to his fellow citizens? How does he demonstrate that he has arrived? He will almost never learn to speak the language well enough for acceptance; he is unlikely to change his religious beliefs (and would be no better off if he did in all probability, at least at first); he is usually unfamiliar with the processes of democratic politics, and his aspirations therein are limited (even by the very terms of the Constitution in some degree); citizenship itself is so easily obtained for the most part that it is *per se* no great

o

prize; the careers open to him may be limited, by his education, or, in the case for example of trade union activity, by jealousy of the newcomer — all these ways of proving himself in the land of his adoption may be closed to him. But he *can* fight to earn money; with it he can purchase, not only the sense of security which he above all lacks, but the goods which will earn him the recognition and esteem of his fellow citizens.

More than that, this readily understandable cleaving, in a society all the members of which (or their ancestors) had been immigrants, to the only solid and universally recognizable and recognized standard of social judgement, is one of the secrets of America's unique and prodigious wealth. The Swiss historian, Rappard, who is among the most penetrating students of America, has argued most convincingly that what is economically unique in the United States is the depth of uniform consumer demand. What is necessary, in order to take the maximum advantage of the economies of modern industrial mass production is, not merely a very large market, but one with a high degree of uniformity and predictability in its demands. This the American market pre-eminently provides, for it is no good saving the money you make if you are to impress your fellow men; you must spend it on commodities which they can see, or services which they can recognize. (It is no accident that Thorstein Veblen evolved his theory of conspicuous consumption in contemplation of the American scene.) Yet more, it is no good spending your money on things, of which your fellows do not know the value, or even which they do not or would not themselves desire; here indeed is a solid groundwork for a uniform and predictable mass demand. And on it, to make assurance doubly sure, is raised the great structure of modern advertising, in the techniques of which America leads the world. Not merely does it provide the masses with guidance as to what they should buy, and as to what will be acceptable to their neighbours as symbols and manifestations of wealth, but, by stimulating yet more the desire to earn, it once again stokes the giant machine of American productivity. Firm adherence indeed to other standards than the material is necessary to resist the money standards which are unshakably rooted in the American system of advertisement, as each new exposure, on each new visit, to the hectic blasts of American television and radio make the visitor acutely aware.

But Britons at any rate certainly cannot lay even their relative emancipation in the past from the direct and over-powering domination of the cash box as a flattering unction to their souls, for they have not solved the problem of national leadership in democracy either, but only put it off. America, because she was the pioneer democracy, faced up almost from the beginning to the fundamental question which perplexed the great Utilitarian philosophers of that era and which is at the heart of the democratic process — how can moral, or even aesthetic, standards be maintained in a community where by definition everything must in the last resort be decided by mass opinion? Jeremy Bentham, who described himself to President Jackson as 'more of a United States man than an Englishman', was ruthlessly logical in his answer to this question. Declaring that man is the servant of two sovereign masters, Pain and Pleasure, and that that which they tell him to do is that which he ought to do, he believed that those courses of action were right which promoted the greatest happiness of the greatest number, and that their nature must be determined by majority vote — by the process which he called counting heads instead of breaking them. With equally remorseless logic he asserted roundly that there was no qualitative distinction between human pursuits and pleasures, between poetry and push pin, between Beethoven and boogie-woogie. Here he posed the basic dilemma of democracy, with which the United States has long been grappling and which Britain has long side-stepped, but which, after the social revolution of 1945, she is unlikely to be able much longer to evade.

In other words, even American materialism is democratic, and that democracy is the result of a strain of political idealism which is as old, and as important, as the materialism itself. The democratic fervour of the United States, with its early search for mass education and an informed and intelligent electorate, is indissolubly bound up with the American search for a higher standard of living for all Americans. This persistent democratic passion has been the result of a genuine, and in many respects unsullied, idealism; otherwise, how can we explain the fact that America did not, like so many other societies before it, slip into the easy hands of an oligarchy, or split into manifold tyrannies in the fashion of Latin America? The consistent victory of democratic principles in the United States — albeit they may sometimes have been tarnished in the execution — is a striking witness to the continuous presence of a ferment of the highest principle in the heady brew of American material triumphs.

Thus alongside the unprecedented economic achievements of America, there have always lain her political and social ideals, 'that all men are created equal, that they are endowed by their creator with certain unalienable Rights, that among these are Life, Liberty and the pursuit of Happiness'. At the heart of the American tradition, however far the practice has sunk below the precept upon occasion, has always been the devotion to freedom and self-government. This passion has long overflowed its national banks, and fertilized the other lands, not of the West only, but of all the earth; America has always had a sense of mission at the core of her being, and with her rise to power in a contracting world her democratic ideas have spread far and wide throughout it. She fought her two great wars, as her leader in the first declared, to make the world safe for democracy; 'Our object . . . is to vindicate the principles of peace and justice in the life of the world as against selfish and autocratic power and to set up amongst the really free and self-governed peoples of the world such a concert of purpose and of action as will henceforth insure the observance of those principles.' As Wilson said on another occasion, 'America has a great cause which is not confined to the American continent. It is the cause of humanity itself.'[3]

The Messianic strain in the American people matches the very similar strain in Russian history, though now the vague, mystic sense of destiny of 'the third Rome' has been strengthened and stiffened by the iron framework of Marxist prophecy and predestination. This is one of the reasons for the rigid, almost obsessive, character of the great mid-twentieth century rivalry of the two continental powers, and for its global repercussions. It is not merely the national rivalry of two states of unprecedented grandeur and might, armed with weapons of unimagined destructiveness, but an ideological confrontation of a depth and breadth and intensity unequalled since the religious wars of the sixteenth and seventeenth centuries, and with infinitely greater potentialities for human good or ill.

Hitherto, America's sense of democratic mission has proved in many respects frustrating for her people. Where lands have come under her immediate control, such as her erstwhile colony the Philippines, she has had remarkable successes, as has Britain in some of her one-time colonies, particularly India. The case of the American democratic conversion of Japan, however, must be regarded as still 'not proven'. In Western Europe at the moment, too, after the victory in World War II, democracy is well nigh universal, but it has not yet lasted long enough in every country for certainty that it will endure permanently. But in other parts of the world, such as Latin America and the Far East, where American influence has been potent, democratic self-government is very largely at a discount. So, also, the great world organizations, the League of Nations and the United Nations—in the launching of both, and the maintenance of the latter, of which, the American inspiration was the most important factor—have proved in many respects disappointing as agencies of international justice and peace.

One of the main reasons for these failures has been that American influence has been too widely dispersed. Even for the United States, to persuade all men everywhere of the virtues of democracy has proved too large a task. The dissipation of her influence in distant places has sometimes endangered it nearer home: America had to learn in China in 1949 the painful lesson of the very real, if uncharted, limitations of the power even of so great a nation as herself. This does not mean in the least that she should abandon her world leadership, but that she would be wise to secure a broader base for her operations. This need Atlantic Union would meet with remarkable efficiency. The power for self-government, the influence for democracy, which a great free constitutional Union, of more than 400 million souls and unprecedented resources and economic strength, would exert in the world would be nothing less than enormous. It would be a strong and practical lever for the accomplishment of America's, and the West's, purpose — to ensure that government of the people, by the people, and for the people shall in the fulness of time come to all the peoples of the earth.

It is this democratic purpose of America, as well as her material plenty, which makes her way of life appealing to the many new nations of the world; in particular it gives it powerful attractions for the peoples who are most sensitive to the history of colonialism. This feeling is to a considerable extent mutual; the United States, as the first of modern colonies to break away from her mother country, inevitably has a deep emotional sympathy for other nations struggling to be free. Indeed, one of America's chief difficulties in the last fifteen years has been to reconcile her anti-imperialist feelings with her growing need of intimate association with the democratic, imperialist powers of Europe, and particularly Britain and France. But, with the rapid dissolution of Britain's colonial empire and the growing hope of a settlement in Algeria, this ambivalence of feelings has become less and less important. It no longer constitutes a formidable obstacle to Atlantic Union, for the present multi-racial composition of the British Commonwealth makes it clear that the reputation of colonial powers can be remarkably repaired by subsequent acts of atonement and liberation.

The merging of the United States with the one-time colonial powers would indeed enable the American people to facilitate and expedite the final stages of the Afro-Asian march to independent self-government; this could be accomplished much more successfully with the augmented financial resources which would be at the disposal of Atlantic Union. It would also do much to assuage the soreness of the Europeans, because it would cause America to assume some more direct responsibility in the matter, and that soreness has chiefly resulted from the British and French feeling that American anti-imperialism has in the past few years enjoyed power without responsibility. More than that, it would take away much, if not all, of the sting — or rather the dull, protracted ache — resulting from the British and French sense of declining greatness, by turning their eyes away from the shadows of their departed empires towards the real substance of the growing and dynamic power of the new Union on both shores of the Atlantic.

Per contra it would greatly facilitate the process, almost universally recognized in the West to be urgent and essential, of giving aid to the under-developed countries of the world. In an international society from which the cold war had disappeared this programme might be reckoned the most important activity of the West, for by it, to a considerable degree, the decision of the poor nations for Communism or freedom would be determined. The disparity between the standards of living of the West (U.S. *per capita* income 1948 $1,525; India 1946 $75; Ecuador 1948 $40) and of the rest of mankind is so staggering that it is safe to say no Western nation has yet fully realized its pressing nature. The United Nations has not proved a satisfactory co-ordinator of programmes of aid, and the United States, as she has recently declared, cannot any longer carry so much of the burden alone. An Atlantic Union would contain within it virtually all the powers of the free world in a position — and with an obligation — to give aid to under-developed countries. Not only would it be able to administer a really sweeping aid-plan with efficiency, but it would have at its disposal unprecedented sums for such a purpose, generated by the rising prosperity of the great combine.

It is necessary, though, as we have already remarked, for the West to demonstrate to the uncommitted peoples — and for the matter of that the Communist nations — other advantages and capabilities besides the simply material. One important gain for the prestige of the West arising from the creation of Atlantic Union would be its clear demonstration of Western political open-mindedness and flexibility. The 'new' nations are correspondingly conscious of the antiquity of the old; by their standards as modern states (the racial and even cultural antiquity of some of them is of less practical consequence) even America is venerable. But this does not mean that the older political organisms are revered; rather does it tend to mean that they are expected by the more youthful to show the symptoms of senescence — inflexibility, rigid tradition, crabbed self-centredness. There is in fact no indisputable analogy between the biological old age of individuals and the antiquity of nations, but there does seem to be a tendency for long-lived political bodies to become fixed in their patterns of thought and behaviour. It is highly desirable for the West, not only to show the world that its peoples still have the imagination, virility and limberness to undertake great and novel political enterprises, but also to maintain their own capacity to adjust to new circumstances, for when the species fails to adapt itself to an altered environment (or, in the case of men, to modify that environment) its very existence is cast in doubt.

The 'new' powers, their codes of conduct as yet inchoate, their precedents yet unmade, their habits unformed, have shown a notable tendency to coalesce in larger political units. The life, for example, of all the Middle Eastern states has been deeply affected (and, in the case of some of them, rendered insecure) by the potent force of Arab nationalism; in the as yet unproved United Arab Republic, two of them have actually merged their separate national sovereignties. Similarly, in West Africa, Ghana and Guinea, themselves scarcely out of colonial leading-strings, are seriously moved by pan-African sentiment. The widely scattered islands of the British West Indies are in the travail of confederation. All over the world, projects and enterprises for economic and political union — in some cases for supra-national states — are burgeoning and blossoming. In Europe itself such plans are being brought to reality; the Common Market is launched, and the Outer Seven soon will be (swallowing up en route the long sought Nordic economic union). There could be no more convincing demonstration to mankind, not merely of the unity but of the foresight, suppleness and vigour of the whole West than the promotion of Atlantic Union.

The number and variety of these closer regional groupings destroy one argument, which has been raised against an Atlantic federation in the past — that it will arouse the jealousy of other powers. The process of regional consolidations has gone too far to be stopped, and to attempt to do so would in any case be a grave error, for in the constricted world in which we now live the procedure of greater political aggregation is profoundly important and predominantly healthy. We now have a genuine world community of something approaching a hundred states; the supreme problem of the United Nations is to render such a great number of sovereign governments, each in the grip of powerful external and internal controlling forces, amenable to co-operation. The United Nations has been able to achieve some things, but the day is clearly far off when it can unquestionably guarantee international peace, let alone even remotely resemble a world government. Meanwhile we must live through these dangerous times, and one way to do it is by encouraging the growth of regional groupings.

These have a dual effect. In the first place, they increase the security, and sense of security, of their members (and in this respect one is tempted to proclaim that 'you all know, *in*security is mortals' chiefest enemy'), and in the second place they render international affairs far more manageable. If, by the growth of regional units, the number of member states of the United Nations could be halved (and this would be accomplished by even three or four groupings on the scale of Atlantic Union), the business of that body would be vastly easier to transact. It might necessitate a fundamental revision of its constitution — by altering, for example, the character or size of the Security Council to recognize the existence of new great powers — but this might well provide an opportunity to enable it to perform its functions more efficiently.

But the growth of new political super-units is only healthy if they do not acquire a fresh and violent chauvinism of their own, for to create larger nations which turned out to be more xenophobic than the smaller ones would be to jump out of the frying pan into the fire, if only because little wars which can be localized are less dangerous than larger ones which cannot. Therefore it would be essential from the beginning that Atlantic Union be non-exclusive; it must not earn the suspicion of its neighbours by arrogance, and it must keep its own ranks open to new adherents. Most of the nations of the world will not, in all probability, ever wish to join it; they will prefer to form regional groupings of their own. These groupings Atlantic Union must encourage and foster, and must never regard with a jaundiced eye. On the other hand it must, while always keeping its own doors open to applications to join, begin to build its own Union on a scale which will make success possible; too many international organizations have failed in recent history, by trying to go too far too fast, for unnecessary risks to be taken. A group of North Atlantic states, deriving from the historical source-lands of Western civilization, has a reasonable chance of making a success of Union, and it should consolidate that success before expanding too rapidly. But in due time it should be ready and willing to incorporate new members who are clearly — economically, politically and socially — ready to assume the responsibilities which membership of the Union would entail. By this time the Union will have become a going concern and will be able to judge by its own experi-ence the requirements for entry to it; it should not imperil its own democratic existence and influence by over-rapid dilution, but it should never create for itself, or deserve, a reputation for insolent exclusiveness.

No one can tell how swiftly or how largely an Atlantic — or any other regional — Union would gather new accretions. But such a process of international political growth, step by step, tier on tier, constitutes the surest, and perhaps the only, practical route to international government. The nations of the West have in the past led the world in showing their willingness to fight to the last ditch to prevent any single power from imposing its peace and order on the peoples of the earth by force. The only other way to the obviously essential ultimate goal of world government is by consent, and the democratic example of Atlantic Union would be of inestimable importance in promoting this. It would provide unassailable evidence that larger units of international government can be voluntarily created by free men, who remain self-governing. What the old smaller nations have once safely accomplished the new super-nations themselves may also one day do. Once the process of confederation has been proved possible, in the fullness of time — no one can say how soon or how late — a world united in liberty and self-government will become a real and practical possibility. As a wise European recently wrote, the free world should make a plan ' for endowing itself with a set of free democratic

permanent institutions of a federal nature, which would
ensure between its members the administration of freedom
and peace.

'The trouble today is that the Communist world understands unity but not liberty, while the free world understands
liberty but not unity. Eventual victory may be won by the
first of the two sides to achieve the synthesis of both liberty
and unity.'[4]

This is the challenge to America which European union
presents. But it is not the way that the American people have
been wont to see it in the past; they have thought of the
United States as being on the outside looking in. They
thought of the British as being on the inside looking out —
thought of them, over the 3,000 miles of ocean which separate
the two peoples, as inherently a part of Europe, from which
the United Kingdom is only divided by the 22 miles of
the Straits of Dover. They have been irritated by the British
refusal to see things this way, and by the unwillingness of
British governments to recognize unequivocally that they are
part of Europe by entering unreservedly into a European
union. Yet in fact the challenge of European unity to
Britain and to the United States is the same in kind. It poses
to both the question whether they will recognize the physical
and political facts of the world in which they live by submerging their separate national sovereignties in a wider
unity. Hitherto they have both supported European union
from without: are they now willing to support Atlantic
Union from within? For Britain the challenge is much more
pressing and immediate, but in truth for both of them it is
equally real and in the end equally important.

Let us not suppose — there is little danger that the British
and American governments will do so — that the obstacles
are not formidable for both powers. Neither nation has since
its beginning felt the triumphant tread of a foreign
conqueror; neither nation is accustomed to submit to the will,
or even the desire, of others. Both peoples tend to be suspicious of the works of all governments; both prize their
independence almost as highly as their liberties. Neither state
had in fact ever entered in time of peace into an important

and cast-iron military defence treaty with a leading European power until after World War II; neither state had even found it easy in the last fifteen years to reconcile its foreign policy with that of the other, let alone with those of all the N.A.T.O. countries. The difficulties will indeed be great, but they will not be insuperable. A generation which has seen the miracle of a Franco-German union cannot be too sceptical about the possibility of wider confederations.

The challenge of European union is no mean challenge. But the American people sometimes respond better to greater than to lesser challenges: America was for a brief span paralysed by Joseph McCarthy, but was swiftly galvanized into activity by the Russian threat in the cold war. Nor is she unaccustomed to international challenges akin to this. She emerged from isolation and gave birth to the idea of the League of Nations: she emerged from isolationism and created the United Nations.

The United States, too, is not handicapped, as is Britain, by the habit of gradualism; her pragmatism is capable of braver ventures. America, after all, is a land of bold beginnings. Many of the most vital steps in the history of the United States have been without precedent. The original colonies were heroically new departures; the American Revolution was a great and novel event in the history of empires; each of the fifty states of the Union in its turn has made a fresh beginning with an individual constitution; America actually devised the machinery of the constitutional convention, especially called together for the writing of fundamental law, for the making of a new written constitution. Above all, in the superb achievement of 1789, the creation of the Constitution of the United States, she not only brought a great nation into existence, but also virtually invented modern federalism. And this is the pattern on which most of the great states of the modern world are, in one form or another, organized: an Atlantic Union would have to regard the American federation in great degree as its prototype.

It may be admitted by some critics that the creation of the American Union was a magnificent accomplishment, but at the same time doubted whether it can be repeated, let alone excelled. Have the American people now the resilience, the vitality and the wisdom to redo and to outdo the work of the Founding Fathers? This question only the future can answer. But if they should wish it, they have the constitutional instrument ready to their hands; no revolution will be needed from the purely technical point of view. Just as the United Kingdom, by virtue of the legislative omnicompetence of Parliament, can legally effect any constitutional reform, however radical, so also has the United States, through the wisdom of those same Founding Fathers, the hitherto unused constitutional means of effecting reforms which are too fundamental, complex and numerous for the normal process of constitutional amendment.

'The Congress . . . on the application of the legislatures of two-thirds of the several states, shall call a convention for proposing amendments, which . . . shall be valid to all intents and purposes, as part of this Constitution, when ratified by the legislatures of three-fourths of the several states, or by conventions in three-fourths thereof, as the one or the other mode of ratification may be proposed by the Congress. . . .'

The American people have the constitutional means to enter Atlantic Union if they have the desire.

There is a way if there is the will, and there are increasing signs that the will may come. The Western air has been filled of late with cries that its nations need to grow ever closer to one another, and in particular that the institutions of N.A.T.O. must be greatly strengthened; some of these cries have originated in the United States, many have found an echo there. Very recently the Secretary-General of N.A.T.O., Paul-Henri Spaak, speaking in New York, called on the United States to lead the free world towards true interdependence, which is much more difficult to accomplish, in his view, when it is a question of co-ordinating economic policy rather than mobilizing against possible aggression. The United States had twice saved the free world, first with the Marshall Plan, then with N.A.T.O. 'I think it is necessary for the United States to act a third time and to act quickly. At this moment, when the danger of war seems to be receding, the peoples of the Free World must be given new reasons for remaining united.' On the same occasion, Governor Rockefeller of New York declared that this was the time to think of 'new and greater designs' for economic and political unity in the next ten to twenty-five years. 'We must be planning, not merely how we hope to check aggression, but how we propose to make this Western community of free peoples ever more profoundly unified in the cause of freedom everywhere.'[5]

These are but straws in the wind; they are nevertheless important straws (potential presidential candidates are not reluctant to promise the earth, but are notably reluctant to promise it if it looks like being unpopular). The concept of a democratic Atlantic Union must make a deep appeal to the idealism of the American people, and he who regards that idealism as shallow and ineffective does not comprehend the true America nor yet her true greatness. There are those who believe that American opinion is, at the close of 1959, in the midst of one of its instinctive periodic phases of reconsideration and reformation, which give an appearance of uncertainty, because the people are awaiting a decisive lead, but which end with a great forward drive; Jacksonian Democracy, the New Freedom, the New Deal, the Truman Doctrine, these were the fruits of such periods of hesitancy, of re-thinking. The time is ripe for Americans to look again with clear eyes at their international situation and their relations with their allies and their enemies. If, as a result, with due and proper public preparation and education, the issue of Atlantic Union were in the fullness of time put fairly before the American people, their response might well, I believe, astonish mankind in its receptiveness and even enthusiasm.

NOTES

[1] W. G. Hancock, *Australia*, London 1930, p. 54.
[2] This section is based on my *Great Britain and the United States*, pp. 166-73.
[3] Wilson, *op. cit.*, pp. xii, 110.
[4] Salvador de Madariaga, *The New York Times Magazine*, 11 October 1959.
[5] *The New York Times*, 17 November 1959.

PART III

The Anglo-American Predicament

'Not only the fortunes of this fearful war, but also the happiness of future generations, depend upon the fraternal association of Great Britain and the United States, without prejudice to the larger world structure that will be erected to secure the peace and freedom of mankind.'

Winston Churchill, 1943

CHAPTER XIV

Europe, The Commonwealth and Atlantic Union

BRITAIN and America have thus very much to gain from an Atlantic Union; Britain has the most urgent and obvious interest, but the ultimate stake of America may be quite as important. Because she is more directly and instantly affected by events in Europe, the United Kingdom must take the initiative, but the actual creation of the Union must depend absolutely on the willing participation of the United States. It is therefore the British and American peoples essentially who must take the lead in bringing this new political body to birth, for without their active leadership the Union cannot be accomplished.

This is necessary because European institutions are already in actual existence, and if Atlantic institutions are to supersede them it can only be through, in the first place, the joint efforts of Great Britain and the United States. Even more necessarily must it be so because they are, in differing degrees, 'the outsiders'; they are by geographical fact and political habit, though again to a different extent, the island, the insular, powers. Isolation from Europe, isolationism from its affairs, has been a real and important part of their experience, even if both nations are now quite convinced, and rightly, that it never can be so again. Europeans may be intellectually aware of this British and American conviction, yet they cannot but doubt it sometimes in their souls. In the future, as in the past, France, for example, may have splendour, but she can never have isolation. The European powers are acutely conscious of the English moat and of the great oceans which protect America; they have not always in the past understood fully the doctrine of sea power, but they have been made painfully aware of the effects of the existence of the Anglo-American island bases upon the destiny of Europe. The continent has seen often enough how Britain and

America, after failing to help in preventing its wars in peace while there was still time, have been able to withdraw to these maritime fortresses at moments of defeat, leaving Europe to its fate. Unwilling soon enough to take risks for their allies, because they would not engage the enemy until they themselves were directly threatened, they have been unable to prevent the peoples of Europe from being engulfed.

It is true that they have also in due course returned to liberate the continent, but at a fearful price in blood and destruction, and at an even more awful cost to the European spirit. One can fully understand the agony of mind of 'liberated' France. No wonder that the nations of Europe are upon occasion deeply mistrustful of those whom General de Gaulle calls 'the Anglo-Saxons'. His own *Memoirs* are instinct with suspicion of 'the attempts at Anglo-Saxon hegemony', and his insistence on the French development of nuclear weapons largely derives from his obsession with the idea that France must act as a counter-balance to attempts to dominate the continent by Britain and the United States.[1] France, and other European peoples, are still capable of deeply emotional anti-Americanism, though happily less frequently than of yore, and their dislike of Perfidious Albion and all her ways has a much longer history. At the present time, in 1959, the German feeling towards America is very cordial, but towards Britain is notably cool. There is a basic element of mistrust in Europe's attitude to the two 'outside' powers, which makes it inescapable that they must do the initial spadework in the construction of Atlantic unity, although as the foundations are laid they can reasonably expect increasingly effective and even enthusiastic assistance.

And how much in fact Europe has to gain from Atlantic Union! It gains, first and foremost, the highest possible degree of security against attack from the Communist world. Seen in the global perspective of the Eurasian land mass, the Western European peoples, for all their 250 million souls, are perched on the western edges of the World-Island, potentially subject to overwhelming pressures from the Communist third of mankind. Atlantic Union cannot prevent Russia from attacking Western Europe, but it can make it certain beyond doubt that it will prove a suicidal operation.

It can — and from the European point of view it is of paramount importance — remove effectively and for ever from the continental European mind the lingering fear of being abandoned, left in the lurch, by the 'Anglo-Saxons', or, to use a preferable term (which revives, in a different sense, the graphic phrase of De Tocqueville), the 'Anglo-Americans'. Europe would be as integral a part of the Union as would Canada or the United States herself.

Europe would also gain added strength to prevent what may be in the future the greater danger from the Soviet Union, subversion by Communist infiltration. As the remarkable tonic effect of Marshall aid on the body of an economically sick Europe after 1947 indisputably showed, the prime effective barrier to Communism is prosperity; and the unprecedented opportunities of drastically raising European standards of living, which Union will afford, will be the best possible medicine for warding off the effects of the forthcoming economic offensive of the Communist world. (Europe will indeed profit most from the economic potentialities of a united Atlantic area, for her living standards are for the most part lower than those of Australasia or North America.) Furthermore, the second effective barrier to Communism, strong democratic institutions, would be rendered much stronger than it has ever been in most of Europe by the stiffening and stabilizing effects of the Union. Everywhere in Europe the stimulus, economic, political and social, of participation in the Union, and in its construction, would have an inestimable invigorating effect — a 'toning up' process all too frequently enjoyed by mankind, in its public (as opposed to private) activities, only in time of war.

Apart from these overriding general advantages of Atlantic Union to Europe, it would have special benefits for particular states or groups of states. The little nations of Europe, for example — and worthy members of that society they are, whose effective control even over their own destiny is always strictly limited by their relative smallness — would gain a very high degree, practically speaking an absolute degree, of protection against their great neighbours within the Union, some of whom on past showing they have ample reason to fear. The Benelux partners, for instance, must certainly wonder occasionally how effective France and Italy would be in holding down a Germany which might once more, even if only temporarily, take leave of its senses. So strong would the Union as a whole be, and so considerable would be the protection it would offer, that small states, such as Sweden, and even Switzerland, long devoted to the principle of self-preservation by neutrality, might be persuaded to cast in their lot with it.

Finally, all the small states would gain enormously from the access to larger markets and readier supplies of raw materials which so vast a territorial aggregation as Atlantic Union would ensure. A secure and tariffless market of more than 400 million people for Swiss watches and precision instruments, for instance, could hardly fail to be gratifying to Switzerland, as might also be her unlimited access to the raw materials of the larger countries. Almost alone among the nations, a number of the smaller powers of Europe — The Netherlands, Denmark, Norway, Belgium-Luxemburg and Iceland — are all even more dependent on foreign trade for their very life than the United Kingdom herself, some of them far more so; and the greatly enhanced security of that commerce in an Atlantic Union would be of the utmost benefit to them. Clear evidence of this is the amount of trade which, for example, Australia and New Zealand already have with the small, as well as the large, European powers; to the markets and resources of these Commonwealth Preference members, indeed, they would then acquire a freedom of access which is notably denied to them at the moment. Though the standard of living of most of these small states, particularly Sweden, for example, is very high, and might not therefore grow very much quicker as a result of Union, they would, in this uncertain world, profit greatly from the increased security of those standards.

To each particular state, also, Union would have special, often unique, advantages. Thus, in the case of the great powers, Italy, whose standard of living is lower than that of any other large nation in Western Europe, would stand to gain most from the economic opportunities of Union. France would gain a complete guarantee against domination by Germany, which, even in an era of resuscitated French 'grandeur', must be the secret fear still nourished by most

Frenchmen; France may proclaim her closeness to Germany and her mistrust of the 'Anglo-Saxons', but Frenchmen know in their bones that they never have been in modern history, and never will be, threatened by the insular powers as they were three times threatened in 75 years by Germany. At bottom it is probably French resentments and fears, arising from Britain's refusal to participate in an integrated Europe as a counter-balance to Germany, that are responsible for the recent revival of French mistrust of Britain. Germany will gain from Atlantic Union absolute assurance against a 'sell-out' to Russia which would endanger the free existence of the Federal German Republic. Furthermore, Atlantic Union would exercise an attraction of compelling force over East Germany; nothing could better keep alive in breasts behind the Iron Curtain the desire to be reunited with Western Europe.

All the powers of Western Europe without exception would gain a high degree of certainty that the fearful nationalist wars which have so long been their scourge and which in the twentieth century have twice plunged the whole world into hideous strife, would not arise again in their midst; they would not have any certainty that other wars would not come, but they would be reasonably sure that national strife in their own ranks would be impossible in the future. But, because of the immense power and strength and technical mastery of the Union as a whole, it could not but be, if wisely and freely governed, a potent influence for peace in the world at large. It would greatly add to the possibilities of international stability, which is, of all the public needs of man, perhaps the most pressing in the present age.

Internally, too, all the nations of Europe would benefit immensely from the Union, because, for reasons which we have discussed earlier, it would be the most effective practical guarantee of the continuation, strengthening and creation of free democratic institutions in their midst. Small nations which have long enjoyed self-government, such as Belgium, The Netherlands and Denmark, could be confident that it would not be frequently threatened by destruction from without, whether by overt attack or by subversion and corruption. Great nations, like Germany, would find that those worthy and stable elements in the community which are resolute in favour of liberty and constitutional rule would be immeasurably strengthened. Nations, whether in the Union at first or not, which do not enjoy individual freedom and self-rule, such as Portugal and Spain, would be irresistibly influenced by this triumph of democracy. All the peoples of Europe would experience unprecedented political stability, whether directly as a result of an improvement in their own situation, or indirectly as a result of the improvement in the condition of their neighbours. All Europe would enjoy in greater measure that rule of law which is one of the most significant contributions made by the West to the art of human government.

Europe has indeed much to gain from Atlantic Union.

What of the fourth group (along with the United States, Europe and Britain) which would provide foundation members of the initial Union we have envisaged, The Commonwealth? We are, as has been suggested, concerned here with the inner core of the Commonwealth, probably Canada, Australia and New Zealand. The fact would have to be faced at once by Britain that the Commonwealth as a whole might at first be weakened by the creation of Atlantic Union. If Britain gives up her sovereignty, that free association of sovereign members can hardly fail to be gravely affected; even so flexible, not to say nebulous, a concept as that of the Commonwealth could not readily be stretched to fit comfortably the changed relationship which the new subordinate position of the United Kingdom government would necessitate. At least to the extent that her freedom of action, indeed her very legal power of acting, would be constitutionally limited, she would be unable to adjust her policy to purely Commonwealth purposes in the manner to which she and it have in the past been accustomed. This would not be so serious a difficulty in the case of her colonial Empire, as in the case of the Commonwealth, because of its necessarily subordinate status until each part gains its independence, and because of the speed at which that independence is being granted; the actions of each part after independence would obviously be conditioned by the new circumstances. In other words, the difficulties of adjusting the Commonwealth relationship to Atlantic Union arise from the sovereign independence of the members of the Commonwealth.

And this fact itself really provides the solution of the problem. The whole essence of the Commonwealth relationship as it has evolved over the last hundred, and particularly the last fifty, years is that it is an association of nations which are genuinely and absolutely free. Its members may leave the Commonwealth at any time, as Eire has done; some British possessions, on gaining independence, have not become Commonwealth members at all but have severed all their special connections with it, like the Sudan. This freedom has always been recognized as absolute, and it must apply equally to all members, even Britain herself. Provided that she fulfils, as she can do, her obligations to her dwindling Empire, the overriding duty of the government of the United Kingdom is to the people of the British Isles.

It is vital that Britons should grasp imaginatively the fact that within a very few years their colonies will be remarkably few and far between, for nearly all will have attained their independence. A number of small residual outposts will remain for some time to come; one or two of these, such as Malta and Gibraltar, may wish to adhere in some fashion to Atlantic Union, or to preserve a special direct relationship with the United Kingdom. The problems of any remaining few British colonies, protectorates and trusteeships may in fact be much easier to solve in the context of the Union. But for Britons the essential fact to apprehend is that their old imperial role, apart from their leadership of the Commonwealth, will very soon be at an end. Britain then must, in this day of the super-power, anchor herself firmly to another rock. Already the Atlantic Ocean, not the Mediterranean Sea, has been her life-line for nearly half a century; one thing the Suez crisis of 1956 showed clearly was that Britons were not yet alive to this fact. There are many signs that they now are. The next move in their re-orientation is a full understanding, and conviction of the necessity, of Atlantic Union.

Leading members of the Commonwealth, even including Britain herself, need have no moral, let alone constitutional, qualms about such a move towards a federal Union of the

West; they too are sovereign nations whose own interests are paramount for them, and if those interests dictate a fresh political affiliation of a far-reaching kind, it is the duty of their governments to undertake it. In 1947 when India and Pakistan gained their independence, the bonds of the Commonwealth were drastically modified, loosened in fact, to fit the needs of Indian republicanism; some critics at the time lamented this and regretted that the much closer ties, which the inner states of the Commonwealth might have been willing to continue to accept, were dissolved in the wider grouping. It must be said that what is sauce for the goose is sauce for the gander, and that, if those inner members now deem it necessary to revert to a closer relationship, they have every right to do so. Atlantic Union may justly take priority in British calculations over the Commonwealth, particularly as the latter's leading members, those closest to Britain (Canada, Australia and New Zealand), would themselves be members of it.

But we need not take too gloomy a view of the future of the Commonwealth, for it certainly does not seem that it would be impossible to create a new special relationship, of intimate discussion and consideration, between Atlantic Union and members of the Commonwealth who do not join it. This would be very much to the interest of the Union, one of whose major tasks will be to foster its relationship with the Afro-Asian undeveloped peoples in order to promote their economic development and their democracy. In this process the bridge of understanding between the two which the Commonwealth has come in the last fifteen years to constitute is an exceedingly valuable asset, as Americans are sometimes prone to forget, and one which the new Union would be well advised to cherish. Nor would Britain's colonies be the only ones; to Belgium and France, at least, (with the problems of the Congo and Algeria on their hands) the existence of a special category of powers associated with the Union might prove of inestimable value. It is not inconceivable that a former American colony such as the Philippines might welcome such a relationship. Such an outer ring of associated powers, perhaps even calling itself 'The Commonwealth of the Union', would be immediately valuable, and might also

pave the way in some cases for future full membership of the
Union itself. Nothing, in any case, could be better suited than
such an arrangement to remove Afro-Asian mistrust of a
new super-power of 'white' nations, tainted perhaps by the
colonial past of some of its members.

There is no great reason to suppose that all this would
cause grave offence or serious perturbation among the outer
members of the Commonwealth. India, the most important
one, is firm in a non-attachment which makes her extremely
unlikely to desire any closer relationship with the Union in
the foreseeable future. The African members, such as Ghana,
have their eyes fixed upon a different regional grouping, but
they might be the sponsors of a fraternal association between
Atlantic Union and some future union in Africa. The West
Indian Confederation might well be one of those powers
which would, in the not too distant future, attain the political
maturity to qualify for — and to desire — full membership
of the Union. Pakistan, Ceylon and Malaya would be unlikely
to be affronted by this revolution in the affairs of the
Commonwealth. South Africa alone, though her government
could certainly not complain, might seem, as by so many
trends of the modern world in that unhappy land, to be liable
to be hurt by the new dispensation. And the three oldest
members of the Commonwealth, those closest to Britain's
heart and warmest in their feelings towards her, would stand
to gain enormously from the Union. The Australasian
countries have been fully aware, since World War II and the
rise of Asian nationalism, of their extreme vulnerability;
what Japan attempted in 1941, China, and even other
powers, might very well attempt in the future. The great
spaces of Australia, in particular, deceptive though they are
because of their aridity, must long be a standing temptation to
the overflowing millions of Asia lying off her northern shores.
Her 'white Australia' policy and her vast subsidized immigration programme are both symptoms of this Australian
awareness.

Australia, which is approaching the status of a middle
power at the moment, and which is territorially equal in size
to the United States, will one day be a great power; New
Zealand hardly can ever be. But this day of Australia's great-

ness is distant, and the weakening of British strength in the world in the last quarter century has been recognized in Australia by the A.N.Z.U.S. pact with the United States, which has become an increasingly firm pillar of Australian and New Zealand policies since it was signed in 1951. Both Australia and New Zealand, and particularly the latter, still depend to a very great degree upon long sea communications for their prosperity, as well as upon beneficent sea power for their safety; as far as the eye can see they will depend upon American sea power almost as much as the United Kingdom. Even in mid-twentieth century they are a remote and vulnerable outpost, albeit a large one, of the Western world. Nothing could add more to their strength and security, both directly in defence and indirectly by the stimulus it would give to investment and immigration, than membership of Atlantic Union, inappropriate though the term itself might at first sight seem. And they would be most valuable members, not merely for their democratic stability and experience and their great resources and potential strength, but because they would, by their geographical position, greatly add to the strategic global power of the Union.

Canada, the second Commonwealth power, has also a vital role to play in Atlantic Union and a very great deal to gain from it. Though Canada's relations with her great neighbour have been extremely good and extraordinarily close for many years, she has never quite felt easy about the giant stature of the American colossus. Perhaps the most important reason, apart from a mere desire to change after twenty-two years, for the overthrow of the Liberals in the Canadian election of 1957 was a growing Canadian uneasiness as to whether she can retain her national identity in view of the overwhelming American penetration of the smaller power's economy. This was responsible for Mr. Diefenbaker's sudden demand at the time for a great increase in Commonwealth trade. Atlantic Union, by merging even the vast sovereignty of the United States in a wider economic and political unit, would go far to solve Canada's problem; it would provide an integral counterpoise to excessive American influence.

Canada, however, has even more than this to gain from a Union which would irrevocably cement together the destinies of Britain and the United States, for she has always lived, and must always live, as long as she values the Commonwealth connection, by Anglo-American friendship. In the nineteenth century she was in a sense a hostage for British good intentions in the hands of the United States; in the twentieth century she might suffer the most, at least in an emotional sense, from a rupture between Britain and America, for, as the Suez crisis clearly demonstrated, she has at bottom no choice but to side with the United States. For her, no consummation could be more devoutly to be wished than Atlantic Union; and of all the other powers, not merely of the Commonwealth but even of the prospective Union itself, she might be expected to be the one which would welcome it most warmly and which would exert, proportionate to her strength, the greatest effort to bring it to fruition.

NOTES

[1] *The New York Times Magazine,* 15 November 1959.

CHAPTER XV

Anglo-American Unity

IF the United States and the original four members of the British Commonwealth were once persuaded of the need for Atlantic Union, and tendered a genuine offer of it to the continental peoples, it is hard to believe that Europe would not accept it, however far its own unity had proceeded. A number of the small outer nations of Europe, such as Denmark, which is much torn by the division of its interests between the Six and the Seven, might be expected to welcome it warmly, as also might the smaller members of the Common Market, especially The Netherlands, with its many external economic interests. Germany, with her great industrial capacity and her powerful post-war predilection for the United States, might also welcome it; so perhaps might Italy with her grave economic problems and her strong American connections.

It might well be that France, with her newly reborn insularity, would be the most unwilling European participant. General de Gaulle, indeed, has recently forced the removal of American planes, capable of carrying nuclear weapons, from French soil and has, on nationalist grounds, withdrawn certain French naval forces from N.A.T.O. control. This is not merely a part of the French campaign for nuclear equality, for the General has actually made it clear that he no longer favours the increasing integration of N.A.T.O.'s forces, which, however ineffectively realized in practice, has at least been its ideal since General Eisenhower first set them in full motion in 1951. De Gaulle has often seemed to dislike America's influence over European affairs almost as much as that of Russia; as he wrote of Britain's acceptance in World War II of American leadership, ' Should France be unable to play her traditional leading role on the Continent, this obliteration of England, who had been hitherto so directly involved with that leadership despite her insularity, was a distinctly evil omen of the way in which the affairs of Europe were ultimately to be settled.'[1]

It is earnestly to be hoped that Europe would not refuse the hand of the 'Anglo-Saxons', proffering an invitation to Atlantic Union, but it is not possible to predict reactions to proposals of this kind with certainty, and we must always be prepared for such an eventuality.

What should the attitude of the Commonwealth nations and the United States be if they decide to make the offer, and it is refused by many or all of the European powers? They should go ahead and form an Anglo-American Union, a basic confederation of the United States, Britain, Canada, Australia and New Zealand, to which at a later stage such European states as wished might adhere. Some of Europe's peoples might possibly wish to do so at once, in which case it might or might not be considered wise to welcome them immediately. But if, for example, the French persuaded the Common Market countries that they had too much to lose by sacrificing their concrete present gains to greater potential ones, it is very possible that other nations of Europe might be inhibited from joining the larger Union; Switzerland and Sweden, for instance, might certainly be expected to revert to their traditional neutrality. In such an event the Anglo-Americans should definitely be prepared to 'go it alone', in the hope that in the goodness of time the larger unity might still be possible.

Though such an Anglo-American Union would be, from their point of view and the point of view of the West as a whole, much the less desirable of the two alternatives, it would still be a great accession of strength to the cause of freedom. It would have an initial population of some 250,000,000, compared with the 165,000,000 of the Common Market, as well as a very high degree of economic development, combined with vast natural resources. It would have certain advantages which a wider Atlantic Union would not; it would be a much more easily manageable and workable organization, and, because the first stages of any union are necessarily so important, this would mean that to launch it successfully would be considerably easier than to launch Atlantic Union as a whole.

It would have the inestimable practical advantage of a common language, with all that that implies both for the swift and sure conduct of affairs and for a high degree of mutual comprehension. Common legal habits and a basic pattern of law closely akin would make the inevitable subsequent disputes about the Union's powers far easier to settle; the British would need to accustom themselves to a wider, more 'political', role for the appropriate courts, but the basic respect for law which both peoples have would make this possible. Long experience in kindred processes of democratic government, willingness to compromise, and previous successes in working together politically and militarily, would ease the transition from the old to the new relationship. More closely commensurate standards of living would make economic interlocking less difficult and, in places, painful than in the case of the more complex and larger federation. The wide pre-existing network of social affinities — identical products, shared interests, similar tastes, particularly among the younger generation — would be not only an initial but also an augmenting asset, for the process of unification would unquestionably increase them beyond measure. Such a Union would be a second best, but it would be a very good second best.

An Anglo-American Union would go a considerable distance towards resolving Britain's dilemma. An Atlantic Union alone will resolve it fully, but, though she should not and cannot join a purely European union, she can and should if necessary join a Union of the English-speaking peoples, which would strengthen her bonds, economic and political, with the non-European world — bonds far more powerful emotionally than any that tie her to Europe, bonds economically twice as great as those constituted by her trade with the continent. The Commonwealth countries would gain, not only economically, but, in the case of Australia and New Zealand, by the greatly enhanced security which they would enjoy; Canada's potential nightmare of Anglo-American discord would be finally exorcized. And the United States would acquire an enormous and reliable increase of strength in the protracted and arduous struggle with the Soviet world which lies ahead. Such a tightly-knit Union would have present power, and potentialities of future development, to make it safe against the Communist third of the world for a very long time to come. This would be true even in the event of the neutralism, or outright defection, of other areas of the earth. With the ability, energy and immense power of America, the skill and capacity of Britain, and the vast, virtually untapped resources of the Commonwealth countries, there would be in an Anglo-American Union huge strength now, and room, even if the curve of American expansion (like that of Britain) flattens out, for continued growth far into the future. And this Union would be as solidly united politically and as sound democratically as any possible supra-national confederation that can be imagined.

Whether it is to be the wider or the narrower confederation which emerges, an Atlantic or an Anglo-American Union, the essential element in its construction and operation is Anglo-American unity; without this, neither an Anglo-American nor an Atlantic Union can come into existence or function, any more than in our present state of unfettered national freedom of action the free world can survive in the absence of Anglo-American co-operation. We can afford no more Suez crises. This is indeed, in itself, perhaps the most potent of all arguments for one union or the other, because it would, by the accepted pressure of the new institutions, remove the abysmal dangers which result from Anglo-American discord in conditions of unbridled national sovereignty. No power, not even one as mighty as the United States, is now the absolute master of its own fate; failure to recognize this fact and to embody that recognition in institutional form is a risk that the free world, and the British and American peoples in particular, can no longer afford to run.

Anglo-American unity, too, is one of the most hopeful instruments for the building of any union of liberty-loving nations. For the last fifty years co-operation and cordiality of feeling between the two peoples has grown persistently and powerfully, from the era of dawning recognition of common interests at the turn of the century through 'association' in the First World War to intimate alliance in the Second. Historians have become increasingly aware of the importance of the fundamental ties of language and culture, economic life and racial stock, as well as of legal, political and social outlook. But this intellectual appreciation is not all, for vigorous efforts at the social, educational and political level to improve on this state of things have continued and expanded since 1897, when Mahan, greatest of American strategists, wrote in words quoted above: 'When we begin really to look abroad, and to busy ourselves with our duties to the world at large in our generation — and not before — we shall stretch out our hands to Great Britain, realizing that in unity of heart among the English-speaking races lies the best hope of humanity in the doubtful days ahead.'[2]

Very right and proper is this intense promotion of the unity of the English-speaking peoples, for in the last resort great political movements, like great religious conversions, are the products of passion rather than reason, of the heart rather than of the mind. Emotional forces alone are a strong enough solvent to dissolve the habits, prejudices and rigidities of Western nationalism, and thus prepare the way for a broader Union. All too often such passions are engendered only in the fierce flame of war; thus it was in the white heat of events between 1941 and 1944 that Anglo-American friendship was forged for a time into true unity. Emotion of this kind, however, can be created also in time of peace, or at least the near-peace which is the best that the mid-twentieth century can achieve. An Anglo-American passion for Union can be created only by the constant efforts of those, albeit they are at first few in number, who believe, with fervour and to the roots of their being, in Anglo-American unity. Only such a vocal minority can impart that impulse which will bring an Atlantic or an Anglo-American Union into being.

Their number must necessarily remain limited by many factors, and particularly by the natural and inevitable limitations on the opportunity for the two peoples as a whole to get to know one another, even in this age of swift travel and mass media of communication. It is this fact which makes the post-war imbalance in trans-Atlantic travel, arising from the dollar shortage and the relative wealth of the Americans, so serious, and which makes so necessary the further development of schemes for transatlantic interchange at all levels of society, and particularly among the young. All too often, because they do not know and have not seen with their own eyes — because indeed, even in these days of undreamed of plenty in the West (for such, by the standards of all history, they are), life is frequently too short — the two peoples are aware only of the deficiencies of the other rather than their merits.

Not that covering up the other's vices, let alone harbouring fundamental illusions about them, is in any way a desirable preparation for further unity — although recognition of our brother's weaknesses does not necessitate constantly shouting them from the roof tops. Nothing could be more catastrophic than the disillusion, and consequent disruption, which would result from an Anglo-American unity which had not looked with a level gaze at the serious vices, the grave weaknesses which each of the peoples displays, and particularly perhaps at those most feared or despised by the other. Only a real insight, not merely into the failings of ourselves as well as the others, but also into our own deficiencies as the others see them, can allay mutual sensitivity sufficiently to make domestic life together tolerable. For there are vices in plenty to give both peoples pause.

The American who looks at Britain — even the percipient American who can make allowances and who will avoid the stereotyped caricature — will find many things that will make his blood boil. A lack of energy and enterprise, in many spheres of life, which amounts to lethargy, a traditionalism and conservatism which clings insensately even to those things from the past which are a positive hindrance to future development; a lack of economic and social foresight, as for example in the matter of road planning and construction, which is positively stunning; an unwillingness to carry anything in life to its logical conclusion, which is maddening to the thorough-going mind; a smug satisfaction with 'muddling through', which attributes to inherent skill and virtue what is in fact all too often just astonishing good fortune; a periodic international perfidy of great ruthlessness, masquerading

Q

under a mask of incompetent innocence; an astonishing degree of social and political hypocrisy, which shows itself so clearly in colonial affairs, which pretends, for instance, in Whitehall that there is no British colour bar, which acquired an Empire predominantly for profit, and which now makes a great virtue of giving it up on grounds of principle when it has in fact no other choice; a wooden addiction to understatement, a behavioural reserve, which are in part attributable to a certain insensitiveness and to a considerable lack of ready cordiality; an insufferable and arrogant complacency, all the more galling for being haughty and largely unexpressed; and, perhaps worst of all, a sickening social sycophancy, a nauseating and ineradicable addiction to social inequality, which has survived even the social revolution of 1945 and which in great degree makes nonsense of fifty years of vaunted democratic social progress.

But if the American finds much in England to make his blood boil, even the sympathetic Briton will, as one American noted, find many occasions in America for his 'blood to run cold'.[3] He cannot but be aware of the undercurrent of violence in American life, when the United States had in 1957 6,920 cases of murder and non-negligent manslaughter compared with 151 cases of murder known to the police in England and Wales; he must also be aware of the fearful problem of juvenile delinquency; of the collapse of family life, with an estimated 382,000 divorces in 1956 compared with 28,700 in the United Kingdom; aware of the enervating and in some ways anarchic domination of 'progressives' in education, and psychiatrists and tranquillizers in adult life; of the naiveté of many of America's views of the outside world as well as her views of herself; of the gulf between practice and vaunted precept in so many problems, such as that of the Negro; of the braggadocio and the addiction to overstatement; of the ruthlessness of the economic system; of the widespread and deep corruption of political life; of the restlessness and apparent instability of many American individuals and the periodical intolerance of the American masses; and, perhaps, above all, of the persistent posturings, both private and public, before the ubiquitous altars of the golden calf.

Because of the failures in communication and the immense

inherent difficulties of two peoples (even literate peoples who share a language) really getting to know much about each other, these painful impressions are, all too often, the predominant ones in American and British minds, and they form a disastrously incomplete foundation on which to build a real and lasting intimacy. But there is a small, though growing and highly articulate minority, in both countries, who know the whole scene, and who can depict it in a balanced fashion. They must be the nucleus of any movement for Anglo-American association, for they know what is good as well as what is bad in each society, the virtues as well as the vices, what to love as well as what to hate. And there is a plenteous bounty of things in America that Britons who know her admire and respect, and which arouse the warmest feelings of affection in their hearts.

The infinite and magnificent variety of that great land; the splendid achievement of its people in creating in so short a time out of such diverse human materials a deep and potent patriotism; the superb economic achievements of that people, which have opened up before all mankind the promise of the actual abolition of poverty; their remarkable efficiency and their endless energetic dynamism; their unwavering and unhesitating practical logic, which shows itself in their willingness forthrightly to back any good idea to the uttermost; their economic enterprise and flexibility; their supreme technological skill and mastery; their genuine and profound belief in equality of opportunity and in the equal dignity of all men and women; their maintenance, in circumstances of enormous difficulty, of the full constitutional freedoms of the individual; their persistent and unrelenting pursuit of objective truths, however disturbing or painful; the uninhibited and thorough-going reality of their democracy in practice as well as in theory, in the organization of schools in the local township as well as in taxing themselves there to pay the price; their willingness to trust the people at all times and in all places, with detailed execution as well as general control, with the recall as well as the election of officials; the wonderful fountains of American voluntary effort and individual initiative in every branch of life; the unrivalled freedom and scope of their lavish hospitality; their unequalled private philanthropy; the unsurpassed nobility of much of their international policy, combined with its quite incomparable generosity; their sense of humour, their good humour, their essential humanity; and, perhaps above all, the spontaneous embracing warmth of their everyday but lifelong kindly good nature, which has enabled them — alone, so far as I am aware, among the peoples of the earth — to make the term 'stranger' into one of welcoming and cordial greeting.

And Americans who come to know Britain can find as much as this in her people to stir their admiration and affection. The intimate and delicate loveliness of her green countryside; the man-made beauty of her ancient and mellow buildings; the placid patience of her undemonstrative people; their fundamental kindliness; their practical public as well as private toleration of individual opinion and eccentricity; their feeling for inherited and dignified pageantry; their political good sense and maturity; their self-sufficiency and their cohesive national homogeneity; their orderliness and respect for the law; their remarkable social discipline; their dogged pertinacity and fortitude; their basic reliability; their sense of public duty and service; their profound patriotism; and, most difficult perhaps of all political achievements, their combination of an active and effective political democracy with an extraordinary and quite unrivalled political and social stability.

Upon the shoulders of this minority of Anglo-Americans, who have developed a real understanding of, and devotion to, both societies, there must rest the chief responsibility for the promotion of Anglo-American unity. They alone have the ability to generate a passion for Union which is capable of breaking down the barriers of prejudice, habit and vested interest which stand in its way. But they should not be dismayed by the task: far more difficult feats have been accomplished by men with far less promising material, and a solid groundwork for Anglo-American unity has long been laid. It is, after all, sixty-five years since Mahan — most hard-headed of American patriots — published his essay called *Possibilities of an Anglo-American Reunion*, and it was in 1920 that the phenomenally successful practical man of business, Andrew Carnegie, wrote,